BLUE WATER, BROWN WATER

Stories of Life in the Navy and in Vietnam

Randall Gray Cook

For Heido,
Who Lives in my Heart

iam seges est ubi Troia fuit

now corn grows where Troy was

Virgil

CONTENTS

Foreword

The origin of this book lies in the fall of 1994. During a dinner party, one of my oldest friends, Dick, and I began telling Vietnam stories to his parents, his wife Jennifer, and my mother. They had never heard these stories before because neither one of us had ever told them to anyone in all the years since the war.

The stories just came tumbling out, one after another, as our family sat, transfixed. They couldn't believe that their "boys" had done such things, or had had such adventures. We unconsciously, or maybe consciously, left out the darker things, and kept it light and funny. It was such a relief for both of us, to get some of this stuff out, and everyone enjoyed it so much we agreed to do it again. Regrettably, that never happened.

But that evening triggered something deep inside me. Memories, repressed feelings, a longing to talk to somebody, somebody who understood what I was saying. In the years since Vietnam, I had several times started telling of an experience or incident there to friends, and had received in return nothing but a blank, uncomprehending stare. They couldn't relate, it wasn't their fault, so I learned to just shut up about it and put it in storage.

Now I became more interested in meeting some other veterans, so I joined the local Vietnam Veterans of America (VVA) chapter. I also began doing some reading about the origins of the war, which meant I read a lot of books about the politics of the time. Then came many combat books written by veterans from all the services, as I was curious about what the Army and Air Force guys, the Marines, and even other parts of the Navy, had done there.

It was good to be around veterans again, there were no blank stares here. Stories would come out over coffee, and I gradually came to see all of them as heroes. And there were some genuine heroes among them. One of them loaned me an inscribed book entitled "*A Rumor of War*," by Philip Caputo, a memoir of his experiences as a Marine Officer in Vietnam. It has been called one of the books that really defined the Vietnam experience to those who were never there. And it is a very good book. This Vietnam author and many others had been appearing in the VVA Veteran, the monthly magazine for vets, urging them to get their experiences down on paper, and telling them what a cleansing experience it could be.

Psychiatrists from the Veterans' Administration were saying the same things, as one way of trying to get out the anger, frustrations and hurt that we all carry to one degree or another. The general idea was that, whether you eventually just put it away in the bottom drawer, or kept it for your family to read, or tried to get it published, just do it and see how much better you will feel.

I took note of that, pardon the pun, and began to think that, though I enjoyed and learned so much from other guys' books, I would like to tell my side of it to *them*, and to Vietnam Veteran families, and to anyone else who is curious about that period in time. And then I read another book, this one written by Sebastien Junger,

"*The Perfect Storm.*" It had nothing to do with Vietnam, but it was a very good read, and was obviously well researched. What impressed me most was that this was Mr. Junger's very first book. I then thought, well if he could do it, I could certainly give it a try. It would probably end up in the bottom drawer somewhere, but that didn't seem to matter.

Once I had made a firm commitment to myself to try writing a book, I had to get up the nerve to tell my wife. It felt so *presumptuous* to even have such thoughts. And then one of those incomprehensible things happened, one that told me I had made the right decision. She was in the computer room, and I stuck my head in and announced that I had something important to tell her. I said, "Heide, I think I'm," and here I got a big lump in my throat. Trying again, I said, "I think I'm going to," and I broke down crying! I went into the bedroom, sat down and cried my eyes out. It was so bizarre! I never saw it coming. I am not a big crier, never have been, only on very special occasions. She rushed into the room, really alarmed, and asked me what was the matter? When I was able to tell her, she became instantly supportive and encouraging, and was always so.

That crying thing, it happened again not long after, when I was reading the VVA magazine, and came to the "Reunions" section. There was a listing for the Mobile Riverine Force Association, which included those who served in LST's in the Brown Water Navy. Tears began streaming down my face without my realizing it, and Heide again asked what was wrong. I said, "I've found my old outfit," and had to leave the room for a while.

Writing this book, I have come to tears several times, and I guess what the authors and the psychiatrists had been saying is true. I have tried to empty my head of all of these things, and to alleviate my huge anger at what happened to the men and women who served in Vietnam. I will always remember in my heart, but my head is clear. Well, almost. Somewhat. Not really.

Prologue

This book is **not** about heavy combat in Vietnam, for the simple reason that I saw none there. Combat, yes, but not so heavy. My destroyer threw a lot of lead at the enemy, and we had to return fire several times on the LST, but I leave it to the ground troops, fliers, and other Navy Riverine guys to tell their stories. There were some awesome people in Vietnam.

No, I am just going to tell you about what the Navy looked and sounded like then in day-to-day operations, about some of the best men I have ever known, and about how the world looked through my eyes, while traveling from point A to point B during a 3 1/2 year hitch, in a very turbulent period for the United States.

This is a memoir, and I have tried my best to be honest and accurate in my recollections. It is non-fiction, and so should be taken as the truth by the reader. In cases where my memory, being 40 years removed from events, is not as great as I think it is, at least the substance is sound. I have re-created many conversations and comments, when if not verbatim, are very close. If I have made a mistake on terminology or timeline or geography, it was certainly not intentional. In some instances where I have researched a subject for clarity or have quoted another, the sources are noted.

Some of the stories herein are rated "R," or even worse, for language and situations. I could have cleaned them up, sanitized them so to speak, but then I would not have been able to tell the whole story. At any rate, I apologize in advance if anyone is offended, particularly Vietnam Vet family members who are still trying to learn about the war. But this is the way it was, good and bad, high and low, and is just one of the 2,700,000 stories that could be told.

Brotherhood

When I travel by air, I wear a sports jacket, and on the lapel I wear a pin that is a facsimile of the Vietnam Service Ribbon, which we who served there all wore. I do this to signify to other veterans that I would like to shake their hand and say, "Welcome home."

I travel standby and therefore am often one of the last few passengers to board the plane. In July 2003 I was waiting for my name to be called at Washington National Airport, headed for Miami. Everyone else had boarded, and the agent at my gate got on the PA and said, "Will Barry McCaffrey please see the agent at gate ten?" The name was familiar to me and I thought this could be General Barry McCaffrey, whom I knew had done a couple of tours in Vietnam and had been the nation's "Drug Czar" under President Clinton. The agent repeated the call for him, and this fellow in a brown suit walks up to her to pick up his ticket and *bingo*, it's General McCaffrey. He was instantly recognizable, as he had appeared frequently on national television as a military commentator during the war in Iraq. He boarded the plane.

Finally my name was called, and I gratefully picked up my boarding pass and walked down the jetway. As I entered the plane, making a right turn into the first class section, all I saw was General

McCaffrey, and his eyes were riveted on my lapel pin. His eyes are rather intense. We then locked eyes in mutual recognition and I nodded to him and said, "Sir." As he got up from his seat, we each offered our hand and introduced ourselves.

He then said, "I'm glad to see you are wearing that pin."

I replied, "Well, we need to do a little advertising for the guys."

And he replied, "Yes, we do."

And that was it.

I took my seat in coach and felt as if I were glowing. I just had a real good feeling. Not because of who he was but because we were bound by events that had occurred so many years before. He retired a four star general and I left the Navy as a lieutenant, but that didn't matter. He is a highly decorated combat soldier who commanded the very aggressive 24th Infantry Division in Desert Storm, was the President's Drug Czar, and has performed many services in the highest echelons of the military and government. Yet, for an instant, all of that fell away and he became a company commander again out in the bush somewhere, and I was operations officer on an old ship again, up some river.

It's amazing. Anyone in uniform who ever set foot in that place is bound to everyone else who did. It's an indescribable bond, more like an understanding. It's as if, two people who have never met before but see that the other is wearing the Vietnam Service pin, they need do nothing more than look each other in the eye and simply nod. It's a recognition of all that went before. It is the memory of our collective experience over there, and of the return to an ungrateful country. It is something that ties us together and always will until the last one of us is in the ground. It is a Brotherhood.

General Hershey

I could have stayed out of the draft and out of the military altogether. As a kid I had had a rather serious eye operation involving the removal of my right eye for a while so that the surgeon, who was also my cousin, could remove a tumor about the size of my thumb, which was wrapping itself around the optic nerve and was about to blind me. (By the way, my cousin was Dr. Craig Johnson who had recently retired as Chief Eye Surgeon of the Navy as a Rear Admiral). The operation was successful but left a muscle, which had been scraped free of the tumor, stuck to the eyeball. This left me with double vision in all of my peripheral sight, up, down, left and right.

Craig offered to go back in and repair the problem but I said uh-hunh, thanks anyway. He then said that the double vision would do two things: it would enable me to see two pretty girls instead of one, and it would make me eligible for 4-F status, therefore not subject to the draft. He asked if I wanted a deferment when the time came and I said no, I didn't want to do that, and we dropped the subject.

Of course that small decision came back to see me in 1967, in the form of the U.S. Army, which was now fighting a war in Vietnam and needed fresh recruits to fill the ranks. General Lewis B.

Hershey, Director of the Selective Service System, was looking for me and my friend Richard Cooke. We had been to the draft board in downtown Houston often and had to see a lady named Sylvia each time. Richard swore that Sylvia kept calling us back because she had a thing for us, there was no question about it.

One day in September I happened to be sitting in an office there when a man came in and asked someone in the room if they knew how he could get hold of Jimmy Robinson, because his brother Frank had just been killed in Vietnam. I just moaned to myself, "Oh, no." These two guys were friends of mine, and all I could think of was poor Frank. And poor Jimmy. They were very close.

That was my second personal brush with anything having to do with Vietnam. The first was when my friend Mike Driscoll was killed there in June of that year. A group of us had met in kindergarten and had grown up together. Poor Mike. Poor us.

On another occasion I was in a waiting room sitting with a couple of black guys, and they were talking about Muhammad Ali. They had actually been in the line with him in April when he had refused to step forward and take the oath. They said they urged him, "C'mon man, c'mon brother, step forward, it ain't worth it," but he wouldn't budge. They also said he was shaking. I would have been, too. Guess he really didn't have anything against those Viet Congs.

I liked these guys and enjoyed talking to them. I told them about a friend of mine who had used one of many tricks to fool the draft board and stay out of the service: an hour or so before going for his physical he stuck a bar of soap in each armpit and held them there. By the time he appeared before the doctor, he felt terrible, was sweating profusely, and had turned a kind of gray color. He was sent home.

The Army was getting too close for comfort, so Richard applied for Army OCS (Officer Candidate School), and I applied with the Navy for OCS. My step father was Rear Admiral Edwin J. Zimmermann, and he had always said he wouldn't try to influence my choice of service. Of course, courtesy of the Admiral, I had toured just about every ship on the East Coast by then, and had lunched in a number of wardrooms (officers' mess). But the Navy actually was my own choice; at least I think it was.

Once accepted to OCS, I paid a final call to the draft board for a physical, receiving my first military shots, my first "short arm" inspection, and having to turn my head and cough. My next assignment was to report to Navy Officer Candidate School, Newport, Rhode Island. So now it begins.

Note: Victor Michael Driscoll, Corporal, USMC, was killed by small arms fire on June 3, 1967, Quang Tin. He may be found on panel 21E, line 44 of *The Wall*.

Frank Eugene Robinson, Navy Corpsman, was killed by artillery/rocket/mortar fire on September 8, 1967, Quang Tri. He may be found on panel 26E, line 37 of *The Wall*.

OCS

So, in February of 1968 I reported to Officer Candidate School in Newport, Rhode Island, for training. Luckily, Captain Stan Ohlin, a close friend of my step father's, lived nearby, so I was able to leave my car with him while in school. In fact, Captain Ohlin was the one who dropped me off at the school's gate and wished me good luck. The campus itself looked like a small college with the addition of parade grounds and minus any landscaping whatsoever. The day I reported with hundreds of other guys was very disorienting.

We were first assigned to companies, mine being D-6801, or Delta-6801. We were then issued our uniforms and told to pack away the civvies. That was the least of our traumas that day, as they then ran us into the barbershop to be sheared like sheep. You will never know how that feels until it happens to you. All of that great hair dropping to the floor. They seat you in front of a big mirror so you can watch. In thirty seconds you become a different person, with this round, bristly dome where your head used to be.

After we were all sheared we had to form up in line and wait awhile. A guy behind me said, "Man, I can see the back of your brains," which made me feel a whole lot better. Off next to a meeting room, where we met our company officer, Lieutenant Salemi. Dark,

Mediterranean-looking guy with a good sense of humor. He asked if any of us had been leaders of any kind in the scouts or school or whatever. Most of us avoided eye contact with him and slunk down in our seats, but the one or two who volunteered that they were scout leaders back home, became temporary Officer Candidate company commander and assistant. We are now led to our new quarters in King Hall, named for Admiral Ernest J. King, Chief of Naval Operations during World War II. Second deck, two to a room assigned alphabetically, so I get a roommate named Cox.

During this day of orientation we are led twice to the mess hall for chow, where besides eating fairly good food, we are able to size up our "shipmates" and begin to get acquainted. I must say I was thrown together with a good group of guys, a real cross-section of society from across the country, all college graduates, and not a bad egg among them. We were going to get much, much closer to each other in the next 16 weeks.

The psychology of this first day was just brilliant. They took hundreds of personalities from every background imaginable, with their individual tastes in clothes, hairstyle, food, women, cars and friends, and changed them into a homogenized bunch of bald guys dressed all alike and living in a cubicle. The shock of all this sudden change in one day was crude but effective. In order to get through this school, we were going to have to pull together as a team. Teamwork. That's what the whole thing was about, though we actually didn't see that at the time. We would learn a little about this and a little about that along the way, but we were here to learn to trust and rely on each other, and in that the school was quite effective.

While we were Officer Candidates our official status was Petty Officer 2nd Class, an enlisted rating with commensurate pay. So we were enlisted until graduation, and those who failed remained enlisted and were sent to boot camp.

The second day set the pattern for all of our subsequent days here:

Reveille at 0530 (which became known as O-Dark-30)

½ hour to do the three "S's," (shower, shave and whatever else you have to do)

Police your space, make the bunk, everything put away, nice and neat

Fall in for chow

Fall in for morning formation. The whole battalion formed up on the parade ground for instruction from company officers, and then this, which I can hear to this day: Some guy without benefit of a loudspeaker but with a huge set of lungs and a foghorn-hoarse voice, blared, slowly, *"Plan of the day, Tuesday, 10 March, 1968,"* and would proceed to call out any special events for the day.

Fall in for classes

Fall in for chow (we fell in a lot)

Fall in for classes

Back to King Hall for study

Fall in for chow

Back to King Hall for study

Lights out at 2230 (10:30 PM)

Blessed sleep, unless you were assigned a watch during the night. The watch consisted of minding the "quarterdeck," which was the reception area of the Hall, and of a roving patrol of all of the passageways (hallways), to make sure all of those Officer Candidates weren't acting up. We also had to maintain a log, same as on the bridge or quarterdeck of a ship.

In our first few days here, two things became very apparent. One was that you were never able to get enough sleep, and we will discuss that later. The other was that we always moved about the campus as a group. You never saw an Officer Candidate walking by himself. We had to march everywhere, sometimes at double-time, and as a consequence, were never lonely.

* * *

Physical training started right away. Now we were *really* intimidated. We were waiting in the gym, when this *giant* walks in and announces he will be our PT instructor for the duration. You could hear the muffled exclamations, like, "Jesus Christ", or "Goddamn!" He was a Chief Petty Officer who was 6'5" of solid muscle on top of maybe a 34" waist, and one of the biggest men I have ever gawked at. I have seen both Arnold and Andre the Giant up close, and this Chief would not have felt uncomfortable around them.

Now, most of us were in pretty good shape, or we thought we were, but this guy proved the fact that we weren't. You couldn't help but marvel at his size and physique, but soon enough he had a nickname, "The Sadist." He expected us to do all of the things that he could do, you know, Herculean things. Here we are a bunch of college boys, for example, lifting and carrying around telephone poles. We figured he could probably carry one under each arm. Of course there were also wind sprints and laps and pushups and pull-ups and calisthenics no end, just to keep us warmed up for more exotic tortures.

The gym had a 30-foot ceiling, or at least it seemed that high, from which dangled a number of 3-inch thick ropes (in the fleet called 3-inch hawsers). We had to climb all the way up and touch the ceiling. If you couldn't do it, you were marked down in PT, and being marked down in any subject was dangerous. I was able to do it on the second try, motivated by that fact.

The obstacle course was designed for totally fit people like the Chief. It was a real killer but I rather liked it, not because I was so fast getting through it, but because it worked on every muscle in your body, and just getting through it without collapsing was an accomplishment in itself. Within a few days everyone was so sore, no one could move without moaning in pain.

Marching drill and swimming were taught by other instructors but we all thought about the Chief because of the agony we were going through. Swimming was actually a relief due to the lack of gravity pulling on sore muscles, while marching only exacerbated our misery. But, miracle of miracles, within a few weeks we stopped hurting and began feeling that particular rush of being stronger and more fit than we had ever been before. Hatred for the Chief subsided, replaced by grudging admiration for his very basic but effective program.

There was an Officer Candidate named Ford in another company who was completely unaffected by all of these tortures, mainly because he was another of these perfect physical specimens. A real nice guy, he was about my height but had every muscle where it should be, and each was of perfect size. He was something of a "ringer," as he was a world-class rower and the Navy wanted him for their Olympic rowing team. He didn't have such a hard time getting through OCS, and wasn't going to the fleet anyway, just back into training. But there was no jealousy on anyone's part because he was so likeable. And what an athlete!

* * *

Swimming was used for exercise and competition, as well as learning survival skills at sea. For exercise, there were always laps to swim because in order to pass PT you had to swim the minimum number, freestyle. There was also water polo, which was pretty rough because of all the flying elbows. (Later, in Sasebo, Japan, officers from my ship and other destroyers played a bunch of carrier pilots in a famous and bloody game of water polo). Water volleyball was a little less of a contact sport, but great for the body.

We also did some water wrestling, where one guy is in the water and another sits on his shoulders, and you wrestle another pair. Well, there was one black guy in Delta Company named Mr. Hayes, and I was paired up with him for a match. So I ducked underwater and came up with him on my shoulders. All of a sudden I was completely shocked with the realization that I had a black man sitting on my shoulders! It really freaked me out!

Naturally, growing up in Houston I had had plenty of contact with black people, but the only physical contact had been a handshake here and there. And of course I used to hug our "mammy," Ermagene. She was family. I had never been this close to a black guy before and was in total confusion until we entered combat and I had to concentrate on the other team.

From then on Mr. Hayes felt just like any other guy would, and I subliminally learned an important lesson that day.

The instruction we received for survival at sea was at once interesting and sobering. We were told that when the water temperature was at 45 degrees, you could survive for only 5 minutes or so. Since then, hypothermia has been invented, and we now know that in 32 degree water you can go in less than 15 minutes, whereas at 45 degrees you can last up to 3 hours if you do things just right. We knew nothing about "core temperature" or the fact that cold water reduces body heat 30 times faster than air. I think the idea was to avoid being in cold water altogether, which was all right with me.

Forget about the shark repellant. It came in a small, flat rectangular box, and we were given instructions as to its use. But the sailor who was instructing told us on the QT that word around the fleet was that it actually attracted sharks, and to throw it away whenever you see it. No problem!

We were introduced to the "Mae West" life jacket, the one that is orange, called international orange, and stuffed with kapok, which is fibers from the fruit of a number of tropical trees, especially the Ceiba plant. The Mae West is a little bulky and our training vests were really ripe after having been used by so many Officer Candidates over the years, but it keeps you afloat, and it was drilled into us over and over to always keep one handy. That was good advice. The downside was that if you were ever in water for 3 or 4 days, the kapok became waterlogged and you sank to the bottom.

I guess in order to get into the cold water or into shark-infested waters in the first place, you had to jump from somewhere. So this evolution involved a platform atop a 15-meter tower beside the swimming pool. Again, every Officer Candidate had to make a successful jump in order to continue in school, so it was very important. From the pool it didn't seem so high, but once you climbed the ladder up to that little platform, it was *very* high. Since it was a single jump, you just take a leap and point your toes for a smooth entry. I didn't particularly enjoy the experience but it was over quickly enough; however, from that height you fall like a sack of potatoes, with a lot of acceleration, and impact is harder than you think it is. There were of course some guys who tipped forward or backward too far and hit the water at a bad angle. It knocked the wind out of some of them, and others tried to laugh it off as they got out of the water with large red areas where they smacked the water.

And then there was "Tower Charlie." Tower Charlie was an unfortunate fellow from Charlie Company who got to the top of the ladder and couldn't jump. He worked up the nerve to get to the edge of the platform but couldn't do it. He was so scared you could see his legs shaking. The instructor told him to jump, but he said, "No sir, I can't," and backed up to the far end of the platform. He tried to get back down the ladder but the instructor stopped him with a sharp command. He was told to let a few more guys go past him, and to watch them, then it would be his turn again. You felt truly sorry for the guy, knowing he was just terrified. Soon enough everyone had jumped but him. He knew that failing to do this would wash him out of the program. So with hundreds of eyes on him, and the instructor gently (really!) coaxing him, he worked his way up to the edge again, legs shaking violently. And after another minute or two, he jumped. With a not-so-elegant entry into the water, he came up to the cheers of everyone in the building, those around him slapping him on the back in congratulation. He was a very happy man, but had earned the nickname "Tower Charlie," which stayed with him through graduation and probably beyond.

Those Officer Candidates who were paying attention that day learned a little lesson from Tower Charlie. It took a lot of guts for him to jump off of that tower in the face of sheer terror, and that seemed to me to be a pretty fair description of courage.

There were two other survival techniques to learn: treading water, and making a flotation device out of your pants. Treading water wasn't so bad, even with t-shirt and trousers on, at least for the first two minutes. But you had to do it for 5 minutes, and by that time, regardless what shape you are in, you are in pure agony, your arms feel like lead and your legs are on fire. You just did it because you had to and that was that.

If you end up in the drink and don't want to tread water, you can get your cotton pants off, take out the belt, and tie a knot near the bottom of each leg. Then by holding the waist open behind your head, bring the pants over your head with a strong move. The legs will fill with air, and actually it makes a pretty good pair of water wings. Since cotton breathes, this isn't good for a long day in the water, but you can repeat the maneuver, anything to avoid the alternative.

* * *

There were some wonderful guys in my company. My roommate, as I have mentioned, was a guy named Cox from up east. I believe he went to Princeton, was very bright, smoked a pipe and had a wry sense of humor. The guys immediately bestowed on him the name "Sux." Sux Cox. I thought he was a pervert and he thought

I was a clod from Texas, and we kept each other laughing throughout the ordeal. In fact, that whole group was funny.

There was Jim, below average height and a little plump. When reveille blew at its unearthly hour, he would yell, "I hate this fucking place!" Or, "Like I used to say when I was a kid in church, *shit!*" Everyone would yell at him to shut up, then get up with the first laugh of the day.

Warren Dold was also from Houston, and he got a lot of ribbing because of his heavy East Texas accent. When he introduced himself, it came out "Warn," so of course he became known as Warn Dold. And in a small world kind of way, it turned out that he was married to one of my old friends from school, Kitty Wright.

Tim was a real trip. Son of a congressman from Boston, you would think he would be well behaved and decorous at all times, but he was the silliest bastard in the company. His forte was mixing up his uniforms into an outlandish mish-mash, and posing for heroic pictures.

Dan Heck was a big boy from Tulsa. Big as a pickup truck. No trouble when he was around. Dan and I would have many adventures in the Orient, but I am getting ahead of the story.

George was a red headed guy who seemed okay at first, but as the program progressed he began exhibiting some traits that would not serve him well as an officer.

And there were Ralph and Joe and Steve and Roger and Framp and so many others. I was given the nickname "Stick," I guess owing to my physique, 6 feet and 145 pounds, straight up and down. After awhile I only answered to that name because everyone had forgotten my given name.

What a great bunch. I can sit here and look at pictures I took all those years ago, pictures of many of the guys in the company. And I recognize all of the faces immediately, but it is sad and frustrating that I can't remember most of their names. I hope they all survived Vietnam and are now hanging out getting old and mellow like I am.

* * *

As I said, we marched all the time. Any movement outside was in formation, marching to and fro, fro and to. There was the marching to get from point A to point B, and then there was precision marching, or drills, out on the "grinder" (parade ground). The grinder was also used as the punishment ground: extra marching time carrying the 9½ -pound heavy M-1 rifle. I did my time out there for one perceived infraction or another.

While marching you needed a guide-on, who called cadence and who carried the company pennant while marching on parade. The position was rotated among us and I enjoyed doing it. There were many ways to keep cadence: Navy songs, the old standby, "I don't know but I've been told" ditty, the simpler, "Your left, your left, your left right left," and the simplest of all, "somf, somf, somf."

That last was concocted by Delta Company. It is an acronym, or a word made up from the first letter of several words. Acronyms make up 99.9% of the terms used by the Navy. Anyway, one of the most popular songs then was "*Young Girl,*" by Gary Puckett and the Union Gap. It was a great tune. The first line was, "Young girl, get out of my mind." One of the guys changed those words somewhat, giving the tune a sexual connotation and began singing it around the dorm. The revised song became so popular that the words became the acronym *somf.* Therefore, we were marching and smiling in perfect time and no one was any the wiser. (Really, it is just too crude to put into print, right Jim?).

When marching to the mess hall, we often had to halt and stand at attention while waiting to go in. As soon as my roommate learned what a Section 8 was (discharge based on mental instability), he began trying to hold my hand while we stood at attention, hoping an officer would see him. He never got his Section 8. This kind of behavior, though, known as grab-assing or skylarking, would certainly earn you a quick trip to the grinder with an M-1.

If you weren't exactly in formation but were hanging out waiting for something to happen, someone would officiously bark out the order, "Now men, mill about smartly!" There was a smart aleck in every crowd.

* * *

Since it was still winter, we were issued blue uniforms to wear until spring, then we got summer uniforms, both white and khaki. We were taught how to wear and maintain them. We were also issued two items I shall never forget: boxer shorts and boondockers.

I have always hated boxer shorts, but while at OCS we had to wear them. There was never a shorts inspection, but somehow they *knew* if you were cheating. The California guys called them "baggies," and for good reason: they just hung there, doing nothing, letting you dangle in the breeze. I had always preferred the tight Fruit of the Looms, which gave some support and actually some protection. They were known as "supermans" in California, but were *verboten* at OCS.

The boondockers were a pair of ankle-height, black work boots nicknamed "boonies." These we wore most of the time during the week, and they actually became an integral part of our feet. The problem was keeping them shiny. We put so many miles on them, they would require a shine every night, which no one had the time or inclination to do. So someone came up with a spray varnish, which put a shiny surface on them and smelled awful. Along about 2200 hours (10:00 PM) each night out came the spray cans. All you could hear was aerosol sounds, and everyone got dizzy from the chemical odor. This practice was illegal, and the spray cans were always confiscated. If they could find them, that is. And the boonies were shined.

Our underwear, t-shirts and socks were laundered, courtesy of the Navy. You threw them all into a net bag, closed with a giant safety pin, and they were picked up, and returned to you folded. A pretty good deal. It turned out to be the same aboard ship.

The uniforms were a different story. They had to be cleaned or washed and starched, by an outside vendor, and at our expense. At an appointed time, we would gather up dirty uniforms and take them out to the back of King Hall, where the most bizarre scene awaited us: a fleet of cleaners trucks, backed up to the curb, with the drivers waiting for us like spiders, each trying to entice you by shouting louder than the next guy. The names were great, like "Mike's-I'm a Vet," or, "Sailor Bill's," or "All-Navy Cleaners," or "Fleet Cleaners." They did a good business at OCS.

Uniforms would come back in a day or two, and they did a pretty good job, with one exception: a pair of my gabardine khaki slacks had been washed and starched as if they were cotton. They were shrunken by 3 or 4 inches around the waist, were 5 inches shorter, and were as hard as plywood. So I had to shit-can them (throw them away). Problem was there were so many cleaners I couldn't remember whom to complain to. I think it might have been "Mike's-I'm a Vet" who did it.

The winter uniforms consisted of dress blues and a sort of blue working uniform. That was good, because the winter got very cold there. How cold did it get, you may ask? During a particularly brutal cold wave, a destroyer had been operating out in the Atlantic and had run into some rough weather. As the snow, sleet and sea water hit the superstructure, it quick-froze until the ship was encased in a layer of ice. As this layer began to thicken, the ship became top-heavy, a dangerous thing in a bad sea. There was real fear that she would capsize. But with the crew frantically working with chipping hammers out in that awful cold, she was able to make it safely into port. I was able to see her shortly after she tied up, and it was a miracle that ice palace was still afloat. Must have had a really good captain and crew.

Anyway, that was the kind of winter we had. Boy, was it cold. Made me appreciate the wool greatcoat we were issued, as well as the dark blue wool shirts. We all worked very hard to look sharp in these things, and during one inspection I was singled out for how I pleated and tucked my wool shirt, and was given merit points for it. I was kind of proud of that until one fellow remarked that the only reason that had happened was that my father was an Admiral. I think I told him where to stuff his wool shirt.

* * *

Lt. Salemi, our company officer, was okay, we thought. Not much older than we were, he was funny and had a semi-irreverent attitude toward the Navy. He gave lectures on what being a Naval officer is all about, and to him we listened. Since he knew, and we knew, that most of us would end up in Vietnam, there was a recurring theme in his talks, that the South Vietnamese were our allies and should always be treated with respect. No derogatory nicknames, no jokes, no condescension, etc., etc., etc.

In general, we found the OCS officers to be pretty much sub-par. As a group they didn't seem very sharp or interested, and they seemed to have a lackadaisical attitude. It was plain they would rather be somewhere else. We decided that they must have been sent here as a punishment.

In contrast, the Chiefs and Petty Officers who taught us various subjects were of high caliber: they knew their subject and wanted us to learn. Their demeanor gave us an important lesson in respect for the enlisted man.

There was one guy I will never forget. He would have been a Hollywood casting agent's dream of the perfect sailor for the movies. A 1st class Petty Officer, he was teaching us about boilers and steam turbine engines, and knew his subject inside and out. No taller than about 5'8", he was one of those bantam rooster kind of guys, tough as nails, with a Boston accent and very colorful language. He looked sharp in his dress blues, and had many hash marks running up his sleeve, one for each 4-year hitch he had done. His hash marks and rating chevrons were a crimson red, instead of being gold, and that meant that he had had some kind of disciplinary problem along the way. Long Navy service and had been in some trouble. You could easily imagine him brawling with the Shore Patrol in Hong Kong after raising hell all night. Then going back to his ship as an exemplary crew member.

He illustrated his points with stories, such as one involving a whore in his hotel room last Saturday night, and he couldn't get the window open for a breath of "fresh air."

There was a movie, *"Don't Go Near The Water,"* which was set in the Pacific during WWII. Glenn Ford portrayed a Navy Officer in public relations, who had to locate a sailor improbably named John Paul Jones, serving on the USS Ankletooth. The idea was to have him do War Bond tours and speaking engagements across the USA, the problem was his constant use of expletives. Our 1st Class Petty Officer would have taken home the Academy Award.

He was the real deal, and we loved his class. We discovered a new word, "salty." Besides describing some of his stories, it meant he had long sea service. Actually we learned a lot about the Navy in that class.

* * *

Supplementing the sleeplessness, inconsistencies and sore muscles that we lived with daily, came the upperclassmen. Although our tenure at OCS was somewhat shorter than a stint at the Naval Academy, the upperclassmen played the same role: yelling, taunting, and totally unreasonable. They were in charge, through us, for maintenance of the dorm buildings. That included all of the hallways (passageways), stairs (ladders), reception area (quarterdeck), and bathrooms (heads), along with the attendant walls (bulkheads), ceilings (overheads), floors (decks) and oh yes, doors (hatchways). You can see the psychology here. Everything we were familiar with became something different, the equivalent of the environment we would find aboard ship. We were getting a total immersion course in a new language simply through everyday living. Very effective.

My first experience under these tyrants was being led with a group of others to one of the heads in King Hall. This little upperclassman guy, yelling at us, "Okay men, let's get after them *pubes!"* Which translated, meant, "Clean those Urinals!" It was a lot of fun.

Another learning experience in maintenance included the use of the electric floor polisher. The big one, with maybe a 30 inch polishing wheel, under which you put a flat towel and let 'er rip. I was thrown from bulkhead to bulkhead trying to use that thing, and never did get the hang of it. I left it to other, bigger guys to keep the decks as shiny as a mirror.

* * *

Other than physical fitness, we began to get into the academics of officer training. The curriculum was well rounded, but there were so many subjects, and you had such a short time to master them, that everything got very intense. The pressure was on to learn everything you could about every subject. And this pressure sat right on your head up until the very last day you were there.

The courses were:

Engineering

Tactics

Military Indoctrination

Naval History

Navigation

Seamanship

Damage Control

Leadership

Naval Administration

Military Law

Engineering was easy for me since I had always been mechanically inclined. However, Tactics made my head hurt. My mirror image was Mr. Cox, who "sailed" through Tactics but stunk in Engineering. So we made good roommates, supporting each other in these and other subjects, and I am sure the same thing happened up and down the passageway.

I could handle everything else pretty well, except that Navigation gave me some problems. Shooting sun lines and stars, and even the moon with a sextant may have made sense to some of the guys, but not much to me. I was able to get through the course, but never felt like I learned enough. These basic methods were still used at sea, in fact I finally did some successful drills out in the Pacific. But more often you could use radar to navigate in coastal waters, and you could use the LORAN out at sea, when it wasn't broken. The Long Range Navigation System used radio signals, three of which crossed at the same point to give you a position. This was the rudimentary precursor of the GPS, or Global Positioning System.

Some of the courses had interesting "hands-on" evolutions, designed to train you as well as scare you to death, in order to demonstrate how serious things could get at sea. Two of the most memorable were part of Damage Control: the Engine Room Fire and the Sinking Ship.

We were taken to an out-building, a low brick affair, and were given fire-fighting suits, with hood, and positioned in a crouching position behind various low concrete barriers. The room was fairly large, very black on every surface, and no lights. They left one garage door-sized opening at one end. Then they set it on fire. Nothing has ever frightened me much, but *that* was scary. Claustrophobic. That was incentive enough to put out the fire, which we did with high-pressure hoses. Everyone was a black mess when we finished, and we all smelled as bad as the inside of those fire suits. But we got the message: there is nothing worse than a fire at sea.

The Sinking Ship was a real piece of work and must have cost millions. It was off base, so was used to train damage-control teams for the Atlantic Fleet. We were put down into the hull of a ship, which then began sinking and taking on water. It was very realistic. There was a large hole in the hull below the water line, and it was shooting water at us under high pressure. We had to plug the hole or sink.

The water began rising as we scrambled to organize and decide what to do.We were able to locate the things we needed to start work on the problem: mattresses, some wooden beams, and heavy mallets. You couldn't help but notice that the water was a dirty brown color and had a really bad odor. That might have been more motivation to act quickly. Anyway, a few of us began trying to stuff some mattresses into the hole while the others tried to position the beams. We tried twice to make a patch but failed, and found that the water level rises quickly on a sinking ship. On the third try, we got a couple of mattresses into the hole, and wedged the beams against them. Two guys pounded them into place against the opposite bulkhead, and the water stopped. It was up to our shoulders. And for just a little while there, we had forgotten this was just an exercise, and were frantically working to stop that leak. To this day I don't know how far the instructors would have gone, had we not been able to make a patch. As we were leaving, my roommate said what was on everyone's mind: "They ought to change the water in that thing, for Christ's sake!"

One aspect of Damage Control that interested me was the ability of the Damage Control Officer to actually change the center of gravity of his ship, regardless of its size. This could be done in order to correct a list, prevent the ship from capsizing, compensate for the weight of water being used to put out a fire, and a myriad other reasons. He could move ballast water or even fuel oil around the ship to accomplish this. I have even read of instances where the crew were used by grouping on one side of the main deck or other. There were infinite possibilities.

The Tactics course offered us the chance to be attacked by a submarine. The BZ Trainer was a precise mockup of a Destroyer's bridge, and teams of us manned it for the Anti-Submarine Warfare (ASW) exercise. We had thought the Sinking Ship was expensive, but this was even more incredible. It was all electronic, and was on the leading edge of technology for the day. We began by turning on our sonar to search for a sub that we knew was in the vicinity. If we did not detect him in time and he got close enough, he would kill us. We had conventional homing torpedoes to shoot him with (no nukes in the training class). After a long game of cat-and-mouse with this electronic guy, we finally located and destroyed him. This was a great exercise for ship handling, sonar, radar, coordination on the bridge, and decision-making. When we were finished and had dispatched the bad boy, the screen of the simulator lit up with a big "BZ," or Bravo Zulu, naval code for "well done." I am sure that if there were a Difficulty Dial numbered from 1 to 10, we were clicked to number 3 or 4, and the real professionals played at 9 or 10. But we enjoyed the moment. (In a later chapter you will read about an episode involving a Russian submarine. The real thing is much more impressive and frightening than the BZ Trainer).

For Seamanship we got to sail around the harbor for a while in a little putt-putt called a YP, for Yard Patrol. About all it offered was a morning in the outdoors. It would have been more fun and more informative for us if one of the destroyers had put to sea for a day and let us observe everything from the signal bridge down to the engine spaces. But the YP had to suffice for now. I guess they figured we would all be at sea soon enough.

* * *

At some point during the myriad lectures, we learned the basics about biological and chemical warfare. Part of the exercise, while in a sitting position, involved stabbing yourself in the thigh with a pretty good sized needle and squeezing an "antidote" into the muscle. The whole thing really hurt, but the *anticipation* of stabbing yourself was worse. I think everyone finally did it to avoid being the last chicken in the room.

* * *

I remember fondly the old Army movies we were occasionally shown in class. I say Army, but they were actually old Department of

War and Department of Defense movies with mostly Army guys in them, many in vintage uniforms, circa WWII. These pictures were great, either in black and white or sepia, all showing their age, and with the stilted instructional language of the day. It was funny because here was a roomful of college graduates, being talked to on about a 4th grade level, or as if we had just fallen off the turnip truck. The most popular films covered the subject of venereal disease. Some were just awful! Trying to scare us to death, they showed very graphic pictures of what could happen if you contracted various diseases from evil women. There were boils and pustules, and something called a canker. Or was it a shanker? It didn't matter much because our friend Jim soon adopted these terms as his own, and we began hearing his lament at reveille, delivered in the drawl of an old Southern plantation owner, "Ohhh, ah got a cankah on mah shankah," or "Ah got a shankah on mah cankah!"

But the main reason we loved the movies was it gave us a chance to *sleep!* Even 15 minutes was heaven! You could never get enough of it. Lights out, and most heads hit the desk. You would be surprised at how deep a sleep you can achieve in such a short time. The instructors knew exactly what was happening but they always let it slide and never called anyone on it. It's not like we were going to be tested on cankers anyway.

* * *

As far as personal weapons go, I don't remember ever qualifying on the M-1 Rifle. We learned how to clean one, and how to disassemble and reassemble it, but never got to the shooting range with it. Possibly because the M-16 was now in general use and the school hadn't gotten their allotment yet, or more likely an Officer Candidate with a loaded rifle was something they didn't want to think about.

We did get to know and to love the old .45 Caliber Automatic Pistol, though. This thing was, and is, a real cannon. Used by the Army since 1911, approximately 2,000,000 were produced by 1945, it's last year of production. It was very popular up through Vietnam because it was so reliable and so lethal. (I was to carry one later, whenever I transported classified documents, and always felt well protected. It tended to give you confidence). It was also very heavy, at 3 lbs. with a full clip.

This was part of the problem: it was so heavy, it was hard to aim. You couldn't linger on the target for long, it would start moving around on you. You had to put it on the target and fire right now, or bring the sights slowly across the target and fire. And if you didn't caress the trigger with slowly increasing pressure, but jerk or just pull it instead, you would hit something 20 feet to the right or left of the mark. This was the technique most of us used.

And there wasn't much of a follow-through, like you get from a golf swing, where you fire and contemplate the shot while still aimed at the target. That's because that gun kicks like a mule, and ends up pointed at heaven. It is difficult to use, even for a big man, but many thousands would agree that it's a lovely weapon. The affection that service people have had for this gun is well illustrated in the book and movie, "*We Were Soldiers Once...And Young*," by Lt. Gen. Harold G. Moore (Ret.) and Joseph L. Galloway. This is a true story about a desperate battle fought in Vietnam in 1965. The part of Sergeant Major Basil L. Plumley was masterfully portrayed by actor

Sam Eliott. The Sergeant Major's choice of weapon in battle was the .45 Automatic.

The M1911A1 pistol had kind of a famous quirk: the safety feature. If you don't need the weapon for immediate use, simply do not chamber a round. If you want it "at the ready," chamber a round. The pistol is then cocked, with the hammer back. The thumb safety can then be engaged. If you were not thoroughly familiar with the .45 and well trained on it, unintentional discharges could result. Numerous unintentional discharges were reported annually, and you can imagine that feet and other body parts were damaged. I always wore my .45 with an empty chamber.

I have a friend, let's call him Rob. He was in the Army about the same time I was in the Navy. Not a big guy, he would have made a great lightweight or welterweight boxer. But he could handle a .45. He not only qualified on it, he was a marksman. He was so good at it, his buddies paid him to go down to the range and qualify under their name. Go figure. He was the one in a hundred or a thousand who could actually hit what he was aiming at.

* * *

In our time at OCS we came to realize that everything we did or learned was represented by a box, and that box needed to have a check-mark in it before we could proceed to the next box. It wasn't so much how much information went into our heads, or what percentage of it we could retain, but whether or not we could get by that particular problem or evolution. So when it came down to the quality or quantity of the education we were receiving, we knew after awhile that quantity was what counted most, and that was a little disheartening.

Ask most anyone who went to OCS in those days, what was the main thing they learned there, and they would tell you it was the meaning of the word "ambiguous." *Am big u ous*, adj. 1. having two or more possible meanings 2. not clear, indefinite, uncertain, vague. Whether it was the things we were taught, the orders we were given, or anything else we were exposed to, there always seemed to be at least two ways of looking at it, two or more interpretations. It was very confusing until we caught onto it, and then it was only half as confusing. Try taking a multiple-choice test sometime, where 2 or 3 of the answers could apply! Maybe it was just the way things were done in that society, because the ambiguity continued on into the fleet. That was the reason that I tried very hard to be precise and concise in the way I communicated with my guys aboard ship. I always wanted to leave room for them to use their own judgment, but never to leave them confused and guessing at my intent.

An answer that popped up frequently in multiple-choice was "pelican hook." A pelican hook is supposed to resemble a pelican's head. The "jaw" is a spring-loaded clasp. If the pelican hook is at the end of a wire or line, it can be hooked over a ring, and the clasp snaps closed to keep it from coming loose. They were in wide use in the Navy, and we knew a lot about them. In fact we heard so much about them, we didn't want to know any more. So, it became our own SOP (standard operating procedure) that, when taking a test, regardless of the subject, and didn't know the answer, write down or choose pelican hook. We figured to be correct at least 50% of the time.

* * *

Our weekends were not like they used to be. First of all, we were not allowed off the base for the first six weeks. That meant no social life, and you got to spend weekends with the same ugly mugs you just spent the week with. No women. You see, in those days there were no women at OCS, and consequently no women on ships. In fact, we now know that the leading edge of change then were the few black guys in the battalion. I guess there are women all over the place by now.

I take that back, there was one woman on the base, whom we would see only occasionally, and she was really cute. Drove everyone crazy. She was a WAVE (an old acronym for women in the Navy) and was the Commanding Officer's secretary or personal assistant. Ah, the PERKS (prerequisites) of command!

Anyway, the highlight of our "fun" was the inspection and parade in review (PIR) on Saturday mornings. First came the inspection, where we were to be absolutely perfect in appearance: spotless and wrinkle-less, standing at attention in perfect rows with perfect spacing, eyes straight ahead. I remember the ordeal of getting into "dress whites," which were stiffly starched cotton, one Saturday. The pants were like a board, and to avoid wrinkling them, you had to stand on a chair to put them on. Then, try to march to inspection without bending your knees. We looked like a bunch of robots.

The inspecting officer was normally a full Captain, and most judged the uniform as a whole. But we got to know a few of them who had an abnormal obsession for only certain parts. There were the Hat Man and the Shoe Man.

A classic incident occurred during one inspection. Big Dan Heck was next to me in line, and the Hat Man was several rows away, working his way toward us. Suddenly something went "plop," and Dan let out a string of obscenities under his breath. No one knew what had happened except the guy in back of him, who nearly choked trying to hold back his laughter. A seagull had dive-bombed him, dropping a big gooey one on top of his white hat, which then proceeded to slime down to his collar and down the back of his uniform. So Dan is cursing and the guy behind is dying laughing, and we were all wondering what was going on.

Now here comes the Captain, who stops in front of Dan, inspects him up and down, especially up, and moves on. To his enormous relief, the Captain never noticed the damage because he was average height, and Dan was so tall! Thus began Dan's lifelong vendetta against all seagulls.

The PIR was not so bad. We marched to some great Navy music, which tended to inspire one to march smartly! Past the reviewing stand, with the reviewing officer and the CO of the school. It actually was an impressive show, and was over about noon, then back to King Hall to hit the books and maintain uniforms.

At least, that's how it went for the first six weekends. On the seventh Saturday, at about 1:00 PM, we burst forth from the gates like a plague of locusts. Poor Newport, having to endure this attack of testosterone-laden and alcohol-deprived young gentlemen, all dapper in their dress blues. There were plenty of places to find a drink, but the local ladies were in short supply. In fact, there didn't seem to be any. Between the Naval Base personnel and the civilians, not much was left over. So, like generations of Officer Candidates before us, we looked to the nearby college for girls, Salva Regina, also known by generations of Officer Candidates as "Slippery Vagina." We found some dates from there, me and Ralph and one other, and had a forgettable evening at someone's apartment. But at least we were able to spend time with some females of the opposite sex.

I was more fortunate than most: my step father's friend, Captain Ohlin, besides keeping my car, made me feel welcome at his home anytime. He tended his own lobster traps, so there was always fresh lobster, and his wife Jane and lovely daughter were always nice to me. So I had an escape hatch when I wanted to get away from all those guys.

But there were also great times to be had with the fellas. A group of us went to Boston one weekend to study architecture and history (joke). We learned how to properly pronounce such things as "Harvard Square," and " park your car," and "follow the arrow." That last gave us the biggest problem: one of the guys asked a bartender where the men's room was. He said, "Follow the arrow." But it came out something like, "Fow de aoh," like his mouth was full of marbles. None of us could understand, and our guy asked him 3 times to repeat it. Finally, the barkeep made it simple, pointed, and said, "That way."

We somehow ended up in a downtown dance joint, Dante's Inferno. Huge.

Great rock and roll music. And real girls. I mean good looking girls, and they liked us. It must have been the uniform. Things get a little hazy about the rest of the evening, except that it involved a very pretty blonde, a cold ride out on a country road in her car, and her boyfriend, not necessarily in that order. But all of our guys had a wild night at Dante's Inferno, and I would recommend going, but it probably disappeared long ago.

The Navy sponsored a trip for us to the Mystic, Connecticut Historic Seaport, where, decked out in our dress blues, we visited a replica of an old 4-masted Man O' War, which had a lethal arsenal of 14 guns or so. We milled about smartly for a while, enjoying the old port and paying tribute to all of the "old boys" who had set sail from here so many years ago.

One of our guys' mother owned a house on Cape Cod, and graciously offered it to us for a weekend. A dozen or so of us went, and it changed our environment so much that by the end of the weekend we felt almost human again. The moment we arrived we jumped into swimsuits, except for two of the guys who wore the most outrageously psychedelic beach pants you ever saw. It was enough to make you go blind. (Looking at these pictures now, I am thinking, as my wife would say, how young and cute we were then). Cases of Bud iced down in a wheelbarrow, and we were in business. A nice, sunny day, the water way too cold to swim, it didn't matter, we had a mellow time out of uniform.

In the evening, we did our best to look like civilians, all wearing khaki pants and t-shirts, and went into Provincetown, Mass. Turns out it didn't matter how we looked because the denizens of Provincetown looked so *weird!* First thing we saw was Abraham Lincoln walking toward us, stovepipe hat and all! It seemed everyone was in costume, and we asked what the special occasion was, and were told that there was no occasion, this was a normal Saturday night in P'town. We boys from the provinces now began to have our eyes opened to the rest of the wide, wide world.

* * *

One morning the battalion stood at attention waiting for the Plan of the Day to be read. All of a sudden, one of the fellows dropped like a rock, out cold. (This wasn't that rare: guys had dropped before, usually due to the heat. Or, if you stood at attention for too long and locked your knees, you could cut off blood circulation and down you go). But then another, and then another went down. Pretty soon the field was littered with Officer Candidates and we were ordered to help them to the infirmary. The formation broke up pretty quickly. I was feeling queasy and picked up some anti-nausea and anti-diarrhea pills, but lost it both ways. Several times.

It turned out that food poisoning had been served for breakfast. There had been a green tint to the bacon rind that morning, and it smelled a little off, but I and most others had eaten it anyway. My opinion of the food in general had gone downhill since the first few days of school, so much so that my portions had been getting smaller and smaller. With this episode, I stopped eating food altogether. I and many others went to the only alternative: ice cream. Three meals a day of ice cream. It came in those little red and white, oblong cardboard cartons, Carnation brand, I think, and my favorites were chocolate and the triple vanilla/strawberry/chocolate. You had to fight to get there first but it was worth the ordeal. I had weighed 145 lbs. since I could remember, but under this diet plan I ballooned to 164 lbs. All of the excess weight came off as soon as I left OCS.

* * *

One day I got a call from a friend at home, telling me that my friend Kay had died. We had dated in high school and college. She was so pretty, small with dark hair and perfect porcelain skin, a beautiful little figure, and so feminine. She was a sweet girl, and we always had a loving and laughing relationship.

For some time she had been treated for Hodgkins Disease, then called the "young man's disease." The cobalt treatments had been hard on her, and left a dry white patch of skin, about the size of a silver dollar, just below the hollow of her throat. I had no idea things had gotten so dangerous for her, and I was really brought down by the news.

She had been married for a short time, to *Bobby*. In college I was not ready for marriage and she was, I'm sure to get away from her parents (they made her cry a lot). So she became engaged to *Bobby*. I asked her once what was so good about him, and after thinking for a minute, she replied, "Well, he's a good dancer." (We were all so young then). I knew the marriage would be a short one, and it was, and deep down I had had some thoughts of a future with her.

Later in life I lost another beautiful girl, Mickey, to Hodgkins Disease. I hope they are no longer calling it the young man's disease.

* * *

One evening in April it was announced over the PA system in King Hall, that Martin Luther King had been killed in Memphis, Tennessee. Killed by a white man named James Earl Ray. Immediately on hearing this news, and in a knee jerk reaction I jumped up and yelled, "Yahoo" several times. And the silence I received as an answer shut me up right now, and I stopped my antics in hot-faced embarrassment.

It gave me pause to think. Our black Officer Candidate, Mr. Hayes, whom I had grown to like, lived down the passageway. I very much hoped that he hadn't heard my outburst, as I didn't want to hurt his feelings.

It was a little confusing for me. Growing up in Houston, I had worked beside black people since my early teens. In junior high school, one of the few Latinos there was my friend, Mike Carillo. I have mentioned our mammy, Ermagene Russell, who was as much a part of our family as we were of hers. From her we learned the goodness and graciousness and dignity that a human being could be capable of. As a consequence, I really had nothing at all against black people, or Latino people, or anyone else. (I do remember, though, hearing so much about Martin Luther King, that he was a troublemaker and lightning rod for violence).

But I could turn right around and go out with my friends and use the "N" word and the "S" word (for Latinos), all day long and not think about it. Sounds strange, I know, but that's the way things were then. I was still young and ignorant about many things.

In college I became close friends with a Latino, Mario Silva, and learned that if all these people were as intelligent and good and downright silly as he was, what's the problem? At the same time, there were no black people at my college, and only one hippy with long hair (who received a haircut courtesy of the football team).

So by the time I got to OCS, I had received very mixed signals about different peoples and diversity and racism. And that day in April 1968 was the real beginning of my education. My years in the Navy completed that education.

* * *

In June of 1968, Senator Robert F. Kennedy was shot dead after a speech in a Los Angeles hotel. Word spread through OCS like wildfire. So much was going on in the outside world, it was hard to keep up. We weren't directly affected by this event except that Tim disappeared from school around the time of RFK's funeral. You might remember his father was a congressman from the Boston area.

Well, the evening he got back, he asked if we could speak in private. I said sure, and went down to his room. He closed the door and said, "I just need to talk to someone about this, and since your step father is an Admiral, you will understand." He knew that our conversation wouldn't go past his door. (I don't think that Tim would mind my relating this story 40 years hence).

It turns out his family were very close to the Kennedys, and that he had, indeed, gone to the family gathering and then the funeral. He proceeded to tell me about people that the rest of us just read about or see on TV. He told me about different members of the family, and how torn up they were about this death. Tim was very saddened just by being around them, they took it so hard. He was still very shaken from the experience.

But Tim, being Tim, could not help but find something funny in all this. During the actual burial, he and his family were at graveside. Now, as an Officer Candidate, he had to attend in dress uniform. Our uniform was identical to that of regular line officers, with two exceptions: the hat insignia had a gold anchor rather than the eagle and shield, and there were large gold anchors on the lapels rather than gold stripes on the sleeves. In other words, one look at Tim and you knew that he was a just a lowly Officer Candidate, if you were in the Navy. And there were Navy men there, all right. From graveside, Tim was looking over the crowd, and turned around to see all of the top Admirals in the Navy, who had to stand behind a rope, some distance away. And they were all glaring at him, lowly Officer Candidate Tim at graveside. He said he gulped and turned crimson and turned back around, avoiding eye contact, feeling the heat on his back, along with the darts and arrows. And yes, he said that if looks could kill, he would now be a former Officer Candidate.

* * *

Finally, time began to get short as we approached graduation day. We had been tested so much that our Cumulative Scores now became very important. There came a point where you could "cume out," in other words, your total score had surpassed that required for graduation. Some of the brighter guys cumed out early and could have coasted the rest of the way, but no one did. It took me somewhat longer, but I finally was able to relax and enjoy things a little more.

Actually, I was under more pressure than anyone else because it had been announced that Admiral Edwin J. Zimmermann would be the Reviewing Officer for graduation, and would speak and administer the oath to the new officers. Gee, what a coincidence! Not only that, but my mother and grandparents would be there, too. So it would behoove me to actually graduate.

One of the guys in my section, George, was a study in human nature, the wrong kind. Early on, when he had discovered that my step father was an Admiral, he had arrogantly told me, "That doesn't impress me, not at all." Actually I couldn't have cared less if it impressed him or not. But now that it was announced that he would be our Reviewing Officer, all of that arrogance fell away and he almost begged me, "Can I meet him, can I meet him?" I thought, sure, George, I'll arrange it right away. I just hate it when that happens.

About this time our company officer, Lt. Salemi, got orders for transfer. When we asked him where he was going, he said, "I gotta go babysit the fucking gooks." This from the guy who had preached to us about respecting our allies and not making fun of them. Another case of "do as I say, not as I do." That kind of thing was better than learning from a textbook about good leadership.

We were ordered to fill out a "dream sheet" with our first three choices of duty station after graduation. The top performers automatically got their first choice, the rest of us could only keep our fingers crossed. My first choice was Destroyer-West Coast, and the other two were inconsequential, including a chance for the White House to grab me for their staff. Destroyer-West Coast translated into Vietnam duty.

I knew my first choice was a long shot (that's supposed to be funny), but guess what? On the big day we fought each other to get to the bulletin board to see what the future held for us. I ran my finger down the list, and there it was:

"Randall Gray Cook   USS Bridget (DE-1024)   San Diego Communications."

Actually seeing it in print really gave me a thrill! My orders package said I was being sent to Communications Officer School in San Diego, then on to the Bridget, which was slated to leave soon for Vietnam. That suited me right down to the ground.

Close to graduation now, and we hear that two of our guys didn't make it, both good people. Everyone felt pretty bad about it, and each of us made it a point to drop by and say goodbye and shake hands for the last time. They would go immediately to basic training and enter the fleet as enlisted men. No shame in that, except that they had worked very hard to be officers.

* * *

Rear Admiral Edwin J. Zimmermann was so pleased! To have his step son become a U.S. Naval Officer was almost more than he could take. He loved the Navy and was most interested in the development of its young officers. He had gone to the trouble of arranging to be Reviewing Officer, just so he could be there. And he brought my mother and grandparents along so they could see their boy at an important moment in his life. It was very touching.

He had also arranged with the school's Commanding Officer, that he would swear me in, in a private ceremony before any of the official ceremonies started. The C.O. graciously loaned the use of his office for this, and he, my family, and a Navy photographer witnessed my crossing into manhood. Zim held a bible in his left hand, and read from a paper he held in his right. I placed my left hand on the bible and raised my right. As he read to me the oath I was swearing to uphold, there was a sort of crackling sound in the room and no one could figure out what it was. But I and my mother caught it at the same time. Admiral Zimmermann, commander of ships and men, was so nervous that his hands were shaking and the paper was rattling! I guess he was about to bust his buttons with pride.

After I was officially an Ensign in the United States Navy, he presented me with a brand-new Hilborn-Hamburger Navy Sword, the finest in the world, made of Toledo steel and absolutely beautiful. Many pictures were taken in the office and in front of Nimitz Hall. My family were so proud.

I am sitting here looking at these pictures and thinking that all four of those wonderful people are gone now. But they are part of me and what I am, and so they will never be forgotten. I have come across an official Navy photograph of Zim shaking my hand, congratulating me just after he swore me in. My mother had sent it to my grandmother with a note, which she closed with the words, "Life is good." Oh, my, my, my.

An hour or two later we did a Parade in Review for the Admiral. It was a beautiful sunny day, the band played well, and our marching was superb! He presented a certificate to the top graduate, a tall guy who already looked like he had the makings of a lifer. We then went back to the dorms to change uniform for the graduation ceremony.

We all had a seat, everyone both nervous and happy at the same time. I happened to sit just behind Warn Dold and his wife Kitty, my old school chum from Houston. We hugged and kissed and she told me how handsome I looked, and I told her how cute she still was, and I wasn't kidding. As usual, Zim gave a stirring speech in his booming baritone, and left the audience impressed and highly motivated to go to the fleet. He then administered the oath to everyone but me, and pronounced us the newest Ensigns in the Navy. And thus, the ceremony, and Officer Candidate School, came to an end. We did not toss our hats in the air, leaving that to the Annapolis boys.

We did continue one tradition, though. The old Chiefs had advised us to carry a silver dollar in our pocket, to be given to the first enlisted man who salutes the brand new officer. There seemed to be a gaggle of young enlisted guys waiting for us as we exited, one of whom gave me a snappy salute. As I returned my first salute, I laughed and he laughed, and as I handed him my silver dollar, he said, "Congratulations, sir."

Back to King Hall for the last time, no more marching, thank you, to finish packing and *change into civilian clothes!* We had said our goodbyes over the last few days, and all of us were so happy that there were no sad moments in leaving each other, brothers all, after having endured so much together. We were different men, now. I changed into jeans, cowboy boots, and my old cutoff college sweatshirt, turned inside out. There was but one thing left to do, and that was to deal with the hated boonies!

Remember, the boondockers were the black boots that had become one with our feet. There were so many layers of the shiny spray varnish on them, they weighed about 5 lbs. apiece. I took one, turned it upside down, and smashed it over a bedpost. It shattered like a pane of glass. We got to laughing and I smashed the other one as my roommate smashed his. We both had to clean up the mess, throw it away along with the boonies, say goodbye, and leave OCS in the rearview mirror, headed for a new life.

Fort Omaha

I was in such a daze induced by the sudden freedom, that my next conscious thought after leaving Newport was of driving down the Garden State Parkway in New Jersey, headed for Fort Omaha in Nebraska. My parents were stationed there; imagine the Navy in Omaha. He was now Deputy Commander, Naval Reserve Training Command. They welcomed me home to Quarters 15 in grand fashion, along with their faithful steward, Fellino Torres, and Schnapps the wiener dog.

The respite from the Navy was to be short, as I was to report for duty on the west coast in one week. So I was looking forward to sleeping late and lounging around and enjoying being home. But no such luck, as I was requested by Admiral Zimmermann to "report" for luncheon the next day, in uniform, that there would be senior officers present along with a dignitary. I said to myself, "Uh, oh." At the appointed time I donned the uniform and, looking in the mirror, couldn't help but notice the one little ribbon, nicknamed the "geedunk," that they give you for just breathing. And the lonely little Ensign's gold stripe on the cuff.

I went downstairs, stopped outside the door of the formal dining room to take a couple of deep breaths, and walked in. It was as I had feared. I have never seen so much gold in one room. There were four Admirals and three Captains, not to mention the Assistant Secretary of Defense for Reserve Affairs.

Their uniforms were covered with gold up one arm and down the other, not to mention their fruit salad that extended from the collarbone down to the belt line. These were professional military officers who had cut their teeth during World War II. They had all been out there and back, and then some. And sitting down to lunch with them made me feel like a pipsqueak.

I suppose they guessed how they would have felt in my place, and engaged me in conversation as an (almost) equal, asking about OCS and my new duty station. (I always had the feeling, when talking to very senior officers, that they would gladly give up some of those stripes just to get back into a war zone). And Admiral "Ace" Parker began pulling my leg by telling me that in his day, they used Ensigns as ballast in the motor whaleboat.

He also told a story on himself, when he was a young fighter pilot making his first takeoff from a carrier. In those days there was just a straight-ahead flight deck, not a second, angled deck like today. So Ensign Parker revved up his engine, got the go-ahead for takeoff, powered down the deck, lifted off, flamed out, and crashed into the sea right in front of the oncoming carrier. The speeding ship missed him. But he said they had to talk to him for a *long* time before he got back into the cockpit. I guess that worked out because he had a long and distinguished career in Naval Air.

If this luncheon weren't enough for a green Ensign, the next evening my presence was requested for a dinner party at Quarters 1, home of Admiral George Muse, Commander, Naval Reserve Training Command. I liked Admiral Muse; he was a quiet, dignified, very impressive man. I was again in uniform and let me tell you, I ended up sitting down for dinner at a card table, and seated across from me was the very famous four-star General Bruce K. Holloway, Commander in Chief, Strategic Air Command! He didn't crack a smile all night.

After these really humbling experiences I was more than ready to head for San Diego, where I could again associate with my own kind: the lowly Ensigns I would meet at Communications School. Prior to my departure, my step father sat down with me and we talked about the Navy. He didn't preach to me, just gave some very good advice. The one thing he said that I appreciated a number of times during my "career" in ships was, *never underestimate the power of the sea!* How very true that was.

Note: As young officers in WWII, these heroes made their mark as follows:

Admiral Edelen "Ace" Parker flew off of the famed carrier USS Wasp and the USS Manila Bay. Won the Air Medal for actions against Japanese forces on Sakashimo Gunto.

Admiral "Zim" Zimmermann, as gunnery officer of the USS Ault (DD-698), was commended by Commander Destroyer Force, Pacific Fleet, for defense of his ship and those in the Task Force against multiple Japanese Kamikaze attacks.

Admiral George Muse, in destroyers, took part in the battles of Coral Sea, Guadalcanal, Leyte Gulf, Surigao Straits, and many others.

General Bruce K. Holloway was a fighter pilot with the famed "Flying Tigers" in China, where he earned status as a fighter ace by shooting down 13 Japanese planes.

32nd *Street*

I flew out to San Diego and went right to the famous 32nd Street BOQ (Bachelor Officer Quarters), which would be my home until I joined the USS Bridget. There are many good memories associated with my stay there.

Next day I reported to the Fleet Training Center, and began the Communications Officer course. During the 5 or 6 weeks there, I made friends with an Ensign named Donald Murphy. We palled around some, having dinner or a drink once in awhile. Murphy was also going out to WestPac (Western Pacific) on a destroyer, and little did we know under what tragic circumstances we would later meet on the other side of the world.

There was another guy in class, with thinning blond hair, gold rimmed glasses, and not a lick of common sense. But he was very funny and we hit it off right away. One Saturday we were sitting around the BOQ not doing anything in particular except lamenting the fact that neither of us had a car. All of a sudden we had a revelation, "Let's go buy some cars!" So we went to a nearby lot, one of those that just loves to see young officers and sailors come in, and bought cars. I got a real nice little Alfa Romeo convertible, black with rolled red naugahyde seats. A real beauty and in the long run, one of the worst buys of my life. My friend bought a beautiful 50's Mercedes convertible. After completing the deals, we headed out of the used car lot, and I followed him back toward the BOQ. The silly bastard was so enamored of his new wheels, he was looking all around the cockpit of his new car and not watching the road, drifted across the center line and nearly had a head-on collision. He looked up just in time to swerve back into his own lane with screeching tires and a lot of smoke, and I am sure, scared the life out of one San Diego citizen.

In those days you could drive along the waterfront and see long rows of mothballed ships, including some aircraft carriers. I never liked seeing those big beautiful ships just sitting there, doing nothing. If you wanted to go over to Coronado Island, which is across the bay from San Diego, you had to take the ferry. (Later, the bay bridge was built, and another small bit of charm was lost forever). Anyway, on the trip over, you would see the old USS Bunker Hill (CV-17), a carrier in her permanent berth on the other side. She was just two years old when, in 1945, she was hit by two 500 lb. bombs dropped by Japanese planes. Besides exacting a terrible toll on the crew, one of the bombs bent her keel so badly that it was not repairable. So she became a testing platform for electronics and other things. (Her official history reads a little differently, but this is what the common knowledge was at the time).

Sometimes going over, you would see a cruiser parked near the ferry terminal. It was a very large ship, and served as flagship for one of the major commands in San Diego at the time. I saw the USS Oklahoma City (CLG-91) there several times, and she was a real beauty. One time, going over, I saw what I thought was the Oklahoma City or one of her sisters, in the normal berth. But when we came even with the ship's bow, I looked again to see that she was as fat as a football field, and her 16-inch guns looked like the Holland Tunnel! It was the USS New Jersey (BB-62), which had been re-commissioned for Vietnam duty. She was a big, big ship. Her sheer size took your breath away, and everyone on the ferry said, "Oh my God!" almost in unison. (Later on, when I was serving in the Tonkin Gulf, word was that the New Jersey had been bombarding a target on an offshore island, and her massive guns rained down projectiles the size of a Cadillac until the island just disappeared. Completely. She had incredible firepower).

There was a reason I went to Coronado so much, and that was the Mexican Village. The Mexican Village was known far and wide among Navy officers and young ladies as being one of the best "body exchanges" on earth, along with McCrud's in San Diego. You could go out there on a Saturday or Sunday afternoon, hang out on the large open-air patio, get zonked on beer or tequila, and most likely meet the girl of your dreams. I did, several times.

McCrud's, as it is affectionately known, is in reality the MCRD, or Marine Corps Recruit Depot. It was a much larger version of the Mexican Village, and hosted a dance on weekends. If you couldn't score at McCrud's, you couldn't score at all. There is a nice memory of a really lovely redhead taking me home in her '55 Buick on a chilly San Diego night. In those days, youth wasn't necessarily wasted on the young.

At any rate, regardless of the great social scene there, I had a lot of homework to do, and was quite serious about learning all I could at Comm School, and finished 12th out of a class of 30. Once class ended, I bade farewell to my new friends and went back to the BOQ to wait a couple of weeks before I could join the Bridget. She was out operating somewhere. To fill my time, the Navy used me for various small tasks, and then gave me an assignment that was a real eye opener: *shore patrol*.

This, I felt, was my first real job as an officer. The assignment was to cruise the establishments in the sailor bar district. Things could get pretty rough there sometimes, and the bars were rough themselves. An obviously new and inexperienced Ensign wouldn't have lasted two minutes there, but bless the Navy, they assigned me a great big Chief for protection, I mean as my teammate. He was a black man, nice as he could be, and at 6'2" or 6'3" and 225 lbs. or so, was a formidable guy. When we got out on the streets, his demeanor changed and you could tell that he was a professional and had cracked a few heads with that nightstick he carried. No one gave us any trouble in some pretty mean places.

Finally, the day came for me to pack up, say goodbye to everyone, and head over to meet my new ship. I went with some trepidation but a lot of excitement.

USS Bridget

It was a beautiful, sunny morning in San Diego when I first set eyes on the USS Bridget (DE-1024), all 314 feet of her. She was over 10 years old by then, but looked like she just came off the ways: so neat and clean you could eat off of her decks. I checked in at the quarterdeck and was escorted to see the Executive Officer.

The XO was a nice guy, checking my records and welcoming me to the ship. I was to be the Assistant Communications Officer, and normally would bunk in "officers' country" with the rest of the wardroom. But the ship was presently over its complement of officers, so I was assigned a bunk in one of the Chiefs' quarters, way down below near the stern, until things were sorted out. No problem for me. I was just happy to be there.

Then he dropped the bombshell on me: the Navy had just notified the Bridget and the rest of her division, that there would be no Vietnam cruise, that they were being reassigned to the Reserve Training Fleet, my step father's operation, and would be making a Permanent Change of Station (PCS) to Seattle, Washington. My heart sank, and my face must have also, because the XO asked me if I wanted to stay aboard. He explained that if I wanted to leave, he understood, and it would not reflect badly on my record. He also requested that I not make a decision now, but notify him of my intention in 24 hours. I guess I already knew what that would be, but I said, "Yes, sir," saluted and left.

The Bridget was a destroyer escort (DE), meaning she was built for escort duty. For this reason, she was not very fast, with a flank (maximum) speed of only 27 knots. Also, she did not have very much firepower with her 3" guns. She did have a good ASW capability. But for duty in the Gulf of Tonkin, on the gun line, you needed heavier, 5" guns for shore bombardment and gunfire support, and on Yankee Station you had to keep up with the fast carriers for plane guard and other duties. She could do neither and therefore the mission had been scrubbed.

I met the guys in the wardroom and they were really a good bunch. Laid back, friendly, helpful to the new guy, and, I was to find out, very competent. The Captain was the same way, in fact these officers were so impressive that I formed the mistaken impression that all wardrooms were of this caliber. I was very young then, of course.

I was shown to my quarters so I could unpack and get squared away, and met my bunkmate, Chief Electrician's Mate Phil Hess. Chief Hess and I liked each other right away. He had a world of problems on his plate at the time, and without my realizing it, he became the first Navy man that I ever gave counsel to. He certainly wasn't the last. His problems all stemmed from the breakup of his marriage. His personal life was a mess, and he was drinking and eating too much.

I knew he had a weight problem the first night we turned in. The bunks were stacked one on top of the other, and were made of canvas that was lashed to a metal frame with webbing all around. Mine was the bottom bunk, and the Chief stretched that poor canvas so far, it nearly touched the tip of my nose. I thought that if it ever gave way I would be crushed to death.

The next day I knocked on the XO's door and requested transfer to a DD (destroyer) that was going to WestPac. He was very nice in saying that he wished that I would stay, but said he would put the papers through right away. Meanwhile I was to act as Assistant Communications Officer, familiarize myself with the ship, and stand regular watches.

It was only a matter of days before new orders came through, transferring me to the USS Herbert J. Thomas (DD-833) as Prospective Communications Officer. The XO explained that I would have to ride the Bridget up to Seattle before detaching, but that would give me the chance to stand some watches underway. I had begun standing in-port watches as Officer of the Deck on the quarterdeck, and was beginning to tune in to the rhythm of life on a ship. And my first watch underway as Junior Officer of the Deck (JOOD) would prove to be one I would never forget!

The day came when the four DE's got underway for Seattle. Since this was a PCS, some of the officers brought aboard personal gear for the move. That included the Captain of one of the other ships, who also brought along his rather high-strung little dog.

Things were uneventful on the cruise up the California coast. The water was pretty calm and I found it was easy to get used to the movement of the ship. My very first watch was to be the mid-watch (midnight to 4:00 AM) as we entered the waters off of Oregon. I now know that the Continental Shelf along this coast is almost flat and very narrow. If an ordinary storm should blow in here, the flat and relatively shallow bottom multiplies its effects and makes it a very hazardous place to be. And as we were sailing within eyesight of the coast, over this Continental Shelf, I was about to learn what my step father Zim meant when he said, "Never underestimate the power of the sea."

The ship's movement began to change as the storm blew in. By the time I went on watch we were beginning to roll a bit but it was nothing serious. But during my four hours on the bridge, the weather and the sea turned violent. The Officer of the Deck (OOD) handled the ship well, and I did everything he asked me to while holding on to whatever I could.

The ship began to take some pretty bad rolls, and you could hear things crashing to the deck down below. The surface radar showed that the four ships were able to keep formation on one another, but not without having to work at it. She then began to "pound." A destroyer-type ship could slice through a sea of heavy swells, or waves, with its sharp bow, giving you an up-and-down motion, and that is called pounding, or pitching. Old destroyermen describe the movement as "over one (swell) and under two." Well, as the bow rose and then thrust down into the sea, it began to feel as if we were running into a brick wall. And that meant that solid water, called green water, was coming up over the bows and slamming into structures on the main deck. This could get serious because you now begin taking damage.

And then the unbelievable happened: we took green water on the bridge! I'm telling you that you could see solid green water smashing into the windows. It hit us like a train wreck and made the same crashing sound. The OOD slipped and fell, hit his head on a "navigator's ball" and dropped unconscious to the deck.

So, here I am, a new Ensign standing his first watch at sea, in the middle of a violent storm, the ship taking damage, and the OOD out cold on the deck. Now I did what any new JOOD would do in that situation, and that was to go directly to the PA system, punch the button and say, "Uh, Captain to the bridge, please, Captain to the bridge."

The Captain appeared in moments, in his bathrobe, and took the deck and the conn. The OOD came to in 3 or 4 minutes, and there was no permanent damage, just a good-sized lump on his head. I managed to finish the watch and then went straight down to my bunk and hit the sack, uniform and all. I had not gotten sick during the wild ride, but I was feeling a little nauseous.

No sooner had my head gratefully hit the pillow, than the door opened and in came the Engineering Officer, smoking a big cigar. He sat down and very affably asked how I liked my first watch, and made the most inane conversation while puffing on that damn cigar. He was enjoying the moment, watching the new boy turn different shades of green. He finally said, "Well, get some sleep, I just wanted to check and see if you were all right." I had been much better before his friendly visit. (The Navy has many rituals, and this is one of them, to fool with the new Ensign's mind when it comes to getting seasick. This guy was good at it, and on my next ship I was able to observe one of the true masters of the art).

The day dawned nice and bright with only gentle swells. We had indeed taken some damage, with smashed gun tubs (circular armor plate around .50 caliber machine gun positions), bent or missing stanchions (steel posts) and railings, and either twisted or missing antennae. The other ships reported almost identical damage, and one reported injury to property unique in Naval history. That was the one whose Captain had brought along his dog. During the storm the Captain had locked the dog in his cabin, as he needed to be either on the bridge or in his ready room, adjacent to the bridge.

Evidently, when the ship started rolling and pounding, it scared the hell out of the poor dog, who went ballistic and in a frenzy, started running around the cabin, shitting all over the place, tearing apart all of the bedding, ripping apart uniforms, peeing everywhere, and running through all of this stuff again and again, spreading it everywhere. When the Captain was able to return and opened the door, he thought a grenade had gone off in there, and the stench nearly knocked him down. One thing he said later, he couldn't believe how high up the walls the dog's paw prints went. He must have really been terrorized! With counseling, the dog made a nice recovery, and I'll bet they had to hose down that stateroom.

We arrived in Seattle without further incident, and delivered the ship to her new home. I was on board for another week or so before my detachment, and was privileged to witness a formal burial at sea. A retired Navy man had requested it, and one of the other ships took him out, with us in company. Out into Puget Sound, we watched the solemn ceremony, and saw the old sailor, who was sewn into a weighted canvas bag, slip from under the flag and into the sea. The only way I can describe it is that it was quite lovely.

I was on the Bridget for only 40 days. In that time I had made a real friend in Chief Hess. His attitude had brightened, and he had cut way back on his drinking. As we parted, he promised again about the drinking, and said that he was getting help and support from the other Chiefs. He, too, was detaching soon for a WestPac destroyer, and gave me the name and hull number in case we should run across each other "over there." It turned out to be the same ship as my friend Murphy had gone to, so I asked the Chief to give him my regards.

With some reluctance I said goodbye to a fine group of officers, and for the second time, headed for San Diego to meet a new ship, this time the USS Herbert J. Thomas.

Note: A knot is a measure of speed at sea, equal to one nautical mile (approximately 2,000 yards) per hour, or about 1.15 statute miles per hour.

Note: I have always been amazed that the windows on the bridge were able to withstand such a blow without giving way. It would be interesting to know the pounds per square inch that were exerted on them. The windows were approximately 40 feet above the water line. In succeeding ships I always checked the thickness and soundness of the bridge windows before going on first watch.

Note: The "navigator's balls" are two black iron balls, about the size of a large grapefruit, set on either side of the magnetic compass to protect the compass from being influenced by the steel of the ship around it. They were (and are) a source of much fun at sea, as periodically a brand-new sailor would appear on the bridge to polish the navigator's balls as ordered.

USS Herbert J. Thomas

By now I was getting used to reporting aboard a new ship, so I didn't feel like such a neophyte when I arrived at the USS Herbert J. Thomas (DD-833). She was good-looking, though she was much older than the Bridget, with the classic lines of the WW II destroyer. I reported to the quarterdeck, and was escorted to see the XO.

Not knowing anything about the ship, I was surprised to enter the superstructure through a large stainless steel revolving door, rather than a standard hatchway. The interior was cool and comfortable, and as I walked up the passageway, a huge apparition appeared in the form of Big Dan Heck, my good friend from OCS. We both laughed out loud and gave each other a bear hug, and despite my newly cracked ribs, I continued on to the XO's cabin.

Lieutenant Commander Roger Aydt greeted me and gave me a talk about the ship, the officers and the crew. He was slender, with piercing blue eyes, a military bearing and a friendly manner. He told me I would be the Assistant Communications Officer under Lt. Britton, eventually relieving him to become Communications Officer.

The ship was slated for a WestPac cruise, but not before we went through a scheduled overhaul in Long Beach, got a new

Commanding Officer, and completed a rigorous round of Refresher Training. So my trip to Southeast Asia was coming, but not for a while yet.

LCDR Aydt took me across the passageway to the wardroom where we found Jon Britton, my new boss. The wardroom was not so spacious, with a dining table (equipped with a raised rim for catching food in heavy seas) that seated ten, an alcove that seated four or five for social time, and the galley at the far end, behind the Captain's chair. I would eventually learn that if casualties were ever taken during battle, the wardroom would double as an operating room, and our dining table would become the operating table. Bon Appetit!

Jon turned out to be a good guy, knowledgeable in his job, thoroughly relaxed, and very funny. While we were talking, he popped one of those square red nicotine tablets into his mouth, saying that he was trying to quit smoking. Before he finished the tablet, he lit up, explaining that at first, he would take a tablet, smoke cigarettes in between, take another tablet, smoke more cigarettes, etc., etc. Since nothing seemed to be happening, he made matters simpler by just doing both at the same time. I don't think he was following the instructions so well.

Anyway, after talking for a while, he took me to meet our boss, the Operations Department Officer, Lt. Norm Davis. Norm looked like Mr. Clean without the earring. He was built compact and muscular like a Sherman tank, his short-sleeved shirt fairly splitting at the seams over his biceps. On his left forearm was a large tattoo. He also had a shaved head, and the whole effect was quite intimidating.

Norm was a "mustang," an officer who came from the enlisted ranks. This gave him an unusual perspective on the Navy, and automatically put him in good stead with the enlisted guys on board. In my first meeting with him I decided he was a guy that you didn't want to fool with, but also seemed genial and a real professional. Over the time we served together, those first impressions evolved into real admiration for one of the finest officers I have ever known.

I was now given over to one of the other Ensigns for a tour of the ship. The Herbert J. Thomas was commissioned in 1945, and was named for a Marine Sergeant who was awarded the Congressional Medal of Honor, posthumously, for falling on a grenade to save his comrades' lives in 1942. The Thomas was fast, with 60,000 shaft horsepower, highly maneuverable, and had plenty of firepower. She displaced 3,100 tons of water, was 390' long, 42' wide at the beam, and had a draft of 19', in other words, that's how deep she rode in the water.

For armament she had two dual 5" 38 caliber gun mounts, an anti-submarine rocket (ASROC) missile launcher with nuclear capability, and six torpedo tubes. There had once been a third 5" gun mount but that was gone now. In the armory were .50 caliber machine guns, automatic rifles and .45 caliber pistols. When I reported aboard she also had an unmanned Drone Anti-Submarine Helicopter (DASH) system.

The Thomas had another system, making her unique in the fleet, the Shipboard Toxicological Operational Protective System, or STOPS. This was installed during a 1964 overhaul period, as an experiment in Cold War defenses. Everyone at the time was concerned with Atomic, Biological and Chemical (ABC) Warfare, so she became a floating laboratory. STOPS was designed to make the interior of the ship an air-tight envelope to protect personnel from any contaminants in the outside air. Air was drawn into the system through special filters and driven through huge air conditioners to the inside of the ship at a pressure of plus-3 or 4 lbs. per square inch. Due to this positive pressure, no infected air could enter the ship through cracks in the superstructure, so no contamination could find its way inside. STOPS turned a surface ship into a submarine, a closed environment, with access to and from the outside only through two revolving doors, one forward and one aft. The 5" gun mount that had been located directly in front of the bridge, had been removed to make space for filters and air conditioning units.

The ship had served her country well since 1945. She made three deployments to the Korean war zone and earned six battle stars there. She generated some excitement, when, on radar picket duty she detected a flight of unidentified aircraft and reported them to a group of Corsair fighter planes from the USS Valley Forge, who happened to be passing overhead. In the ensuing air battle a "North Korean" plane was knocked down, and the Thomas recovered the body of a *Russian* pilot. They were also involved in another action, of which crews of combatant ships can only dream. On May 11, 1952, while doing shore bombardment on Wonsan Harbor, she was taken under fire by shore batteries. In the ensuing gun duel she took one hit, but with no casualties. By the time I joined her crew, the Thomas had already made three tours to the Vietnam war zone.

During my tours of the ship and at meals. I began to meet the rest of the officers, including the Captain, Commander W. J. Kennedy. He was an energetic, straightforward guy whom, you could tell, was held in high regard by everyone, both officers and enlisted. I was in luck again, as the Captain and XO were both so impressive. Of course I already knew Dan, and the other guys welcomed me aboard, and all were helpful to me in getting used to the ship's routine. Over the next 18 months I would learn just how well a wardroom could work together. We all drew very close to one another, as is inevitable.

My living quarters were right next to the wardroom, in "officers' country." There were four bunks, again with high rails to prevent your rolling out of the sack in heavy weather. I also had a fold up desk with a safe, and a locker for my things.

Even in the lowly world of Ensigns, there is, or was, a hierarchy. I found that I was the Junior Ensign, as opposed to the Senior, or "Bull" Ensign. Dan Heck was now Bull Ensign, even though I was technically senior to him by a couple of hours, he was senior to me on this ship. Anyway, the Bull passed on to me the unenviable task of polishing the massive ashtray in the alcove, which was made from a brass 8" shell casing from a cruiser. That thing took 2 hours to polish and weighed a ton! Other Junior tasks surfaced when, around a group of officers, some SLJ (shitty little job) needed doing. In fact, the Junior Ensign was also known as the SLJ Officer.

During morning Officers' Call and Crew Call, and as Jon Britton showed me around, I began to meet the 40 or so enlisted guys in the Communications Division. Foremost among these was the division Leading Petty Officer, Signalman 1st Class George Faust. My luck was still holding, as Faust was well liked and respected by the entire crew for his proficiency as a Petty Officer and as a Signalman. And he had one other attribute: he took me under his wing and taught me the Navy, taught me about handling men, and taught me how to run a division. I have always put it this way, that when I went into OCS I didn't know anything, and after I graduated I still didn't know anything. The learning came on the ship.

Every new Ensign, whether out of OCS or the Naval Academy, needs a George Faust. I feel sorry for those who never had one. George gave me the education I needed, while somehow letting me feel that I was running things. He was a genius. And when it came to the point where I *was* running things, our relationship didn't change one iota. Though we always went by the book in our dealings, we developed a great mutual respect and genuine fondness for each other.

Our "gang" consisted of Signalmen and Radiomen. Plus, I had administrative control of the Quartermasters, Yeomen, Personnelmen and Postal Clerk, who, operationally, worked for the XO. But my work was centered on the radio room and the signal bridge. I couldn't have asked for a better bunch of guys. Most of them were just kids, who were led and taught by the most professional Petty Officers. I did not have one person with an attitude; well, maybe one or two. But I suppose every entity does. One reason the division performed so well, though, was that it was such a cohesive group.

The radio shack, or Radio I, was located up in the superstructure, handy to the bridge. And the Signal Bridge with its signals shack, flag bags and signal lamps, was out behind the bridge, in the open. Faust got me familiar with all of our spaces, including our crews' berthing area. It was pretty good-sized, with the familiar racks stacked one on top of the other, down both sides of the space, and a locker for each sailor. I toured the crews' mess as well as our Auxiliary Radio Room, used if Radio I were knocked out, and our storage spaces.

The radiomen checked me out on bridge communications, the various radiotelephone (R/T) sets up there, and while I was looking and listening, I checked to see how thick the window glass was. It was very thick. Little did I realize the thousands of hours I would spend here during my stay on the Thomas.

The bridge was unusually big for a destroyer, very wide. It looked like it belonged on a cruiser. The reason, as was for most of the abnormalities of this ship, was the STOPS system. A normal bridge was smaller, with a "wing" on either end where you could walk outside and use your binoculars or check a compass reading, or whatever. STOPS negated any open-air activities, so the bridge was expanded and the wings disappeared. To compensate for visual loss, a large plastic bubble was placed in the overhead where each of the wings had been, and you climbed up into it on a ladder for a look around. As you might imagine, these bubbles were the source of many jokes about the Thomas around the fleet.

There is an old saying in the Navy, "If it doesn't move, paint it." Well, nothing much moved on this bridge so everything had been painted gray. Including all of the brass fixtures that made a ship truly beautiful. Fewer things to polish, I guess. There was also a lot of fancy woodwork that had been added during the last overhaul period. Very pretty, you could put your coffee cup on it or lean on it or just look at it, but if you ever took a shell or gunfire to the bridge, everyone would be skewered by splintering wood.

As Communications Officer, I was responsible for all message traffic coming to, and leaving the ship, whether by telecommunications, radio/telephone (voice), signal lamp, signal flags, semaphore, and in emergency, telegraph key. I had to make sure all of the equipment and men were in perfect working order. This included the implementation of the brand-new Preventive Maintenance System (PMS).

Other than Communications, there was almost nothing to do. Well, except for the glamorous duties of the Junior Ensign. Oh yes, and there were my collateral duties as assigned by the XO and by Norm, the OPS boss:

Junior Officer of the Deck (JOOD) for the Special Sea and Anchor Detail. That is, the detail set for getting the ship underway from a port or anchorage, and returning to same.

JOOD for General Quarters, or battle stations. One reason I was concerned about glass thickness and wood decoration on the bridge.

JOOD Underway. I was inserted into the regular watch rotation, which meant I could be on the bridge anytime, day or night while underway, for a four hour watch. With all of these duties as JOOD, I spent an inordinate amount of time on the bridge, which was not a bad place to be at all, in order to learn ship handling skills and to be at the center of everything that happens on a ship while underway, which is considerable.

Officer of the Deck, In port. Assist the Command Duty Officer in his tasks while the ship is tied up to the pier.

Registered Publications System (RPS) Custodian, which meant I "owned" all of the classified publications and communications codes, was responsible for keeping them up to date, and for disposal. I also had to pick all of these things up, wherever in the world we might be, and get them to the ship safely.

For this I had a canvas and leather bag that could be locked, and a .45 caliber automatic that I carried. For emergency destruction of documents, I had thermite bombs, very nasty little devices.

Crypto (Cryptology) Security Officer, responsible for all encoded message traffic. I had to change the communications codes, making sure I had the right codes at the right time. Also I was the officer designated to manually encrypt and decrypt the most important message traffic, using the super-secret "rotor" machine. (I guess the machine itself had been compromised somewhere along the way, but the daily codes were the key). I had one backup officer for this job, and both of us had a Top Secret-Crypto clearance.

Postal Officer, sort of a nominal post which I didn't have to worry about too much.

SAS Agent & Courier/Armed Forces Courier, qualified as an armed courier of classified documents worldwide.

There were various other small duties, not so memorable but each an integral part of the operation. I would find that shipboard life left very little private time, particularly when you were underway. You just gave yourself over to the ship. And that was why, when you were in your homeport, none of the officers lived on board. Rather, most had homes or apartments off base.

* * *

Speaking of which, I was almost immediately asked if I would like to go in on a house on Mission Beach with three of the other officers, Bruce Douglas (Weapons Dept.), Gary Upper (Damage Control), and Porter Powell (Gunnery). They needed a fourth, and after having a look at the place, only a few doors from the water, and within walking (or crawling) distance from one of the world's great bars, I accepted. The nickname for our den of iniquity was the "Snake Ranch," and it was well named because it became a center for the single officers and their ladies on weekends. Now I had this Snake Ranch with a bunch of great guys, and my little black convertible, and the world looked pretty damned good.

* * *

I had made another friend at OCS named Frampton E. Ellis III. Framp was a great guy, and a lot of fun, and also based in San Diego. He had somehow endeared himself to a rent house full of girls in town. He called one day and said I should come on over, there was someone he wanted me to meet. I drove up to a plain frame house, and parked out front was this huge motorcycle. On the porch was Framp with his girlfriend, Eileen, the cutest little thing with brown eyes, long blond hair, and still dressed in her "babydoll" jammies. In no time, he sat her on the back of that motorcycle, she was screaming and laughing in her babydolls, and almost doing a wheelie, roared off down the street, leaving me alone with Linda. Man, what a vision! Linda came with short red hair, the most beautiful porcelain skin, and a figure I can't even begin to describe. She also came with high intelligence and a rapier wit. What a package. From that moment on my social life was taken care of for the foreseeable future.

I was driving in downtown San Diego one afternoon, and happened to see Linda walking across the street. She had on a tight skirt and high-heeled boots. I just sat and watched her all the way across and marveled, "Now, that's the way a woman ought to walk." Gorgeous. Reminded me of Marilyn Monroe's famous "long walk" in the movie "*Niagara*."

Framp's big motorcycle was a Spanish bike known as a Bultaco. Even though he drove it on the streets, it was meant to be a dirt bike so we tried it out in the sand dune hills outside of San Diego. He, his girlfriend and I met out there and took turns riding: first, he and his girl, and then me. It was a lot of fun and a lot of noise, but it really was big and heavy and I kept turning it over and falling off. It weighed a ton and I had a hard time getting it back up again. I think we went just the one time.

* * *

The bar near the Snake Ranch is still the greatest beach bar I have ever seen. It may have been called the Beachcomber. We only went on weekends. It was pretty basic, with a concrete floor always covered in sand, open-air windows all around, and a long bar. The crowd was pretty raunchy and rowdy, so much so that few women dared come in. There was one who was there every Saturday, though, and the guy who brought her always made sure that she wore a great-looking bikini and outrageous shades. As you can imagine, she was *very* popular with the crowd, even though she had no arms or legs. Well, to tell you the truth, she was a mannequin, but the Saturday wasn't complete unless she showed up.

* * *

Back on the ship, part of my learning process included doing odd jobs for the ship as a whole, where an SLJ officer's presence was needed. The first of these became my first Command at Sea, a little landing craft called an LCVP (Landing Craft, Vehicle, Personnel) with a bow door that drops down. This was one of the boats that won WWII in the Pacific. Anyway, my crew were the coxswain (pronounced COXUN- the driver), and another sailor. Our mission was to sail across the harbor to pick up parts or supplies. I know I heard some of the older sailors snickering as we pulled away from the ship, you know, giving the new officer something to do. But that was okay, I had to start somewhere. And we did complete the mission with no casualties.

I would otherwise take a truck and a sailor to do errands. Through this I began to see how the Navy supply system worked. You could go through channels and do all the paperwork to get an item, but if you needed something fast and couldn't cover it with paper, you'd better have a 5 lb. can of coffee to trade for it. You could get almost anything in exchange for that shiny can of coffee, parts, services, you name it. I even saw it traded for a parking space on base once, something so precious you could normally only get one by inheriting. That was one of my first valuable lessons: the old axiom that *the Navy runs on coffee!* It was perfectly true.

* * *

Jon Britton took me along to the wardroom for my first Captain's Mast. It is an administrative legal hearing where the

Captain can mete out non-judicial punishment for lesser offenses than would require a Court Martial. It is authorized under the famous Uniform Code of Military Justice (UCMJ), and is a swift and sure way to maintain "good order and discipline" in a ship. No one wants to go to Captain's Mast, and I found out why.

In this case, one of the sailors in our division had gotten himself into some kind of trouble. The accusation was read to the accused, who was then allowed to give evidence, and could have witnesses testify in his behalf. Then the accused was allowed to testify. The problem in this case was that the sailor told a story that the Captain knew for a fact was not true. And Captain Kennedy erupted.

He completely lost his temper, turned red in the face, and flung the case file across the wardroom table. He yelled, spittle flying, something like, "How can you dare to stand there and lie to your Commanding Officer!" He scared the life out of the accused, who seemed to shrink from the onslaught. Besides throwing the file, the Captain threw the book at our sailor both for the offense and for lying about it. Honesty went a long way with Captain Kennedy. He was a good man, who could not countenance deceit in his command.

I, along with everyone else present, was suitably impressed. I am sure that my eyes were as round as half-dollars, particularly as I was aware of the fact that officers can go to Captain's Mast, too! I might mention that there is also a more pleasant version of this proceeding called Meritorious Mast, which the Captain uses to recognize meritorious performance by sailors and officers.

* * *

One evening I was walking out to the ship on one of the large piers, when I came across the most amazing scene! For a moment it looked like a gang fight, but it turned out to be a gang of one, in the form of a Marine versus six shore patrol. This guy was very strong and very drunk and he wanted to fight. And the SP guys were trying to take him down without hurting him. You wonder sometimes where this enormous strength comes from. This went on for a couple of minutes. He was swinging and wasn't going down until these sailors finally just overpowered him, got him down on his chest and cuffed him. He had been trying his best to hurt them, but to their credit, not one SP used his billy club. I still admire that, as they could have subdued him much more quickly with a couple of whacks with a club.

* * *

You know, Marines are called "jarheads" by sailors and by other Marines. The Marines call sailors "swabbies" or "squids" or perhaps something worse. It all comes mostly from a kind of intramural rivalry between the sister services, like two sisters who bitch and gripe at each other but truly love one another. The origin of "jarhead" is a little fuzzy but the main choices are 1) the haircut, with white sidewalls, and just enough hair on the top to look like a cap---makes their head look like a Mason Jar. 2) Some kind of cap they used to wear, or 3) maybe Mason quit making jars during WWII and turned to making Marine helmets. Take your pick, I think it's the haircut. Whatever derogatory meaning I had ever given to that word, abruptly and permanently stopped one day.

I had to go over to the brig to see one of our men who had been hauled in the night before for one reason or another. While I was waiting to see my guy, the SP's brought in a very tall guy, a real hippie, with long and scraggly red hair and beard, and dirty clothes that kind of hung off of him. He was obviously AWOL, and had been living the hippie life for some time. He started talking to anyone who would listen, that he had been out demonstrating against the war and against poverty and against discrimination and against just about everything else. When one of the guards took his arm to lead him to a holding cell, he became belligerent and refused to go. I think he was really ripped on something.

As a couple of guards went to grab him, he started yelling that he had been out on the streets, "fighting for you people." No one seemed to be impressed by that fact. He started struggling, and through a door comes this little Marine; I call him little because he couldn't have topped 5' 7" or so, and this hippie was so big!

He told the SP's that he would take care of it, and just as this guy was yelling that he had been out protecting him, the Marine made a quick move on him and had him immobile and unable to speak in the blink of an eye. He then asked the guy if he wanted to do this the easy way or the hard way. With that, all of the fight drained out of him, and he hung his head and was led away without another word. Man, was that impressive! This fellow was unbelievably fast and strong.

After that, any time I used the word "jarhead," it had a little more respect attached to it. By the way, as a sailor you never called a Marine a jarhead to his face, that is, if you wanted to live. That privilege is reserved for other Marines only.

Note: The Marines do have their moments. General Louis H. Wilson, then Commandant of the Marine Corps, on the occasion of the 203rd Marine Corps Birthday Ball held at Camp Lejeune, NC in 1978, gave the following toast and caused a near riot:

"The wonderful love of a beautiful maid,

The love of a staunch true man,

The love of a baby, unafraid,

Have existed since time began.

But the greatest of loves, the quintessence of loves,

Even greater than that of a mother,

Is the tender, passionate, infinite love,

Of one drunken Marine for another."

* * *

Not too long after I reported aboard, we had a Change of Command ceremony, wherein we said goodbye to Capt. Kennedy, and welcomed Commander Jack W. Bowen as our new skipper. He was fresh from the Carrier USS Ticonderoga (CVA-14) where he had been Engineering Officer. He made a good first impression on all of us, and put us at ease about losing such a fine man as Kennedy.

The ceremony called for us to wear full dress uniforms, and that meant swords. As we were getting all of this equipment out, you could hear Dan swearing a blue streak. Come to find out that he had gotten married shortly after graduation from OCS, and had worn his uniform. Well, when it came time to cut the cake, he did it in style using his Hilborn-Hamburger sword, and then returned it to its sheath. Without wiping it off first. The next time he even looked at it was this day, and he had to struggle to pull it out. Man, what months of wedding cake can do to a blade. It was horrible, and he was sweating bullets thinking we would have to do a sword drill of some kind. Lucky for him we didn't!

Dan could be a very funny guy, but I found out that he was a man who could really hold a grudge. I came to the ship one day, I'm sure it was on a weekend, and here was Dan on the fantail (main deck at the stern, or the back of the ship), holding a makeshift fishing pole made of a mop handle and some string, and he appeared to be fishing. As bait, he had a chunk of white bread floating on the water, with a hook stuck through it. I asked him what on earth he was doing, and he said he was going to catch a seagull. I burst out laughing, and said, "So you still hate seagulls that much?" He just said, "Yep."

I guess I never wanted him mad at me. He was still angry about the seagull who had shit on his hat during that inspection at OCS. Boy, what a temper! By the way, he never did catch one, but maybe just the exercise gave him some satisfaction.

* * *

Back at the ranch, one of my roommates, Porter Powell, made his own wine, and was generous in handing it out to whoever would drink it. It came in gallon milk cartons and was colored dark purple with a kind of reddish tinge. It was a little raw, so what we did was start out on a more premium wine like Red Mountain or Ripple, and then switch over to Powell's Best. After lying out in the sun one afternoon and drinking this stuff for a while, several of us got up the nerve to get into the cool Pacific waters off of Mission Beach.

There is much truth to the fact that the California Current brings frigid water from British Columbia, and pumps it down to San Diego so you will freeze your cojones. Everyone has the idea that California means sun, sand and surfing. And it does, just don't forget your wetsuit. We were out of the water in no time, shivering, goose bumps on goose bumps, and the same shade of purple as the wine. It is the only time I ever got into the water, and I lived in a beach house! The water there averages 56 degrees F during the winter.

* * *

On a Saturday night a group of us decided to go down to Tijuana, Mexico. Framp and his girlfriend, Linda and a guy she was still dating at the time, and me. Linda asked if I would mind taking her sister, Mary, who was visiting from Modesto. I told Linda that I would rather be taking her, but it was okay. Well, we all piled into one car and went to Tijuana for a Mexican dinner.

Sister was the cutest little thing I had ever seen. She was really petite and so pretty, and was wearing this little trench coat that would have fit a 10 year-old. Linda had said that she was from Modesto, but when I asked her what she did for a living, she answered in this small child-like, bluebird-like voice, "I deal faro in Vegas." You could have knocked me over with a feather. I was in *love!* You couldn't help it. Anyway, we had a great dinner and then went to a dance joint someone had recommended. I don't recall if the music was any good, but it was loud and we were all in a good mood and we laughed and danced and drank beer and smoked and drank tequila. And the band kept playing so we kept dancing, to the point that we were all drenched in our own perspiration.

Eventually someone said we ought to wind it down and think about going back to San Diego, and everyone agreed it was about that time. As we were gathering near the front door one of the guys went out to get the car, but he came flying back through the door, yelling, "Stop! You don't want to go out there! Don't go!" Well, we thought someone had been knifed on the sidewalk or something, but soon saw what the problem was: it was *daylight!* The group let out a collective, "*Awww no!*" We thought it was maybe 1 or 2 in the morning, but not dawn! We were both exhilarated and disgusted at the same time, and all of a sudden we smelled like a brewery and old ashtrays. We were further disgusted when we bought the Sunday papers and headed home. But everyone agreed that we must have had a very good time, not to have noticed our overnight stay at that bar.

* * *

We gave a great party at the Snake Ranch one weekend, one that became famously known as Norm's Pickle Party. It was just perfect: we had barbequed chicken, barrels of iced beer, sun and sand, and a very large kettle full of a very potent punch concocted by Norm Davis. His finishing touch to this masterpiece was to float a big pickle on the top as sort of a signature, and everyone had at it. Everyone also got wasted. We were missing Don, the number 2 Supply Officer, and I found him on a bedroom floor, spread-eagled, semi-conscious, with a stomach so full of beer and punch and chicken, he looked pregnant!

It got so bad that we invited everyone to stay the night, but Linda and I awoke the next morning in someone else's room, to a completely empty, completely trashed Snake Ranch. Even my roommates were gone. I think the new Captain wrecked his car on the way home. To this day I'll bet the people who were there would remember Norm's Pickle Party.

* * *

I almost died one night in a bar that was frequented by sailors and Marines. I was sitting there having a drink, minding my own business, and looking over the crowd, as I usually do. I felt this presence behind me and turned around to see this pretty good-sized Marine standing there in a menacing stance. "Why are you staring at me?" I had noticed him as just part of the crowd sitting on the other side of the room. But I think he wanted to pick a fight. I told him that I had not been staring at him and that I wasn't looking for trouble. This wasn't much different from the time I was backed up to a pickup truck by three snarling junkyard dogs, when I was living at the 32nd Street BOQ. I had simply frozen for awhile, then talked really gently and friendly to them while inch by inch I moved away from them and out of their yard. I recall doing the same thing to that Marine until I just eased myself on out of that club. Not to compare him to a junkyard dog, but he had wanted a piece of me just like those dogs did.

* * *

You know how certain songs can bring back instant memories, good or bad? One of mine is *"Ride Captain Ride,"* by the Blues Image. A bunch of us were out at a joint drinking beer one night and someone had been playing that song almost continuously on the juke box. We had a real cute and sexy waitress whom you could tell had dealt with sailors before. And she came up to the table and asked, "What do you all want?" Whereupon, one of our wise guys asked, "Well, what do *you* want?" Without hesitation she turned, pointed her finger at me and said, "I want him!" I'll tell you, folks, I was having the best time of my life in California! Seems to me we ended up in her car after closing, grubbing until we nearly froze to death and one of the guys came back and picked me up. What great days those were, and what a great song, "*Ride Captain Ride!*"

* * *

There was a place known as the "Black Widow Bar." I don't remember whether that was the actual name or if it was just a Navy nickname. It was a place where lonely Navy wives went for a little action while their spouse was overseas. These girls were known as "war widows." I never did go to this place because I thought it was a little sad. You felt somewhat sorry for them because they were young and healthy and had been dropped into a very different society, and their man had gone off on a 6 or 12 month tour of duty to Vietnam. But still they were married, and should not have been out looking for trouble. Maybe they shouldn't have gotten married in the first place.

Navy life is certainly a different life. Prolonged absences by the member are common, leaving "mom" and probably children alone to deal with life's problems. And despite a support system of Navy Wives Clubs, and Naval facilities themselves, the toll on families is high.

My step father used to always say, "The bane of my existence is young married Ensigns." Wives who were not adjusting to the lot of the Navy spouse eventually made life hell for their husbands, making it difficult for them to concentrate on learning and training. There was almost always trouble at home in these cases.

I remember reading in the San Diego paper, which was heavy on Navy news, that during a deployment to WestPac by one of our carriers, there were fully 600 divorces. Looking up the complement of ships such as the Oriskany and the Ticonderoga, pegged at 3,448 men, that works out to just over 17%. Everyone who heard that thought the number was staggering! Now I read that the nuclear carrier USS Abraham Lincoln (CVN-72) had a 15% divorce rate after a recent deployment, with a crew of 5,680 men and women, making it 852 unhappy families. So nothing much has changed over the years. Happily, though, the majority of Navy families get with the program early, figure out the system and use it for a long, productive career.

* * *

My step father had a friend who was Commanding Officer of the USS Mt. Katmai (AE-16). AE translates to an ammunition ship. The Captain had invited Zim to his change-of-command, but he was unable to attend and asked me to be there as his representative. I was happy to oblige, and attended the ceremony. I introduced myself to the Captain, a tall, handsome man with a big moustache. During the proceedings, I got to thinking what a dangerous job this was, ferrying around a rather large ship full of explosive ordinance. The safety precautions on this ship must be unreal!

Then I found out that Mt. Katmai is the name of a volcano in Alaska. I did not think that this was a very good name for an ammunition ship, sort of like it was tempting fate or something. When I got back to the Thomas I looked up the names of other ammo ships, and Vesuvius caught my eye. I just had this vision of one of these ships blowing up like a volcano. There were others, Diamond Head, and many we have never heard of, all volcanoes except for two newer models, the Nitro and the Pyro. Go figure. It's like naming a nuclear sub the Three Mile Island, or a nuclear carrier the Chernobyl! Same difference.

* * *

An OCS friend had been assigned to one of the carriers that regularly rotated to WestPac, the USS Hancock (CVA-19), and he invited me over one day for a tour. It confirmed the fact that those ships are just too big for me! The wardroom was so large it would take more than a dozen destroyer-sized wardrooms to fill it. It looked like a country club, all done conservatively in various shades of beige and brown.

The hangar deck was so gigantic, you just couldn't tell you were on a ship. There were a number of planes parked there and I saw my first A6 Intruder, a twin-engine attack aircraft, up close and personal, and was really impressed with its looks and aerodynamics. I have always liked warplanes, they are such great machines, just never wanted to fly 'em.

While touring other parts of the ship such as the "island" above the main deck and the officers' quarters, we had a discussion about working on such a behemoth, with so many other people. I told him I really couldn't do it, that I would feel lost in the shuffle. He laughed and said it wasn't so bad, but to illustrate what a large operation it was, he said there was actually a Coke Machine Officer, or CMO, I guess. Now it was my turn to laugh. This guy's only duty was to see that the Coke machines were filled, and the money removed. There were so many of them on this floating city that it was a full time job! Being Coke Machine Officer did not exactly put him on a fast track to make Admiral, I guessed. After this eye-opening tour I became even more fond of my "little boy," and couldn't wait to get back to the Thomas.

A friend of mine, Tommy Gamble, flew the A6 for the Marines during Vietnam. He garnered some measure of fame on April 16, 1972. Taking off from the USS Coral Sea, he was making a bombing run over Haiphong Harbor when his load of bombs became stuck in the rack and failed to release. A friend of his was flying at a much higher altitude and took a picture with a hand-held 35 mm camera, at the instant Tommy's bombs finally released and hit the ground. Except for the first one. That one hit the water very close aboard a Russian freighter. The Russian government was very upset about this, and probably if there hadn't been so much going on with the Paris peace talks, they would have made more out of it than they did. I know that I saw a grainy black-and-white picture of Tommy's near miss (or near hit, as George Carlin would say), on the cover of Time or Newsweek at the time, and Tommy's mother had said she saw it, too. He says he did not exactly get the DFC (Distinguished Flying Cross) from that mission. Which is probably understandable.

If you want to know more about the A6 in Vietnam, a very good movie was made about it, *"Flight of the Intruder,"* with Danny

Glover, Willem Dafoe, and Brad Johnson. It is from a very readable book by Stephen Coonts.

* * *

As the new RPS officer, I had begun making runs to pick up communications codes and other Secret and Top Secret publications. Remember, I had to use a locked security bag, and I wore a .45 with a full clip. This was very scary stuff to be carrying around, the security precautions were many, and I took them very seriously.

I heard about probably the dumbest two officers in the entire Navy. One of them was an RPS guy, and they made a run to pick up a satchel full of classified information. After they had done so, they decided to go somewhere for a couple of beers, no one would ever know, so they threw everything into the trunk of the car and drove down to Tijuana! How stupid can you get? Coming back across, in uniform, obviously had been drinking, they were stopped on the American side and a search of the car turned up the bag full of enough communications codes to temporarily shut down the entire COMM apparatus of the US Navy. My guess is that they are still hanging upside-down by their toes at Leavenworth Federal Penitentiary.

Speaking of Leavenworth, there was one other item that you never wanted to lose, and that was your pistol. The Navy was absolutely *paranoid* about these things, you heard and read warnings all the time about it, along with reminders of punishment. I often thought that you could lose an entire ship and not get into as much trouble as you would by losing your .45.

* * *

We were getting word (also known as scuttlebutt, or skinny) back from Vietnam that a lot was happening on the inland waterways of the Mekong Delta, in what was known as the Brown Water Navy. A lot of fighting was going on there. We had only a passing knowledge of riverine warfare because the destroyer took all of our concentration and energy. In fact, you could say the same about any other facet of Naval operations: we only knew what we needed to know about them in order to get our own job done.

* * *

So here I was in San Diego harbor learning to be a movie projector operator. Oh yes! You had to take instruction, and be certified. You learned never to get a fingerprint on the projector bulb while installing it, lest you create a "hot spot" that would shorten the bulb's useful life. You learned how to properly thread film into the machine in order to avoid breaks, or worse, ending up with a pile of unwound film on the deck. All of this may sound frivolous, but it is actually not. During long weeks and months at sea, there were few things available to boost morale: one was the mail, and the other was movies. They were most important regardless how awful or old they were. So there were several officers, including of course the junior Ensign, and crew who were qualified to show the films on those old Bell and Howell 16 mm projectors. Of course you got heavily booed if the film broke. Which it often did.

* * *

We began getting underway to go out and do some training exercises or other. Though I had some experience with this on the Bridget, I was now a part of the Sea and Anchor Detail, and was on the bridge as JOOD during the whole thing. Norm Davis was the OOD and of course the Captain and XO were there. It was a very busy time. I and a radioman had already checked out all of the voice radio-telephones (R/T's) for the proper frequencies, the "black gang" down below had gotten up steam and were ready for engine commands, and everyone else on the ship were at their proper station.

When the Captain said, "Get us underway, Norm," the commands started flying left and right, in a well-coordinated concert of removing the lines from the dock and maneuvering the ship out into the bay. Norm was good at it and I started watching and learning. I was just sort of there at this point, but Norm brought me into the process by asking for sightings or radar ranges and other things. And once we were in open water, he would even let me "drive" for awhile, so I would take the conn.

At this time we were flying the DASH, the little unmanned helicopter that was supposed to fly out and drop sonobouys to listen for, and locate enemy subs, and to even carry a torpedo to drop. The idea being to destroy it before it could get close enough to destroy us. Bruce Douglas flew it by remote control, and said that it had always been erratic. He had had successful flights before, but it seemed that once it flew out from the ship for some distance, he would have to pray that he could get it back. And I think we had crashed one once, before I was aboard, as it stopped responding to commands altogether when it flew beyond the horizon. Eventually we learned that the system was just not working out Navy-wide, and that it would be removed during the upcoming overhaul period. I believe this news made Bruce a very happy man.

* * *

In those days there were no women on Navy ships, no separate berthing areas, no separate heads, and none of the resulting myriad problems of putting women on ships full of young sailors with raging hormones, particularly on extended cruises. Any officer or sailor then would have laughed at the prospect. Now, of course, it is a reality, for better or worse. I'm just glad that we didn't have to deal with it. I have always found it interesting that there are no women in the submarine service, and am very curious as to why and how they have been able to hold out for so long. Probably a succession of influential Admirals who refuse to budge on the issue.

Anyway, the point of the story is that, though there were no women aboard, we had our very own version of Corporal Klinger. He was just a guy who had heard of a Section 8, and was trying his best to get out of the Navy by acting femme and sashaying naked through the showers with a little wiggle to his walk. His problem was that everyone knew it was just an act and paid no attention to him. He was on the ship the whole time I was, and try as he may, it never worked.

Note: On April 29, 2010, which was some time after the above story was written, the Navy announced that the first women will report for duty aboard submarines in the year 2012. So that, as they say, takes care of that! Now there is just one Naval entity left that is exclusively male, and that is the SEALS.

* * *

There is one smell that is familiar to anyone who has ever served on Navy ships, and that is stack gas. It is emitted from the stacks when the boilers are fired up, whether at sea or in port. It is always there, you never notice it until you leave the ship, and when you return, the familiar odor gives you that "welcome home" (in German it's gemuetlich) feeling of security. I can smell it right now, and you can too, if you have ever sailed on what my step father called the "Gray Funnel Line."

* * *

You may remember the guy on the Bridget who tried to make me puke by smoking a big cigar in my face after my first horrendous watch at sea. Well, the master of that particular torture lived on the Thomas: Bruce Douglas. He tried it on me at lunch one day when we were steaming out off San Diego. Even in a calm sea the ship had some movement. What he would do is amplify that movement in the unsuspecting Ensign's mind. In cahoots with the other officers, he maneuvered me into sitting directly across from him at the table, where I could also see the curtains which covered the door to the alcove. Also, being President of the Officers' Mess, he had arranged the menu to include very greasy pork chops. Halfway through the meal, he began to very slightly move from side to side as he talked. This was in concert with the movement of the curtains, both of which

I could see clearly. He continued to rock back and forth for the rest of the meal, and that, along with the greasy food and the moving curtains, started doing a number on my stomach, making me very queasy. I don't know if I grew pale or not, but I didn't budge from my seat. I would not have dared. But his sadistic nature seemed satisfied.

Over the course of time, as new Ensigns joined the ship, I watched him do this to each one. It was really something to watch a master of subtlety at work. He really wasted one guy, who turned a very pale shade of green, bolted from the table and became another small part of Naval tradition and lore.

* * *

There are many Naval terms and phrases that are used every day and are so funny! Possibly my all-time favorite is the euphemism for payday, which is when "the eagle shits." Of course the eagle is Uncle Sam. So when you wanted to know when payday was, you asked, "When does the eagle shit?" Don caught the brunt of this humor since he was the paymaster. He had such a droll sense of humor, though, he returned all of the derogatory remarks with lightning speed, never taking it personally.

Some of my other favorites were:

Monkey shit- a brown, gooey grease used by the engineers for most of their lubrication needs. The name was a good description of how it looked and felt.

Bug juice- Kool-Aid, a staple of the fleet's food pyramid at the time.

Hero material- an officer or sailor who had watched too many Errol Flynn and Douglas Fairbanks, Jr. movies about heroics on the high seas.

Pis cutter- the little cap we wore with the working khaki uniform when not wearing our regular lid.

CYA- cover your ass. The main lesson to learn if you want to get along in the Navy.

"There is no doubt in my military mind"- the affirmative answer to a question.

And two truisms come to mind:

"Never step into the bight of a line"- this was drilled into us at OCS, and you would want to practice it every day while out on the deck. A bight is a coil or loop of line lying on the deck. It can be a single coil or an entire rope. You never know what that line is attached to, and may at any instant pull it tight with such force that it will separate you from your foot. It made you very careful.

"The chiefs are the backbone of the Navy"- that is the way the truism went; however, I and everybody else knew the "true" truism: the chiefs *run* the Navy.

There are so many of these terms and phrases it would be impossible to list them all. I have used many of them throughout the book, most with accompanying explanation. I imagine that quite a few have changed by now or are considered "old hat" by today's young sailors.

* * *

There is, or was, such a thing as Naval Etiquette. The Navy is a very traditional service, and there are rules of social behavior for virtually everything, including how to properly seat yourself at the wardroom table. If you are coming in late, you nod at the Captain and say, "Captain," and then you take in the rest of the officers and say, "Gentlemen." In our own case, if Don happened to be at the table, you would say, "Gentlemen," and then, "Don." (That one is not in the book). If you left early, you'd say, "Request permission to be excused." The Captain then said, "Permission granted." The shorthand for "permission granted" was "per gra," but the CO would never say that.

If you were walking somewhere and wanted to pass a senior officer who was walking in the same direction, you passed him on his left, said, "By your leave, sir," and saluted as you passed.

If you and your wife or girlfriend paid a formal call to the home of your CO or another senior officer, you dropped a formal calling card onto a silver tray in the foyer, and never stayed longer than 30 minutes. (There were some people who forgot the rules and inadvertently overstayed. My step father had a gentle but firm way to handle the situation. He would say to my mother, "Ruthie, let's go up to bed so these nice people can go home." It was very effective.)

If you were at a party or other gathering, you always knew who the Senior Officer Present (SOP) was. If you wanted to leave early, you were out of luck. No one could leave until he did. If he decided to stay late, well, so did you. But in fact that rarely happened because most senior officers did not want to abuse their perks of command. Notice I said "most."

When my mother married Zim and joined the Navy as a Captain's wife, she quickly realized that her ideas of sociability and civility needed modification. The very real rules of behavior in the Navy were codified in a book entitled "Navy Etiquette" or something similar, which he gave to her as a subtle hint of things to come. Other Navy wives had learned these things while coming up through the ranks with their husband, but my mother was a quick study and soon mastered them, and even improved on a few. Her talents in this area were to stand her in good stead, particularly when Zim made flag rank (Admiral).

* * *

When a ship is not headed for a combat zone, the word is training, training, training! We were out one day doing exercises, and the XO decided to do "man overboard" drills. The "man" was named Oscar, and was a life-size dummy made of sewn canvas stuffed with kapok, so he floated. The drill went something like this: one of the deck hands would heave Oscar over the side and yell, "Man overboard, port (or starboard) side!" Word would be relayed to the bridge, and whoever had the conn had to take *immediate* action and, using rudder commands, swing the stern away from him, make a rapid 360 degree circle and, ideally, bring him down one side of the ship or the other, and slow so that he could be rescued.

Poor old Oscar went overboard 10 or 15 times, each with a more or less successful recovery, until it was my turn. I got the stern swung out all right and made a nice tight circle, and then proceeded to run right over Oscar. He was pulled straight down the keel and went right through the screws (propellers). It was a testament to whoever made Oscar that he came out without a scratch. Of course, a human would have looked considerably different. Thankfully, no one came down on me for killing our crewman, due to my inexperience. And also thankfully, that was the only time I ever ran over anyone, either real or not.

One day there was a drill on the .50 caliber machine gun, and one was brought up and mounted amidships on the main deck. After the Gunner's Mates had done some training and qualifying, shooting at a floating target, the officers were given a chance to see how it feels. After instruction from a GM on what to do, I pulled back on the big slide and pushed it home to chamber the first round, grabbed the handles, and put my thumbs on the trigger, which resembled a two-headed snake. After aiming, I opened fire and came nowhere near the target. What power, though! It is an incredibly destructive gun. After the GM gave me a few pointers, I fired again, and began hitting the target. It was probably beginner's luck, and all too soon I had to give it up to someone else. But what a thrill that was!

* * *

We were leaving port one morning and I showed up on the bridge with a hangover. I was functional, but wasn't feeling so good and Norm picked up on it. Once we were clear of the harbor, he came over to me and said, "Mr. Cook, I'd like for you to do a little cross-training today so I want you to go down and stand an evaporator watch for the rest of this watch."

He was able to keep from smiling as he spoke, and I saluted, said, "Yes, sir," and left the bridge. The evaporator is a machine down in the engineering spaces that converts sea water into potable water using, if memory serves, the reverse osmosis process. It just sits there, and definitely does not need anyone to keep an eye on it.

The temperature runs around 110 to 120 degrees Fahrenheit in that space. So I stand an "evap watch" for 2 or 3 hours in that unbearable heat with a hangover. Man, that really hurt, and felt like a lifetime. Norm had made his not-so-subtle point---don't ever do that again! And I never did, at least on the Thomas.

* * *

Destroyers were coming in or going out to WestPac all the time. There was one sailor who didn't particularly want to go to Vietnam, so he decided to make sure that his ship would not be able to get underway.

There are a series of gears that are the link between the steam turbine engines and propeller shafts. They are called reduction gears because they reduce the high RPM's (revolutions per minute) put out by the turbines, down to the slower RPM's required by the propellers. The last in this series of gears is called the "bull gear," a huge thing whose diameter is taller than a man, which is attached directly to the propeller shaft.

Even though it is so big, its teeth are precisely and finely cut to mesh perfectly with the next smaller gear, with no thrusting (movement side-to-side) or any vibration. Well, this guy knew exactly where to look, so he removed an access cover and dropped a large wrench onto the bull gear where it would carry into the smaller gear when the ship got underway.

Come time to leave the dock, and *crunch!* One disabled ship that wasn't going anywhere for a while. The sailor was caught easily enough and sent to prison for destroying government property or sabotage or something. No telling how many months and how much money it took to replace those gears. But at least that guy didn't have to go to Vietnam because he very effectively pulled a warship off the line.

* * *

I remembered what one of the instructors at OCS had said about the Navy's shark repellent, about how it actually attracted sharks, and I had found some in my spaces. The 1st Class had said to throw it away, which I did. Regardless what it said on the box, I had more trust in the wisdom of a salty sailor.

As I have mentioned, in the radio shack's large safe I kept several thermite bombs. These came in handy in case of emergency destruction of classified codes and publications. About the size of an old-fashioned book satchel (or for that matter, the satchel bomb favored by the Viet Cong), the thermite bomb burned with such intensity and high temperature that whatever was placed under or near it, was incinerated almost immediately. There was one drawback, however, and that was that it burned for quite some time. That meant that if I placed it on top of a pile of papers and set it off, it would destroy that, then burn right through the deck, and the next, and the next, until it burned a hole through the bottom of the ship! So it had to be applied with real care.

I had one bomb more than my allotment, so I decided to test it out. No one had ever seen one work, so a small crowd gathered. We were out in open water and not making any way, so I pulled the lanyard and quickly tossed it over the side. Almost at once, it lit off with a blinding white burning light, and vaporized the water around it. It burned so brightly that you could follow it all the way down with the naked eye. Down and down, until it was the size of a pinhead, then it winked out. It was a stunning display of power, and made believers of everyone who saw it.

* * *

Some of the WWII era destroyers still had the old "Hedgehog" system for killing submarines. The Hedgehog was a smaller version of the depth charges you saw being rolled or fired off of racks at the stern of the ship, in old movies. If you were on the ship's bridge and looked down at the main deck near the bow, you would see a circle made up of 24 of these small bombs. They were mounted at about a 70 degree angle to the deck, aimed forward. The thing was to locate the enemy sub, rush to the point of contact, aim the ship's bow, and fire. The bombs were self-propelled, and hit the sea in a circle 100' in diameter, about 250 yards out. Hopefully, one or more would do some damage to the enemy.

The Hedgehog system was about 25% effective in hitting something, as compared to a poorly 7% for depth charges. I did hear one story about Hedgehogs hitting something. A ship that was in port and tied up outboard of another ship was running a dummy test of the system. That is, just running an electronics diagnostic or whatever. Well, somehow, some real dummy fired the whole salvo of bombs, which made a beautiful pattern as it arced into the air and landed in a parking lot, killing a number of Fords, Chevrolets and Buicks. At least they were training dummies and not armed. Naval myth? Maybe, but probably rooted in fact. Then there was the one about the stray practice torpedo that shot out of the water, slid up onto a beach and scared the hell out of some civilians.

* * *

The time finally came when I relieved Jon and became the Communications Division Officer. I believe he was headed for a communications station (comm sta) in Ireland or some such. He was a good guy and I hated to see him go, except that now I was the boss. Rather, Faust and I were the boss. And it was now sink or swim, and I had to work doubly hard in order not to sink.

Note: My friend Frampton Ellis, with whom I had so much fun, has had some career since then. I am sure he has made several fortunes in the stock market, inventor of sports shoe technology, which most of us are wearing right now, and computer security technology, the last two coming under the heading of intellectual properties that he controls and licenses. Not bad!

Long Beach

Eventually, we had to think about the upcoming overhaul, or yard period, at the Long Beach Naval Shipyard. We would have to vacate the Snake Ranch, and find a place near the shipyard, since no one could live aboard the Thomas while she was being worked on. Bruce and Gary found an apartment in a small complex in the middle of Huntington Beach, and they were very proud of themselves that they were able to get it so cheap! Well, no *wonder!* When I drove in for the first time, the smell nearly made me pass out. Just across the street was a feedlot for cattle! As I was praising Bruce on what a brilliant negotiator he was, he explained that it only smelled like that when the wind shifted toward us. That was supposed to make it all better. Trouble was, the wind blew in our direction most of the time. Man, I can still smell that. The odor was dangerous. Explosive. Any of you who know Huntington Beach today wouldn't believe that we and our cattle were surrounded by countryside and not much else.

* * *

We brought the Thomas up to the shipyard and parked her at the pier. Immediately we were swarmed by yard birds (civilian yard workers) in their hardhats, and by supervisors with whom we met to discuss the work to be done. Radio I was to be upgraded to a certain extent, but the major work on the ship involved the removal of the DASH system, which had been made redundant by the ASROC (anti-submarine rocket system), replacement of one of the gigantic air conditioning units, and installation of an experimental gas-turbine engine to power the auxiliary generator. Plus, there were a million smaller jobs to be done all over the ship. And after all of that was finished, she would be put into dry dock to have the bottom scraped and painted.

I got a small office near the ship so I could do business. The yard took over our comms, so we made several runs a day to give and receive message traffic. A lot of the crew either took leave or were sent out for training courses. I myself was sent to a Nuclear Weapons Orientation course, even though I had nothing to do with weapons. It was sort of like make-work, except that since the ship had nuclear capability, it made some sense to know what was going on. My "diploma," or Certificate of Completion, is decorated with an explosion and a nuclear mushroom cloud above it.

Our stay in the yard was long and monotonous. We could watch the work progress on the ship, at what seemed like a snail's pace. The air conditioning unit to be replaced was located in the superstructure above the main deck, and was so large that a good-sized piece of the side had to be cut out so it could be moved. I wondered about such heavy machinery being located so high in the ship. Wouldn't that make her top-heavy in rolling seas?

I learned a lesson about the effect of salt water and salt air on metal. One of our engineers showed me a chunk of rust that had been removed from somewhere way down in the hold. It was four inches thick and crusty. He said that at one time, it had been a solid piece of steel one inch thick. I was really concerned about it because part of our hull was that thick. I wondered about holes.

Everyone was required to wear a hardhat while on the ship, which looked like it had been turned inside out: just wires and equipment and junk everywhere. Who on earth could bring order to such chaos? Anyway, we found out why hardhats were mandatory when, one day, a large bearing was accidentally dropped from aloft and hit a fellow right on the head. He was wearing his hat. It knocked him down, and we heard later that he had an injury, but that it was not life threatening. He was very lucky, and we were from then on wearing our hardhats all the time, no problem.

There was one other accident. Our paint locker was located way out on the bow, away from any critical machinery or ammunition, in case of fire. The space had been scraped and painted, and to finish it out, two yard birds were gluing down new flooring, the familiar non-slip gray rubber matting. The glue they were using was yellow and about the consistency of molasses, and emitted very toxic fumes. All Navy people know that glue, and also know that it should never be used in a confined space without proper ventilation. Well, these guys didn't do it right, and pretty soon they were very sick and being carried off the ship on stretchers. I think they both recovered but we heard stories about a guy who had died recently from using that glue. A ship is a very dangerous place to be, whether at sea or in port, or in the shipyard. You just needed to be aware of your surroundings and to stay alert.

* * *

To take our mind off of business, and to occupy the guys whose families were back in San Diego, the Chiefs formed a bowling league. They had their own team, the officers formed a team, and the rest were made up from various divisions on the ship. We didn't realize it at first that the Chiefs' team was made up of ringers, guys who could have done very well on the professional circuit. We came to understand that they had formed the league in order to attract new victims to crush. They just beat the shit out of us and everyone else and we didn't mind because of the positive effect it had on crew morale. Any time the officers got whipped the morale meter spiked. And it didn't cost us anything but temporary embarrassment.

* * *

My little Alfa convertible began acting temperamentally; that is, it would only start when it felt like it, which was about half the time. I was forever hitching a ride to work with a roommate. I did some work on it, and had some work done on it, but nothing seemed to have an effect. I got so exasperated with that car that one morning I said to the guys, "If I go out there and that damn thing doesn't start, I am going to buy a new car this afternoon." Sure enough, I cranked and cranked on it, and it wouldn't fire, until the battery began to run down again.

I bought the Los Angeles Times and found a 1964 Corvette convertible being offered by a Chevy dealership and called the salesman about it. I liked what he had to say, but told him that I couldn't get there until that evening or the next day. He said not to worry, if I wanted a glimpse of the car that night, I could come by after they were closed and have a look. I was a little excited about it, so I did. It wasn't on the lot, so I went up to a big garage door and looked through the window. That's all it took. *Sold!* Sitting there, beautifully lit, was the best looking car I had ever seen, a sleek, shiny bright red Corvette that may as well have had my name painted down the side. I am quite sure the salesman had positioned and lit the car so as to hook me like a fish, which he did.

I bought it the next day, trading in the Alfa, for which they actually gave me a decent price (it was running at the time). I was so happy and so stupid that I drove away without checking the gas gauge, and ran out of gas on the LA Freeway! In my new car! You *never* want to run out of gas on the LA Freeway.

* * *

Speaking of cars, Larry, our supply officer, went out and bought the most garish car in California, a red 1960 Buick convertible. It was 20 feet of red paint and chrome and fins, and really looked like it could fly. In fact, I think they called the fins "Delta Wings." Well, someone had gotten hold of some tickets for the dress rehearsal of a new local play, and a group of us went down there in Larry's convertible, of course with the top down. After the play, we partied a little bit and things got out of hand. Larry was not much of a drinker and got a little bit lit, and on the way home, I swear he went up over the curb and hit a fire hydrant in his new Buick. As best as I can recall, everyone scattered and left poor Larry to deal with the police. What a mess, there was water everywhere and the Buick was damaged, but it sure was damn funny.

* * *

The Officers' Club at Long Beach was home to an organization called The Anchorettes. We had heard about them in advance, and thought, well, that's nice, some USO-type little old ladies to hand out cups of coffee and doughnuts to the boys. It was actually a group of eligible young ladies from the greater Los Angeles area who sponsored a dance on weekends to meet and greet Navy and Marine officers who were in the area. What a nice idea. The Anchorettes had been around for many years, dating back to much more innocent times when they really were Donut Dollies, but now it was a great way to meet girls, and I did. Though I don't remember her name, I remember her very well because she turned out to be such an oddball. She was a very good-looking blonde with a luscious body, dressed in a tight navy blue and white suit with a double row of gold buttons, looking like an Anchorette should. And since she seemed to like me right away, I thought things were looking pretty good.

She was an actress (I think she may have actually used the word 'starlet'), she said, and had been in a movie with Lana Wood, Natalie's sister. There was to be a party the next weekend in Hollywood, and would I like to go? Well, yes I would. We made arrangements for me to pick her up, go to the party, then back to her place, where she said I could spend the night so I wouldn't have to drive all the way back to Huntington Beach. Not too bad for one little sailor boy!

Her apartment was one of those you would see in a Jean Harlow movie, a small adobe complex of studio apartments for starving actors and actresses, and it actually came with a Murphy bed. She greeted me and we talked and had a couple of drinks and then it was time to change for the party. I had civilian clothes, and she came out in an outfit that must have been left over from her movie: sheer harem pants and some kind of shiny top. Kind of an odd outfit, but I thought, this is Hollywood and what do I know?

We arrived at someone's house for the party, and when I walked in I was struck absolutely dumb: that was the largest group of absolutely beautiful people that I had ever seen, both women and men. Everyone was perfect, beautifully white teeth, toned bodies, even tans, expensive clothes, plastic. And they were staring at the outfit my date was wearing. I guess it didn't have the effect she thought it would on these people. After a while, word rippled through the Beautiful People that so-and-so had arrived, and he had just been in the movie, "The War Wagon," starring John Wayne. Well, you would have thought it was The Duke himself the way they fawned over him. If there had been a red carpet handy I know they would have unrolled it for his entrance. And he did make an entrance. What a society!

As things wound down one of the Beautiful Girls asked if we could give her a ride home, to the house of her boyfriend, a big-time director. Though it was a tight fit in the Corvette, up into the Hollywood Hills we went, stopping in front of a really large, modern house, part of which was cantilevered out over nothing but air. Inside, the living room was huge and 3 stories high, and looked like a movie set from a James Bond picture. And a real-life Hollywood drama unfolded as this girl found a note from the director telling her to get her things packed and to leave, she had been replaced. There was screaming and throwing things and the tears flowed, and I ungraciously said we had to go. And we went.

Through her sheer pants, I had been watching my date's legs all evening. Arriving back at her bungalow, I just knew where this was going to go, but that was my mistake. I couldn't get past first base with her because all of a sudden she became very virginal with the excuse, "I'm shy." She was about as shy as a bull elephant, but I wasn't going to force the issue. I guessed she didn't care much for men (it couldn't have been *me*), but had just wanted an escort for the party, you know, someone new and exciting on the Hollywood scene. Ha ha ha. I left very early in the morning.

* * *

We heard that the USS Long Beach (CGN-9) was in the yard for a short stay. The CGN means a nuclear powered, guided missile cruiser. Many of us had never been on a "modern" combatant ship before, only on our WWII era destroyers. So a group of us went over for a visit. She looked so majestic as we approached, at 720 feet long, and she was sleek and bristled with missile launchers. They were very obliging at the quarterdeck and gave us an officer for a tour. We learned that she was the first nuclear powered surface ship in the Navy, and that she *was* big, needing 80 officers and 1,000 enlisted to run her. One thing we did notice, while touring the spacious and confusing interior, was that, even though she was less than 10 years old, she really looked worn and beat up inside. Long Beach had made a number of WestPac cruises lately, but looked oddly unkempt regardless. Our ship was 25 years old with plenty more miles on her, and looked much better. Never figured that one out.

* * *

Finally, when all of the dockside work was completed, the Thomas was taken to a dry dock. It was strange to see the ship sitting up on blocks, high and dry, like an old Chevrolet out in back of the garage. Inside, you had the feeling of plenty of space and size, but in dry dock she looked like a model built by some kid. And when you took a walk *under* her, she really looked small. It was hard to reconcile the images and feelings from so many different perspectives.

In contrast, the two propellers looked very large indeed. Each was solid brass, had four blades, was 12 ½ feet in diameter, and weighed many tons. The propeller shafts were also solid brass. You can imagine the enormous power it took to get these things turning at 350 rpm in solid water, pushing the ship to 35 knots. Thus, the need for the 60,000 horsepower engines.

Just forward of each propeller, attached to the ship's bottom, was a plate made of some exotic metal, and it showed wear and tear. At sea, as the water was drawn back toward the props, it was ionized or electrolyzed or something like that. The charged water could begin to eat at the ship's bottom and on the edges of the propellers. So these plates were positioned to take the wear instead. Made sense, as they were cheaper and easier to replace.

* * *

Once all repairs were made and everything was painted and fresh and new, the ship was re-floated and towed to a dock. There, the gyroscope and the boilers were lit off for the first time in four or five months, and she began to come alive again. We took her out for a series of shakedown cruises in order to test all systems. Once the

Captain signed off on all tests and repairs, we were finally finished with the overhaul period and ready to return to San Diego. And REFTRA!

* * *

The last (and lasting) impression I have of Long Beach, just before leaving, was when I was in the car and needed to make a phone call. I spied a phone booth, parked the car just in front of it, walked no more than 15 feet, made a quick call, and walked back to the car to find my wallet and a very good Buck knife were gone from the console. Man, somebody was really quick! I jumped out of the car and yelled a few ineffective obscenities at no one in particular, and, feeling extremely stupid for leaving these things in plain view with the windows down, just drove away. At least I had taken the keys with me, or I would have been walking away.

REFTRA

REFTRA. Refresher Training. The words still strike terror in my heart. Had I or anyone else known what was in store for us, we would have just shipped for the Brown Water Navy and gotten it over with. REFTRA lasted from March to May 1969, and during that period we had to re-qualify in every single evolution, every minute activity that it takes to make a warship function. It was at times boring, at times frantic, and the longest three months I have endured anywhere in my life.

We spent the first week tied up to a buoy in San Diego harbor, and the rest of the time we were steaming Monday through Friday, maybe coming in for the night, or maybe steaming off the coast overnight. The whole time we had Navy observers on board to teach and judge and grade us. Grudgingly, I will admit that I personally benefited from the experience by seeing what the ship could do under myriad circumstances.

Let's say the bridge were knocked out of action during battle; there was an auxiliary bridge called 'after steering' behind the stacks from which you could still run the ship. If Radio I were destroyed, there was the auxiliary radio room. If the steering mechanism were damaged, the rudders could be operated manually, with a block and tackle if necessary, way down in the stern of the ship. And if any combination of engine or boiler or propeller or propeller shaft were knocked out, there were an amazingly large number of ways to cross-connect the remaining functioning machinery to keep the ship moving. Sadly, the ability to cross-connect has disappeared from destroyers, since the Navy went to a single propeller and shaft. So now when you go dead in the water, you are really dead in the water. Anyway, the WWII destroyers were built to last, and could take a lot of punishment while dishing it out.

Another, more insidious change has recently taken place in the Navy, and that is the rating of signalman has disappeared. *Signalman!* How can you run a ship without signalmen? They have been an integral part of Navy crews since the beginning. Recently I met a sharp young officer who was about to become XO of a guided missile warship, and we got into a discussion of his Navy versus mine. He told me about the elimination of signalmen, and I posed a hypothetical situation to him. What if, I says, you are in action and your voice communications are knocked out. How do you talk to the ship who is in company with you? You can't talk with a signal lamp, or by semaphore, or by hoisting signal flags. He said, "You aren't going to like the answer." I said, "Well?" He said, "You send them an e-mail." I was so dumfounded I just had no answer. I had never heard of anything so stupid, and didn't even bother to ask what if your power were knocked out? There was probably a perfectly good techno-answer for that, too.

This officer had heard of my step father, and worse still, he said that these economy and efficiency moves were based on Zim's very brilliant innovations regarding Navy budgets. Don't tell me that! If Zim had known that his legacy was to be used to justify the elimination of signalmen, he would turn over in his grave. In fact, I have heard about some recent seismic activity at Arlington National Cemetery.

Whether we were tied up to a buoy or to the pier, the Sea and Anchor Detail could take hours since we were always picking up or dropping off observers. As JOOD, it was my duty to go down to greet them and escort them to the bridge. Otherwise it was my job to assist Norm Davis. During battle problems I donned a big gray steel helmet and headset, and became phone talker to the OOD. I would take in reports from all over the ship concerning sightings, radar contacts, damage, and many other things, all of which helped him determine his plan of attack at any moment.

I was pleased with the cohesiveness of my division. They all pulled together and, under the leadership of SM1 Faust and my new leading radioman RM1 Wosika, or "Ski," I didn't have any concerns about performance under pressure. I put a lot of pressure on myself to perform well in front of an audience composed of the CO, XO, my boss Norm and the Navy observers. But I don't remember having too hard a time of it, just that I was on the bridge so much that I started putting roots down.

* * *

There were hazards to be had everywhere. One day we were getting underway from a pier when a Coast Guard Cutter, the Ingram, tried its best to cause a collision by ignoring the Rules of the Road and pulling out in front of us. We avoided hitting her but everyone was pretty angry about it.

One afternoon we had a terrible time coming in to a pier because a short but violent squall blew up just as we were making our approach. Because of its prominent bow and superstructure, a destroyer has a lot of what is called "sail area" in proportion to its size. Sail area catches the wind just as a sail does on a sailboat, and can affect the handling of the ship. Well, this sudden wind blew us back off the pier, and in an instant, the ship was out of control and being blown across the harbor sideways. Bruce was conning at the time, and did a great job of regaining control, but could not get us in to the pier. By happenstance, a tug was underway nearby, and was glad to come to our rescue by nudging up to our starboard bow. Our deck guys got out in a very hard and freezing rain and dangerous wind to lash us to the tug so he could ease us into the slip. Slowly he pushed us in, and the deck crew were out again to tie us up and to release the tug. This was really a masterful performance of seamanship by all concerned, and the Captain gave the order, "Now splice the main brace," the one and only time I ever heard this order given. Translated into English, this meant, "Now break out the medicinal brandy" for those guys who performed so well out on deck in the driving freezing rain and wind. I doubt that that ancient order has been given since. It was great for crew morale.

We were headed out to a designated training area one morning at high speed when Norm gave me the conn while he discussed that day's activities with the Captain and XO. They were huddled in conversation when I shouted orders to the helmsman in quick succession, "Right full rudder," and then "Left full rudder!" As if with one voice, Norm, the CO, the XO, and it seemed like everyone else, turned on me and barked, "What the hell are you doing?" In one of those singularly cool moments in my life, I said, "Sirs, have a look." And they did, as a 60-foot log slipped smoothly (and harmlessly) down the port side. After some "harrumphing" and a "Well done, Mr. Cook," they went back to their conference, and I put 5 points for Mr. Cook up on an imaginary scoreboard.

* * *

We began to notice that when called upon, our brand-new, gas turbine auxiliary generator never seemed to work. I guess that's what experimental systems are for, to try out new ideas, but that generator is very important to the ship's operation, and it plagued the engineers from the time it was installed until the ship was mothballed in '70.

* * *

During training, every division was gone through with a fine-toothed comb by the observers. Everyone got pretty sick of them, even though we knew that they were necessary. Other than radio and signals, which as I have said were no problem, my involvement was on the bridge, and other than Sea and Anchor Detail, that included battle problems.

Anti-submarine Warfare was trained and graded, even though the Gulf of Tonkin was too shallow for submarine activity. The Russians were still around in other waters, though, with their nasty boats so I guess it was necessary. For one ASW exercise, the target was a conventional diesel sub, and I don't remember why, but we just couldn't locate it with the sonar. Probably difficult conditions, such as layers of water of different temperatures where a sub could "hide." Anyway, they had to pop up their snorkel pretty close aboard to give us a hint, and we finished the exercise with some excellent tracking and "killing."

Most of our battle time was spent on gunnery. Other than plane guard and a few other duties, our main job in Vietnam would be shore bombardment, more formally known as Naval Gunfire Support. My first assignment was, I am sure, saved for the junior ensign, because they stuck me inside the forward gun mount as a "check sight observer." I had to squeeze into a space to the left of the guns (with one of the barrels next to my head), and look through a scope to verify that where we were about to shoot, there were no ships or boats or anything else. Before shooting, the bridge would call down to me, "Check sight," and if there was nothing in my scope I would report, "Check sight clear!" Then they would shoot.

It's a very strange sensation, having a 5-inch cannon go off right next to you. Instead of the deafening "boom" you would hear if you were outside, the report was muffled through the steel armor of the mount. What you did hear were all of the metallic, mechanical sounds of the exercise, particularly when the powder casing and projectile were dropped (by hand) into the open breech, the breech was slammed closed, and the gun fired. When the breech was opened, out came the brass shell casing, and the "hot caseman" dropped it through a hole and it clanged to the deck outside.

This was the same gun mount that helped win the Pacific War in WWII. A hot gun crew, then or in Korea or in Vietnam, could put out over 15 rounds per minute from each gun, or 30 rounds per minute from the mount, all done manually in perfect timing and harmony. I am quite sure that a gun crew, as we knew it, is no longer needed to fire Naval guns, and that now everything is completely automated.

We shot at target sleds towed by other ships, and air targets towed by aircraft. I always thought that those people should be nervous despite all of the built-in safety precautions.

As I was on the bridge for most of the gunnery exercises, I couldn't help but notice a small quirk in the system. There was a two-toned warning buzzer that was supposed to sound off immediately before the guns fired to sort of get you ready for the loud noise and concussion. First a high tone, then a low tone, then *blam!* The buzzer worked for some time after overhaul, then intermittently, then not at all. The guys would come up and fix it and it would work for a while and then stop again. The result was that, rather than your being warned and ready, the guns would just fire and scare the living hell out of you. This happened so often that you might think we would get used to it. Au contraire! We never got used to it, and I believe that lesser men would probably develop a case of nerves over it.

They were so loud! In those days, ear protection hadn't been invented yet, at least for bridge personnel. And there was another little problem, this one associated with the STOPS system. I have mentioned that STOPS gave us an air pressure of plus 3 or 4 lbs. per square inch inside the ship's "envelope." When the forward guns were fired the concussion expanded through that pressurized air, and shook our heads like a bowl of jello. So after a firing exercise we would normally come off the bridge with a dizzying headache and with our ears ringing so loud we couldn't think. And as I write this, my ears are *still* ringing that loud, to the tune of $123.00 a month from the VA! (I just got a $3.00 raise.)

* * *

After all the weeks of training and grading and grading and training, it all boiled down to one great, climactic Final Battle Problem. We took her out off the coast, where the "Russians" (the observers) hit us with everything they had. We were attacked by submarines, fighter/bombers and other ships. We fired back (electronically) with torpedoes, ASROC missiles, and the mighty 5" 38's with anti- aircraft and surface bursts. Our job was to kill the enemy and if we took hits, to get them repaired so that we could keep on fighting. It was so intense and so realistic that we could have just as well have been at Leyte Gulf in 1944. At the beginning of the exercise we were attacked by single aircraft or ship or whatever, but at the Big Climax, they came at us from all sides, and I was getting so many reports from all over the ship that I fed them to Norm in a constant stream of information. Somehow he was able to absorb everything while "fighting" the ship and keeping her afloat.

We prevailed. We were able to outgun and outfight the evil observers. I was so proud of my division, which scored an adjective grade of *excellent* and a numerical grade of 89. I scored an 87 or so as JOOD. It was over, and that fact made the whole crew very, very happy. It was like hitting yourself in the head with a baseball bat and it felt so good when you stopped. However, it did leave us with another feeling, and that was of genuine pride that we were now highly trained and looked forward to being tested. For real.

Our reward for getting through the ordeal of Refresher Training was sailing up to San Francisco for weekend liberty. What a great town! We spent our time carousing and drinking and eating well and watching the parade go by. The discovery of the Buena Vista Bar across from the cable car turnaround at the wharf, began what has turned out to be a lifetime connection. The image that lingers, and still kind of defines San Francisco for me, took place just as dawn was breaking and a few of us were walking back to the ship after a great night out. As we were weaving toward the piers, walking toward us was a woman, probably in her early 40's with gray hair in an Audrey Hepburn do, and not unattractive in a very short silver lame dress that just covered her personal items. Nice legs. We were thinking that the evening might not be over after all, but she just kept walking, right through the group, staring straight ahead at something that was 1,000 miles away. I think she was somewhere in La La Land, not to have noticed such fine and handsome young officers. Oh well.

Blue Water

It was time to get down to business. After sailing back to San Diego, we began to sever our lifelines to the mainland and make preparations for the six month cruise. For the single guys, boxes of personal goods were put into storage, and arrangements were made to store automobiles. I helped Porter Powell to store his beautiful vintage Volvo 544. Well, back then it was new enough not to be vintage, but it is now. Anyway, it was white with red interior and was immaculate. Besides his girlfriend, it was his pride and joy. Once it was parked in a garage space, he double-checked the six one-gallon jugs of newly made wine which were stored in the front and back floorboards. The idea was for the wine to mature and mellow for 6 months, and be ready for drinking when we got back.

My mother and step father came up with the idea that I could drive the Corvette out to Omaha, visit with them briefly, and leave it with them. They promised to crank it up and drive it around the fort once in awhile. That sounded like a pretty good deal and so we did it. I always looked forward to being at Fort Omaha because the Navy there were like a big family.

I got Zim checked out on the car, and found that we had a small problem: the speed limit near the quarters was only 10 mph, and the car's engine wouldn't idle that slowly. We had to use a combination of clutch and coasting in order to avoid complaints. Some people said that their houses shook anyway when we went by. While there I needed to call my grandmother in Missouri to tell her where I was going. I approached the subject gingerly, not wanting to scare her. I needn't have worried, though, because when I finally said, "Maw Maw, I'm going to Vietnam," she thought for a moment and said, "Well, honey, be sure to duck." I promised her that I would.

Too quickly, it was time to return to San Diego. By mutual agreement, Mother and Zim dropped me at the curb at Offutt Field for the trip back. Inside the terminal I was waiting for my flight when "Doc" from "Gunsmoke" sat down beside me. He was easily recognizable, and we said hello and chatted a little. Milburn Stone was a very nice man, looked like everyone's grandfather, and in retrospect I realize that I really had to restrain myself from asking how Miss Kitty was. I watched some packages for him while he used the phone, and went to get him when his flight was called. A nice little interlude and a nice man.

* * *

Back in San Diego now, it was "two days and counting" until we got underway, and everyone was very busy. On the afternoon of June 2, though, we got some news that made the world stand still. I was milling about somewhere, minding my own business, when a radioman carrying a message board found me and said, "Sir, you'd better read this, one of our destroyers got cut in half!" I said, "Whaaat?" I was handed the message, it was stamped, *"Urgent,"* and read that the USS Frank E. Evans (DD-754) had been involved in a collision with the Australian Carrier HMAS Melbourne during nighttime SEATO (Southeast Asia Treaty Organization) exercises in the South China Sea. The carrier had rammed the Evans amidships and literally torn her in half.

My heart sank as I told the RM that I had two friends on that ship. I asked him if there was a casualty report yet, and he said, "No, sir, but I'll get it to you as soon as it comes over." Don Murphy (Communications School) and Phil Hess (USS Bridget) were on the Evans and I was very worried. They were good guys. I could not imagine how something like this could possibly happen in this day and age. Later in the day the casualty list came in, and I went quickly through it hoping I wouldn't see anyone familiar. There were so many names. But there he was, missing and presumed dead, EMC Edward Phillip Hess. LTJG Donald Murphy was not mentioned. In my mind I said, "Aw, Chief, I'm so sorry." And I really was sad, I had liked him very much. It turned out that when the collision occurred, the forward section of the Evans rolled over on its side, then capsized and sank within three minutes. Some men actually escaped, but not many; they never had a chance. I still think about Chief Hess.

Later hearings at Subic Bay Naval Base, the Philippines, brought out that the Evans, a little after 3:00 AM on June 3, was part of a destroyer screen, and was located at about the 10 o'clock position off the port bow of the carrier HMAS Melbourne. Ordered to change station to Plane Guard, directly astern of the carrier, she inexplicably turned to starboard toward the big ship. Two more mistaken rudder commands placed her directly in the path of the Melbourne, which was desperately trying to maneuver to avoid a collision. The crash sent shock waves through both navies. Seventy-four men were killed, most in the forward section. The after section remained afloat and was eventually towed to Subic Bay.

Changing station on a carrier is a very dangerous maneuver, as I would be finding out in about a month. On the Thomas it was never, ever done without the Captain or the XO on the bridge, regardless the experience of the OOD. Neither was present on the bridge of the Evans when she died.

* * *

Now came the time to kiss wives and girlfriends goodbye, and make all the necessary promises. So I made a date to take Linda out to dinner. Afterward, we were at her house and sitting on the couch having a nice time when she dropped a bombshell on me. When she said, "I think I'm pregnant," all time stood still for me. To this day, that endures as the longest moment of my life. After the silence, the best I could manage was, "Are you sure?" The question in my mind was, was I the father, because she had still been seeing this old boyfriend occasionally. But Linda was a great girl and a straight shooter, and I could never have asked her such a question. She agreed to see a doctor to make sure, and to let me know. We hugged and kissed (she really *was* a doll!), and I headed for the ship. Turned out later that she was not pregnant, to the huge relief of Ensign Cook!

* * *

At last, we were ready to depart. I was finally going to have my adventure. The ship was fully provisioned, and one by one, services were disconnected from the pier, water, electric, phone, and finally the gangway was taken in, then the last line was slipped. Over to the fuel pier to top off, and then over to the AMMO pier to take on a full load of ordinance for a war cruise. I guess it was at this point that we all realized that this time it was for real. The guys who had been there before knew what to expect, but the rest of us hadn't a clue.

As we headed for the harbor entrance, the Captain ordered that the cruise pennant be hoisted. A cruise pennant, in the past known as a "homeward bound" pennant, was a long, thin piece of cotton or nylon cloth, only 2 or 3 inches wide at the halyard end, and stretching thirty, forty, fifty feet, to a point. The signalmen sew these pennants, and they resemble the Stars and Stripes, with a blue field and a few white stars, changing to a few red and white stripes. Our pennant stayed where it was for the entire war cruise, at the end of which it was hauled down, tattered and dirty, and cut up into small strips to be given to each officer and crewman who made the trip. I think it is a great part of Naval tradition, and it may not even exist anymore because there are no more signalmen!

* * *

Outside San Diego Harbor, we rendezvoused with the rest of our division, the USS Taussig, Renshaw, Craig, Prichett, and Hamner. We formed up into a cruising formation and headed for WestPac. The code name for this operation was "Arrow West."

The crossing to Pearl Harbor was uneventful and took a leisurely 7 days over glassy water, during which the division practiced "tic tacs." Tic tacs are high-speed maneuvers designed for a division or squadron of destroyers that are screening (protecting) larger capital ships. Normally arrayed in a semicircle out in front of a formation, they use these tactics to make quick turns in sync, to either zigzag for ASW purposes, to make a turn toward an immediate threat, or to turn with a carrier during flight operations. It is an excellent drill for the ship handlers and signalmen. Done properly and traditionally, all commands are by signal flag, the flags run up and down the halyard, smartly and correctly, by the command ship, and acknowledged by the others. These drills taught me more about signal flags, codes, and ship handling than anything I had experienced up to that point.

We were testing all of our equipment during this time, and had a drill among the ships with something called the Hydrophone. This was a gadget that you could use to communicate, using water as the medium rather than ether. If you weren't making too much speed, and were within fairly close range, you could talk to the next ship. I used the thing, and it was very funny, because you could just barely understand the other guy due to the constant loud gurgling noise. It was okay as a backup system, but I don't recall ever using it again.

I say that the crossing was uneventful, but I quickly learned that every day at sea was a learning day. There was a signal event that came to define the relationship between me and George Faust and our division, and it centered around Faust. Shortly after we left San Diego, he addressed the guys and told them what he expected of them during this cruise, and laid out his rules of behavior. When he had finished, there was no room for doubt about what he wanted, which included his particular emphasis on keeping our berthing areas clean. There is a Navy term, "Gear Adrift," which means those things, clothes, personal items, or anything else, that are not properly stowed when the crewman is elsewhere on the ship or ashore. There was to be no gear adrift in the Communications Division spaces.

A few days out, Faust requested that I accompany him on an inspection of the OC spaces the next morning after chow. When we met for the tour, I noticed that he had a large garbage bag folded up and tucked under his arm. When we got to our berthing area, it began to dawn on me what he had in mind. Largely deserted of people, nonetheless there was plenty of, you guessed it, *gear adrift*. I had to admit, it was pretty messy. Without saying a word, he looked at me and unfolded the bag, and the two of us proceeded to pick things up off the deck, bunks and horizontal surfaces, that should have been stowed away. The few guys who were there watched in silence, their eyes big and round. When we had finished, we had a space that was neat and clean as a pin, and a bag full of gear that was no longer adrift.

We left with the bag and a couple of guys followed us to see what we were up to. We took it up to the main deck, over to the rail, and after Faust said, "Ready, sir?" we both lifted it and tossed it over the side.

My leading petty officer had made his point. The entire division now knew that Faust meant what he said, about anything! And that he didn't fool around. For the rest of my tour aboard the Thomas, my spaces were always kept neat and clean because the crew knew that Faust was still around, and that he was watching. I don't know if anyone ever said anything to him about this episode, I can imagine that they did, though. There wasn't much they could say, but one of the signalmen, a very likeable guy named Nelson, came up to me and said, "Sir, I know we shouldn't have left all of that stuff out, but that was a *brand new pair of shoes!* I can only see myself shrugging, and Nelson saying something like, "I know, I know."

* * *

Just before leaving San Diego we had acquired two new crew members who would be with us for the crossing: Ensigns Lam Kim Luon and Nguyen Van Be of the South Vietnamese Navy. Even though they were commissioned officers, they remained in training, and our cruise would be a part of that. They were actually very well educated, and were also proficient in hand-to-hand combat using several types of martial arts.

Ensign Lam was tall for a Vietnamese, and quite slender, while Ensign Nguyen was shorter and only slightly more stocky. They had agreed to do a demonstration of their fighting skills for the crew, and it quickly became evident that in a real scrap they could more than hold their own. They were like a couple of snakes: quick and deadly. It was so incongruous to see one of them, relatively small and slight, giving a demonstration karate chop across the throat of one of our muscular young sailors who was almost a foot taller. Their English was good and they learned a lot from us, as we did from them. The last we saw of them was off the coast of Vietnam, where they transferred to the cruiser USS Boston (CA-69) by motor whaleboat. As I write this I wonder what may have happened to them six years later when their country collapsed. Their chances for survival might not have been too good.

* * *

There is nothing on this earth more beautiful or spectacular than a sunset out in the middle of the Pacific. There is no way I can begin to describe the colors and the splendor to you. I have seen nature at work in many far-flung places, but even now I can close my eyes and see those sunsets, so grand and dramatic and fiery. The only thing that I can think of that gives me the same feeling today is to stand in front of a painting by Vincent Van Gogh.

I developed the habit of going up to the signal bridge when I could to watch the sun set, and it was the perfect way to end the working day. It was soothing to the soul. I would also go up there late at night, after a late watch or before turning in. No one else was there except for the dark outline of the signalman on duty. We would acknowledge each other and then I would move away by myself and just look up at the stars for a while. Magnificent. And it was so quiet! Hundreds of guys below me, sleeping or going about their duties, and I was up here alone. Beside the sunsets, it was my favorite personal time of the day.

* * *

I was on the bridge one morning when we got a ship on the radar. We checked with CIC (Combat Information Center) to see if they had it, and they reported that they had been tracking it already. It looked like a freighter and it had maintained course and speed for quite some time. The problem was that our paths would eventually cross and there was a danger of collision. According to the Rules of the Road for navigation, it was up to both ships to maneuver to avoid collision, and so we signaled her our intentions. There was no answer.

We used voice radio and when she was closer, also used the blinker light, to try to get her attention and get her to maneuver properly. There was never even an acknowledgement of our signals much less communication. She just kept on coming, same course, same speed. We of course had to do all of the work in order to avoid this blockhead. And that is where I learned the term "Iron Mike." It is a seafarers term for auto-pilot. Some ships' masters use it when they hit open ocean, where their chances of encountering other ships are reduced, even though they are still in common sea lanes. They simply lock in a course and speed, turn on the Iron Mike, and go to sleep. There wasn't anyone driving the damn ship! I was learning.

* * *

There is a phenomenon that occurs at sea which will always make you do a double or triple take. If you have a contact on your surface radar, you won't necessarily get a visual on the ship because of the distance involved, but sometimes you could look through the binoculars and see only the mast of a ship and not the rest of it, and pretty close, too! It's called "hull down." On a destroyer you stand a bridge watch about 35 feet above the water, and add my height to make it about 41 feet. At this height, the actual curvature of the earth is only 8 miles away, and if the contact is at just the right distance, you can see a pretty large mast or superstructure and nothing else. Maybe you have to be there, but it is a very strange thing to see for the first time. And the second time as well.

* * *

The sea yielded up some surprises: when the sun came up the stewards would frequently find flying fish stranded on the main deck and they would cook them for the Captain's breakfast. And during the day we would watch with fascination as the dolphins played in our bow wave. If there were another ship on our beam (to the right or the left of us), it was easier to see them as they came up out of the water and dove into the wave for hour upon hour. You could spot schools of them by looking for their back fins.

At night we were treated to the most cosmic light show in the water as the little animals named "dinoflagellates" lit up in their greenish blue phosphorescence and streamed from the bow, along the sides of the ship, and out through the propellers into our wake. Sometimes they came in such numbers that they literally lit up the sea behind the ship. Boy, were they beautiful.

* * *

We were to make a scheduled fuel stop at Pearl Harbor. When we entered the harbor and swung around Ford Island, the USS Arizona Memorial came into view. Now, I had seen the memorial before, as a tourist, and it was a solemn enough occasion then. But now, from the bridge of a destroyer, I and everyone there saw it from a completely different perspective. You could have heard a pin drop. The only sounds were muted rudder and engine commands. It was a great show of respect from us to the "old boys" who had fought and died here.

This was only a fuel stop and not a liberty port, and so we were unable to leave the ship. We could only stare longingly at the palm trees and catch the faint scent of fuel oil on the air.

As we entered the port you couldn't help but admire the Admiral's quarters---a large two story white house on the water, surrounded by palm trees and a manicured lawn. As we were leaving, we were not far from this house, when the Captain gave an engine command, probably something like "all ahead 1/3." Well, this produced a big puff of black smoke from our stacks, and the wind was such that it carried this cloud toward the Admiral's quarters, and I swear it went right through his front screen door. We were all horrified, as was the Captain, who kept going, right out of the harbor, as quickly as possible. He did send a message back, though, saying that we were the culprits and begging the Admiral's pardon.

* * *

There is an area way out in the middle of the South Pacific called "Point Nemo," that is the farthest point from any land on the entire planet. When you are on a ship in the Pacific Ocean, you feel small and insignificant enough in the universe, but when you get out beyond Hawaii, the sea is so vast that it feels like Point Nemo, and in this area you feel really lonely. It is the last place in the world that you would expect to have company.

We got him on sonar first. ASW thought he could be a whale or a large school of fish, but then they identified him as a Russian submarine! He was everywhere and all over us at the same time, using us for an exercise dummy, doing firing solutions on us. It was excellent practice for our guys, too, but what became apparent was his eye-popping speed! This one was nuclear because no conventional sub could travel that fast. He was downright scary, and was just playing with us. Knowing that our side had boats just as fast, or faster, told us that their world was much different than ours with our WWII destroyers and diesel subs. What would have leveled the playing field in a battle was our ASROC (anti-submarine rocket) capability, a very destructive weapon. And of course we still had six conventional torpedo tubes, but they would probably not have been much of a threat to him.

After a while the "enemy" tired of the game and left us. We all had the distinct feeling that they had just thumbed their Russian nose at us.

* * *

We were now headed for the US Naval Base at Yokosuka, Japan, a 10 day trip from Pearl Harbor during which we would train, train, and train again. There was some down time, however, which gave opportunity to break in some of the new guys. As I have already mentioned, a joke often played on a new sailor was to send him up to the bridge to polish the navigator's balls. Earnest young men in neat, new uniforms would periodically appear with a couple of rags and a bucket, and ask where the navigator's balls were. After a good laugh, the bridge crew would tell him he had been had, and an embarrassed, but slightly wiser, sailor would leave.

I was on the bridge one day when I saw my first episode of the Sea Bat. An older sailor went out on the main deck to the forward gun mount with a cardboard box, and placed it on the deck, upside down, with one flap used to prop it up so there was a small opening on the bottom. Another sailor holding a large broom slipped around the side of the gun mount, unseen. The first sailor then looked at the bridge and gave a thumbs-up, and another conspirator would get on the PA and announce something like, "Now, attention all hands, attention all hands. A very rare Sea Bat has been captured near the forward gun mount. All hands who have never seen this creature should do so before it is released. Those hands on duty may request to leave their station and go forward."

We now waited and watched for the drama to unfold. It wasn't long before the first young victim appeared, tentatively walking up to the senior man, who explained that he had to be very quiet in order not to scare the animal, and to kneel down and carefully look through the opening. As he slowly knelt down and peered in, *wham*, the other sailor whacked him in the butt with his broom, thus scaring the living shit out of him. This guy, and maybe a dozen other neophytes, went through another rite of passage that all "newbies" had to endure. (I would bet next week's lunch money that this practice is no longer allowed).

The last, and most subtle, initiation for our beloved Seaman Recruits, occurred as we approached the International Dateline at 180 degrees longitude, where the day you are in abruptly changes to the next day. Officially, the information had been disseminated that we would cross the ID during the night sometime between such and such hours. Unofficially, the word had been passed about the International Dateline Watch. I was asked about it by one young man on the mid-watch. I told him that it was a very big honor for a sailor to be the first to spot the International Dateline and report it to the bridge. When he asked what to look for, I had to think fast, and told him, "It's a long string of lights out over the water, you can't miss it." He had the binoculars to his face the whole watch, searching dead ahead. He wasn't the only one, there were a number of guys you could see down on the main deck, seriously watching and waiting. And waiting, and waiting. The sharper the sailor, the sooner he figured out that he had been had again, and just went down and hit the rack.

* * *

Finally we arrived at the Naval Base in Yokosuka. We were to be there for 3 days, and this afforded our younger sailors a chance to see some of the country for the first time. The most popular attractions were nearby Tokyo, the giant Buddha at Kamakura, and of course the beautiful young Japanese bar girls.

The CO and XO were briefed on the mission by the staff of Commander, Naval Forces Far East. Our job fell into four categories:

Naval Gunfire Support- short notice support for amphibious assault and other troops within our gun range.

Naval Shore Bombardment- shooting at pre-determined or fixed coastal targets, within our gun range.

Plane Guard- accompanying aircraft carriers on Yankee Station to assist in aircraft emergencies.

PIRAZ- cruise off of Haiphong Harbor as an early warning radar picket ship. (I now know this is an acronym for Positive Identification Radar Advisory Zone).

* * *

Thus briefed and sated, we sailed for Subic Bay, The Phillippines, which would be our "home port" while overseas. We put in there a total of three times during the tour. On the way we stopped at the big pier at Buckner Bay, Okinawa, to take on fuel.

Our arrival at the large Naval Base at Subic Bay was marked by feverish activity to get us ready to go to Vietnam in a few days. We had hardly any time to go out on base, much less into the notorious town of Olongapo. I did discover a popular place called the Chuck Wagon, a café/restaurant on base where the food was sort of average but the slot machines were very user-friendly.

* * *

Everyone wanted to see the USS Evans, or what was left of her. We walked over to the drydock and there she was. It took your breath away. She was cut cleanly in half between the stacks, like a hot knife through butter. You could see the point of impact on the port side, and how the hull was bent over onto itself until the ship just broke like a plastic toy. There weren't many people around, as the hulk had been there for awhile. We just stared, it looked so unreal and so lonely, trying to imagine the enormous force it had taken to do such a thing. It made you so angry all over again that bad seamanship had caused this and had cost so many lives.

I learned that hearings were still going on at Subic over the accident, and that my friend from comm school, Lt. Donald Murphy, was on base. I got on the phone and found him and invited him to lunch in our wardroom the next day. At the appointed time I met him on the quarterdeck, and took him down to the wardroom. A number of our officers were there to meet him and ask him about the crash. He sat down and I got a good look at him. He wasn't the same strapping fellow I had known in San Diego. He had lost weight, his skin was pasty white, he had red blotches on his face, and his hands were shaking slightly. I wanted very much to ask him about Chief Hess, but I just couldn't.

We never got to lunch. He just started talking. He had been asleep in an upper bunk, and the first thing he remembered was being on all fours in two feet of water, in total darkness. He told about trying to find his way out, and about finally getting to a passageway where he could head to his GQ station, and the forward part of the ship just wasn't there. We were asking him to relive a nightmare, and it was getting him upset, so it didn't go any further than that. But before he left he gave us some very good advice. He said, "Always have a flashlight! Always have a flashlight! Always keep a flashlight with you!" Just like that, in kind of a manic mantra. It was easier then to see what had traumatized him so much that night, even over the other horrors that he must have witnessed. Here was a fine officer and a decent guy whose life had been changed in an instant by the stupidity of others.

On October 10, 1969 the stripped-down remains of the USS Evans were towed out to sea and sunk by Naval gunfire from the USS Cochrane (DDG-21). The 74 men who died in the USS Frank E. Evans have not been forgotten. There is a memorial tree and plaque in Arlington National Cemetery, but there are those who believe that the names of those men should be included on the Vietnam Veterans Memorial Wall. I happen to agree. The naysayers contend that the ship was not within the designated combat zone when she sank. Well, so what? She was pulled directly off the gun line to take part in the exercise, and these men died on a combat tour to Vietnam. Their memory has been highly honored, but they belong on The Wall along with our other heroes.

* * *

I had to make a run to the Communications Station to pick up the new codes and publications we would need to operate in a war zone. We were to get underway again for 3 days of gunnery practice out in a group of islands called the Tabones.

Gunnery went through every drill we had, using each type of ammo we carried. Our gun range was 18,000 yards, or about 10 miles, over which we could hurl a 55 lb. projectile. We also carried a Rocket Assisted Projectile (RAP), on which a rocket engine burned for about 40 seconds and carried the projectile another 3-4 miles. The standard shell was called "HE" for high explosive, and we also shot anti-aircraft and star shells. When we fired star shells, used for night illumination, they lit up the sea in a most beautiful and ethereal way, with the very bright flare descending slowly under its parachute. The white phosphorous shell (WP or "willy peter") produces a dense smoke screen for men or ships in trouble.

Out in the islands was a shooting range, and we put round after round of HE into it. You could set HE for an air burst or to explode on contact with the ground or a structure, and we were shooting air bursts when one somehow flew off the range and, as luck would have it, went off right above a village communal meeting house, completely destroying it. We had to stop firing until it could be determined what had happened, and if anyone had been hurt.

The Navy spotter found that there were no injuries but that the village chief was hopping mad. And the Captain handled the really delicate situation so smoothly that he may have been through this kind of thing before. Maybe the spotter had suggested it. Whatever, the CO arranged to send the chief some cash and a case of gin, and an incident that could have caused real problems was quickly forgotten. Some things are best handled on a local level.

After a few days of this, we returned to Subic for an overnight, and then on July 3rd we got underway. Whether by accident or design, we began a month of Plane Guard and PIRAZ duties in Vietnam on Independence Day, July 4, 1969.

* * *

When you did Plane Guard duty in Vietnam, you became a member of the Tonkin Gulf Yacht Club. There is a very famous and colorful patch that can be worn on a jacket or a ball cap, that is easily recognized by all of its members. Yankee Station, home of Task Force 77, was one of two areas where carrier groups operated off of South Vietnam, the other being Dixie Station farther south, which went out of business in 1966.

There could be two or three groups operating at once, and each group included a number of destroyers. We did several tours on Yankee Station, and worked with the carriers USS Ticonderoga and USS Oriskany. They were flying a mix of planes, including the F-4 Phantom, which was my personal favorite. Our unofficial call sign for them was "Bird Farm" or "Chicken Farm," and they called us "Bubbles" because of our unusual configuration. These two ships were monsters, whose flank speed was classified at the time. These days, in the ships' histories, the top speed is listed as 33 knots, which is very fast, but we on the destroyers had the distinct feeling that they were much faster, and could have run away from us if they had wanted to.

Our job was to take station on the carrier's port or starboard beam at 2,000 yards, or directly astern of her at 1,000 yards. If a pilot crashed or had to bail out, we were right there to pick him up. When the carrier was maneuvering for one reason or another, or turning into the wind to launch or recover aircraft, we had to maintain our exact station. Ironically this is called station keeping, and requires excellent seamanship and the full attention of bridge personnel.

As we have seen with the Evans, changing station with another destroyer is a very dangerous maneuver. You have to figure a course and speed that will keep you out of the carrier's way, avoid hitting the other tin cans, and arrive on your new station without falling far behind the group. The wise Captain or XO is usually on the bridge during this maneuver.

When stationed astern, you steered to stay exactly in the carrier's wake. If she changed course, you were there. Usually the OOD or JOOD gave rudder and/or compass commands to keep station, but as an alternative, we found a modern use for an ancient order. During daytime steaming, you could order the helmsman to "steer by seaman's eye." This delighted the helmsman because it gave him de facto control of the ship. He would literally watch the carrier's stern and its wake, and keep our bow right on it. This is much harder work than it sounds, but they loved it.

I guess my favorite position was here, behind the gigantic ships. And my favorite pastime was going up to the signal bridge to watch them recover aircraft. This was a highly coordinated ballet in which a flight of 4 fighters would come in and circle the bird farm in a wide arc. On each pass, a plane would peel off and head for the flight deck. Of course they would fly directly over us (me), and would be very low and we could see the belly and wheels down and hear this terrific roar, he would continue his glide path toward the deck and then *wham*, he was down with considerable force and stopped. I never got tired of watching this spectacle. And you must remember that the flight deck is always moving, not stationary, particularly in rough water, and the coordination between the pilot and the Landing Signal Officer is literally a life or death situation.

If daytime OPS were fun to watch, night OPS were outrageous! The carrier was lit up like Christmas, and the incoming planes had their landing lights on and their jet exhaust trailed out behind them. We had always heard that a landing on a carrier was literally a "controlled crash." And that was true, because at night the real light show occurred when that plane slammed into the deck in a huge shower of white-hot sparks. And it was one after another, *wham, wham, wham*. The technology and pilot skill involved was just unbelievable, and those Black Shoe Navy officers more than earned the grudging respect of us Brown Shoes. (Once ashore, of course, no one would ever admit this to anybody!).

For all of the time we worked with these two great carriers, we never knew anything about the missions they were flying. Even my communications guys couldn't get any information because we did not have "need to know." Each ship lost aircraft and crews to enemy gun fire and missiles, but we had not a clue to the daily drama which was taking place only 1,000 yards from us. It's probably better that we didn't know.

Our worst day occurred as we were steaming on the starboard beam of (probably) the Oriskany, during her launch of what I believe were F-8 Crusaders. The F-8 was the last fighter plane produced by the US that actually had guns, was a single-seater, and the pilots call themselves Gunfighters to this day. I was on the bridge and we were watching planes take flight one after the other. Well, one of them shot off of the end of the flight deck, and not a second later had a flameout. I'm not sure exactly what happens during a flameout, but the entire rear of the aircraft erupted in a fireball, and it began to lose altitude. The pilot was quick-thinking and brought his nose up and tried to get enough power to stay airborne. It caught us by such surprise that everyone who was watching started yelling, *Come on, come on, come on!"* And as much as that guy tried, he crashed hard into the sea and disappeared. It happened in an instant. Our bridge fell absolutely silent, and someone muttered, "Damn." It was very emotional and sad and cast a pall over our ship. We had just watched someone die right in front of us, and no one knew what to say.

The carrier continued on, and another ship was detached to search the area where he went down. And after a while we heard that a single piece of debris had been picked up, and it was the pilot's white flight helmet with a crack right down the middle of it. None of us could imagine the amount of force it took to crack that helmet almost in two. It was a sad post-script to a bad day on Yankee Station.

Note: In May of 2006, the USS Oriskany, veteran of the Korean and Vietnam wars, was sunk off the Gulf Coast of Florida to be used as an artificial reef. 800 pounds of plastic explosive took the grand ship to the bottom in only 37 minutes.

The great ship USS Ticonderoga, veteran of WWII and the Vietnam war, was ignominiously sold for scrap in 1975.

* * *

There is an evolution called Underway Replenishment, or UNREP, wherein you can come alongside a supply ship or an oiler to take on supplies or fuel oil, much like military aircraft are able to do in the air. The supply ship maintains a constant course and speed, and the destroyer makes the approach from the rear. The idea is to get in fast, quickly put yourself alongside at the same course and speed, replenish and clear off. Tradition says that in wartime, both ships are at their most vulnerable to torpedo or air attack when hooked up, they can't maneuver, so it is always done quickly.

This is a great exercise for a ship handler to show his stuff. We made such an approach one morning, with the XO, Commander Aydt, driving. I had never seen him do this before, and he was really good. He approached the supply ship at a pretty radical angle and at high speed. At precisely the right moment, he whipped the wheel over and reversed engines, ready to place her in perfect sync with our partner. It was a work of art, the prettiest use of a destroyer you can imagine.

And then the Captain panicked. Cdr. Aydt was using superior seamanship, but it scared the Captain and he thought we were going to hit the other ship. He yelled that he was taking the conn, and gave orders that took us away again. Everyone on the bridge was stunned and silent, and I know the XO was terribly embarrassed. And every ship in the area either saw or heard about the incident.

The CO kept the conn and was going to demonstrate how it should be done. We had to come around and make another approach, this time inch by agonizing inch, and finally we were in position, out of harm's way, although it seemed to take all day.

It was an embarrassing situation all around, and believe me, word travels fast around the 7th Fleet. Some time later I was in a bar in one of the liberty ports in Japan. This bar was a hangout for Navy officers and it was full of destroyer and carrier types. I needed to go to the head and there was a guy in there, and over the urinals he asked what ship I was from. I said, "Herbert J. Thomas," and he said," Oh, your Captain's Charlie Tuna!" I said, "What?" And he said, "You know, Chicken of the Sea!"

It made me feel lower than a whale's belly, but all I could say was, "Yeah, that's the one."

* * *

Junior officers will talk, and will give their expert opinions on just about anything Navy. There was a general opinion in the wardroom that, regardless of many fine attributes, the Captain was afraid of the ship. That was 60,000 horsepower down there in a relatively small and sleek hull, making her very agile and very fast. He had just come from the engine room of the carrier USS Ticonderoga as Engineering Officer, a great billet, straight to command of a destroyer, and it just wasn't that good a fit. But to give him the benefit of the doubt, he probably had the USS Evans on his mind every waking moment, and after all, it was his ship.

There is sort of an old Navy axiom, that it is assumed that the Captain of a ship is the best ship handler on board. But it ain't necessarily so. He was very nervous about ever damaging the Thomas, so very few of the officers were ever qualified as OOD underway, and no one but the senior officers ever had the conn during any difficult evolutions.

This makes me think about my step father, who was a pure destroyerman and a superior ship handler. But he was also a true believer in giving junior officers challenges and training so that they may move up and become better officers for the Navy. There was an incident once while he was CO of his very first command, the destroyer USS Compton. He was letting a young officer get the ship underway, when they banged into another ship in the nest. There was an official inquiry, but no action was taken when he explained that there is no substitute for experience if you want to develop young officers. He took many chances like that, and had a legion of admirers throughout the Navy because of it.

* * *

Once we were doing plane guard, and were astern of the carrier at the interval of 1,000 yards, when they did an UNREP. The carrier is such a monster, I don't remember who came alongside whom, but we were watching the smooth transfer of supplies when a very large, white, sausage-shaped container started across. Since the supply ship was much smaller, the transfer lines were angled up to the carrier's receiving deck. I asked someone what that thing was, and was told that it was a replacement jet engine. I was interested, and was watching the transfer, when all of a sudden the lines parted and the engine dumped right into the sea. Someone on our bridge said, "Uh oh, there goes $600,000." Naturally it sunk, but bobbed back up like a cork! The container was Styrofoam, and some genius in the supply chain had foreseen such an accident. It floated right past us and was later picked up by one of the carrier's helicopters.

* * *

Our favorite UNREP was with oilers. Folks, their job was so repetitious, so monotonous, that they found ways to have fun that you wouldn't believe! The human imagination is an amazing thing.

For example, they would send over two fuel hoses, at the tip of which was a huge steel probe that appeared to look like a giant penis. And those sailors would tape to the probe the filthiest, nastiest pictures of women, you can't imagine. I went down to see for myself once, and I still have a memory of those things. They dealt in shock value.

Then there were the movie exchanges. Each time you came alongside, the two ships would trade movies. Remember, back then movies were one of the few things we used to break *our* monotony. Well, we must have been on someone's list, because we kept getting *"The Green Slime."* You can only watch *The Green Slime* so many times. Coming in second was *"The Valley of the Gwangi,"* and third was *"Boy on a Dolphin,"* which had been broken and spliced so frequently that the actors moved in fits and starts like spastics. Alan Ladd was chasing Sophia Loren-splice-they were rolling around on the ground smooching-splice-The End. All within 2 seconds. It was very funny, but only the first time you saw it.

We always looked forward to the USS Guadalupe. I have lived near the river of the same name. With its Spanish name, the Captain or someone in his wardroom got the idea to add a Mexican flavor to the refueling experience. First you would hear the mariachi music blaring out over the water, then as you came alongside you would see the Captain and 5 or 6 of his crew in their serapes and large Mexican hats, waving and serenading you. They would talk on the bullhorn, and when we were pulling away, would wish us, "A Dios!"

* * *

You may be curious as to how two ships connect to each other for Underway Replenishment of any kind: cargo or personnel transfer, or refueling. Or how, coming into a pier, do you get your mooring lines over to the dock. Our Bosun's Mates took this evolution to the level of an art form, steeped in 200 years of Naval tradition. Depending on the job at hand, a BM on the main deck would begin twirling a small line with a "monkey fist" at the end. A monkey fist was a lead weight wrapped in fancy work to about baseball size. Like little David's sling, it got up to tremendous velocity and then was let go at just the right instant, to shoot across to the other ship or the pier. It was a dangerous missile, and the guys at the receiving end normally wore hardhats. An experienced BM could usually place that thing just where he wanted it, and the receiving BM would grab the line and begin hauling it in. It, in turn, would be attached to a mooring line or a steel cable or whatever, which was then hauled across by hand.

Nowadays the art is gone; a shot line is simply fired from a gun. But that's okay, it's probably more efficient, though old-line sailors might disagree.

* * *

After finishing our first tour of Plane Guard duty, we detached from the carrier group in order to head up to PIRAZ duty. As Yankee Station was about 100 miles east of Da Nang, we steamed west to make a stop for supplies. We entered the harbor with the famous Monkey Mountain to our right. There had been a lot of action on and around this mountain during the war, and we heard about a Viet Cong sniper who, perched up on the top, took potshots regularly at people down below. The story was that he was such a lousy shot that he never hit anything, so our side just left him alone. He was simply a local curiosity.

Da Nang was off-limits so we couldn't go ashore. I was curious to see a building called the "White Elephant," which was quite famous for some reason, maybe it was a remnant of the French colonials. It seems that our side had a comm station or something there. I could see it but couldn't get there. Anyway, soon enough we left the harbor and headed north for our new duty station.

Our course took us past the Demilitarized Zone (DMZ) which was about 120 miles to the north, so presently we were cruising off of North Vietnam. And then we entered an area that put us between North Vietnam on our left, and the Chinese island of Hainan on our right. Now, normally a country could claim territorial waters out to a distance of 12 miles. But China claimed a 200 mile limit around Hainan. The problem was that there weren't 200 miles between Hainan and North Vietnam. We had been clearly warned by the Navy to stay at least 50 miles from Chinese territory, and this made the Captain extremely nervous. He was on the bridge constantly and asking our position every 30 seconds or so it seemed. Our LORAN wasn't working as usual, so we used radar to take constant readings. It really was a dangerous area to be in, we didn't want an international incident.

We finally reached our destination and settled into a routine which was a little more slow-paced than we were used to.

PIRAZ duty was damn boring. It meant steaming endlessly in a very large circle at a very slow speed, acting as a radar picket ship for enemy air activity. What kept it a little tense was that we were in enemy waters just off of Haiphing Harbor. So we also had to stay alert for any surface contacts, PT boats that might take exception to our being there. It was so hard to concentrate, though.

You looked for ways to break the monotony. I thought I had found a way, once. Attached to the overhead were two parallel steel handles, about two feet apart and hanging down about 8 inches. It was pitch black outside. On occasion during the watch I would do a couple of pull ups to try to stay sharp. And I took it a step further by bringing my knees up and pulling myself into a ball on the overhead. And dammit if the Captain didn't step onto the bridge in his old brown bathrobe. I couldn't see him but I heard him say, "Mr. Cook, are you comfortable up there?" My brain said, "Oh shit," and I uncurled, eased myself to the deck and mumbled something like, "Oh, hello, Captain." There is not much else you can say at a time like that.

I did like the night watches on PIRAZ because of the peace and quiet. It was so dark except for the red glow of the dials and lights on the instruments. The red served to preserve your night vision. Because we were going so slowly, there wasn't even the customary vibration and sound made by the engines and props at higher speeds. Once one of my guys came up to the bridge in this quiet and dark, carrying a tray of glasses. He said, "Anyone want some bug juice?" Again, bug juice is Kool-Aid. I asked what flavors he had. He said, "Well sir, I've got Goofy Grape and Rootin' Tootin' Raspberry." Maybe you had to be there, but everyone on the bridge just cracked up. Here we were getting a Kool-Aid commercial from this kid, way out in the middle of hostile territory, in the dark. I believe I took Goofy Grape.

The area in which we operated was off-limits to North Vietnamese fishing boats, a point that had been made a long time ago. But Vietnamese fishermen, whether from the North or the South, never paid any attention to rules or regulations or restrictions. They went where the fish were. And these people were the cause of our most memorable moment on PIRAZ.

I was at breakfast in the wardroom one morning, and all of the chairs were occupied. It was peaceful enough, the conversation was normal, that is until all of a sudden the GQ claxon started clanging, and a sailor came on the horn, "Now general quarters, general quarters, this is not a drill, this is not a drill!" As the clanging continued, the wardroom just erupted! From the hundreds of drills, you were trained to automatically react to that sound, you drop what you are doing and scramble and run to your GQ station. In an instant, we were all ass and elbows, coffee and juice flying everywhere, chairs overturned, plates of food falling to the deck. It looked like a bomb went off in there.

Our crew had a good record for manning battle stations, and in a couple of minutes they were ready for combat. I had run to the bridge, and had to get into a life jacket, put on a headset and plug into the ship's circuit, and put on my gigantic gray steel helmet. While doing this I overheard the OOD giving a situation report to the Captain and XO and Norm. The bridge and CIC had been monitoring a number of fishing boats up ahead of us, and both had become concerned when the number of boats increased rapidly and became concentrated dead ahead. That's when they sounded general quarters.

We had been warned about a tactic that the North Vietnamese navy used, where they would move several PT boats in among the fishing boats, and then dash out for a coordinated attack. You know they would have loved to sink an American destroyer. Anyway, when I was suited up I looked at the surface radar and there were contacts just everywhere. And when I looked up ahead of us I was stunned at what I saw. For all these years I have kept that scene in my head, and have always called it "Red Dawn," because the sun was coming up behind what seemed like hundreds of fishing boats. It was both magnificent and scary at the same time, there were so many of them. We and CIC were monitoring the radar for any fast-moving targets among the fishermen, and we just knew that something was going to happen. It felt like there was going to be combat. We had trained for a long time for this and we were ready to fight.

And when nothing happened the letdown was hard. The whole crew were on an adrenaline high, and when we were told to secure from general quarters it was like hitting a brick wall. It was palpable throughout the ship. And folks, this is not forty-years-later bravado, we had been dressed up and taken to the ball, and had no one to shoot at. It was very disappointing.

* * *

After a long month of PIRAZ and Plane Guard duty, we headed for Sasebo, Japan for upkeep on the ship, and a little R&R for the troops. Sasebo is a Navy-friendly place, and we were welcomed with open arms. Along with several other destroyers, we came in with the Ticonderoga, and so were slightly outnumbered by the flyboys.

We quickly found the "O" Club on the base. It's name was the Town Club, but when the locals tried to say it, it came out "Town Crub." So when catching a cab to go there we just said, "Town Crub, please." There was a restaurant and a large bar area, and along with many other amenities, a good-sized swimming pool.

Downtown was rife with excellent restaurants and sailor bars, and though there was nothing official about it, there was an "Enlisted Mens' Club," a "Chiefs' Club," and an "Officers' Club." They were all fun, friendly and really noisy. In fact, it was in the "Officers' Club" men's room that the guy from another ship had given me the unwelcome news that my Captain was known in the fleet as "Charlie Tuna."

A group of us went out on the town one night, starting at the Town Crub for dinner, then off-base to cruise the clubs. At the time, Dan Heck and I favored whiskey sours, so we decided that we were going to have one or two at each club until we found the Perfect Whiskey Sour. It actually ended up being a drinking contest, and I got through nine of them while Dan, who is bigger than I am, topped off at fifteen. Toward the end, we could not have told you the difference between a whiskey sour and gasoline.

The whole group was about eight sheets to the wind, and someone came up with the bright idea to go to a Hotsi Bath. We piled into a cab and asked the driver for a recommendation, and he took us to one that was just perfect! What you did was to undress and, wrapped in a big towel, you were taken to a large tiled room with a number of small, individual hot baths sunk into the floor. You step down and have a seat and let the hot water and steam engulf you and boil out all of the evil things you have put into your body that evening. After a while of soaking, a girl, wearing a little white two-piece swimsuit, came and asked you to step out of the tub. She then soaped you all over with thick white suds, and bathed you with a large, soft sponge. Just like a car wash.

When you were clean you stepped back into the tub, and warm water was poured over your head from a bucket. When you were thoroughly clean and relaxed, she helped dry you off, wrapped you in a towel, and led you to a room with comfortable mats on the floor, and overhead fans blowing cool air. Mind you, there were five or six of us in the same room. They laid us out like corpses and proceeded to give the greatest massage we could imagine. They even popped each finger and toe joint. The "ooh's" and "aah's" came out involuntarily, it felt so good. And then, when we were all as limp as dishrags, came the piece de resistance: we were turned onto our belly and the masseuse stepped up onto the small of the back, walking slowly and massaging with her toes, particularly between the ribs, it sent you to a place you had never been before. (Porter had had so much food and drink that night, that his back walker just squished it out of him and he had to be helped outside.)

When this state of bliss was over, and I felt as mellow and relaxed as I would ever be in life, I exited into an air-conditioned bar and was served the coldest beer I had ever tasted. It was perfect. Those people knew exactly what they were doing, and none of us would ever forget the experience. Somehow we helped each other back to the ship, and regardless of the Hotsi Bath we were all very hung over the next morning. When I saw Dan, I said that I felt as bad as he looked, and he said that it felt like he had been licking ashtrays all night.

* * *

I heard a story about the Japanese Naval Base at Sasebo during WWII, and still do not know if it is fact or fiction, or somewhere in between. The story goes that an area of the harbor had once been drained and concreted in. It was then re-flooded to appear as a natural harbor. In time of war or necessity, giant sea doors could be closed, and the water pumped out, to create a gigantic dry dock that could accommodate a number of ships. Just before the end of the war, the sea doors, which along with their hydraulics were top secret, were towed out to sea and sunk to prevent their falling into enemy hands. The US Navy has been looking for them since, etc, etc. I realize it sounds pretty fantastic, and I can't find any modern references to the story, but that's what I heard there and you never know.

* * *

Back to the Town Crub, most of our activities somehow involved guys from the carrier. As I have said, we were kind of friendly enemies. Black shoes and brown shoes didn't mix very well on land. Some PR or recreation type dreamed up a water volleyball game to foster relations between the two officer groups. Some very good players from the carrier got into the water with some very good players from the destroyers. The play was aggressive, and then got out of hand, with elbows flying, and there really was blood in the water, and the game was stopped.

Four of us walked into the bar, and you could tell it was full of Airdales (another name for flyboys) because of all the hands in the air at various angles, illustrating recent combat missions. We sat at a table and had a beer, and got a little sick of all of this air activity, so we made a plan to stick up for our side, and on the count of three, we stood up, raised a fist in the air, and hollered, "Let's hear it for the brown shoes!" Well, they booed and threw things at us, and I'm telling you the truth, an empty champagne bottle flew through the air and barely missed us. Badly outnumbered, we sat back down and finished our beer, and a guy actually came over and apologized for throwing the bottle.

* * *

The day after we left Sasebo, a US Army helicopter was shot down by the North Koreans over the Korean DMZ, wounding the three crewmen. In April they had shot down an unarmed Navy reconnaissance plane over the Sea of Japan, killing all 31 crew on board. I'm not sure for which action, but probably both, caused us to be part of a battle group on standby to take action against North Korea. Nothing ever came of it, and I have always said that I got my Armed Forces Expeditionary Medal (Korea) while sitting on a barstool in Sasebo.

* * *

After reluctantly leaving Sasebo, we entered into local operations in the Sea of Japan for 6 days. I believe at this time we did some night exercises with a carrier group based on the USS Coral Sea (CVA-43). It was a practice drill only, but practice can be as deadly as the real thing, as we almost found out.

I was not involved, so was in my stateroom or in the wardroom, when I heard a commotion on the starboard side, and someone was saying, "Come on out here, you gotta see this!" A few of us stepped out of a hatchway on to the main deck, and it was as if everyone said,

"Oh, shit!" at the same time. There were the deck lights of the Coral Sea, and we were looking *up* at them. That meant we were way too close to the carrier.

The mistake was corrected and we were clear from them without alarms being raised or any trouble. I don't recall the circumstances that brought us so close, but it is always the "little boy's" responsibility to stay out of the way of the "big boy." We were just very lucky this time.

At the end of these operations, we stopped at Buckner Bay to take on a load of fuel, and went to sea again for another month of PIRAZ and Plane Guard.

* * *

The radiomen monitored all of the message traffic, so we knew what was going on in the Navy, good and bad, at all times. Most of the bad news never reached the newspapers, as the service had a phobia about public relations. That was probably for the best, as ships were a dangerous place to work and accidents happened all the time. One story came across the ether concerning the death of a sailor in one of those bizarre incidents. I believe it was an engineering Chief who was walking along a catwalk down in his spaces, who was hit in the head and killed by a tiny jet of high-pressure steam shooting from a microscopic fissure in an overhead HP pipe. He never knew what hit him, poor man.

* * *

Since we are on the subject, I will relate an incident that took place when we were tied up in one of the ports. Something happened that many of us will never forget. As I have said, way back in Long Beach while the Thomas was in dry dock I took a walk under her, and while there I marveled at how small she seemed to be from that perspective. I spotted a large hole in the bottom that reminded me of a manhole, and it had a steel grid over it, made of steel bars, similar to the rebar that you see in road construction. I asked whoever I was with what that was, and he said it was the main induction pump, which sucked sea water into the ship at unbelievable pressure, to be used by the engineering plant for the boilers and for coolant. A large main induction valve controlled the flow of water into the ship.

While in the Naval Shipyard there were many safety rules that had to be followed, and I guess one of the most important was the use of red tags. Since so many things were going on at once, repairs, testing, etc., you needed to let people know when not to turn on a switch or a breaker, to open a valve, or do anything else that would endanger people who were working on the system. Large red warning tags were tied onto the switch or valve with a string, and were filled out and signed and dated by an officer or petty officer. They meant, *"Do not touch until further notice!"* These rules were supposed to follow us into the fleet because there were repairs and maintenance being performed almost 24 hours a day on these old ships, whether at sea or in port.

Well, back to the present. Tied up to a dock was a destroyer, which was in the yard for upkeep. Part of that involved a visual inspection of the bottom and everything else below the water line. A chief petty officer who was a diver went into the water to make the inspection, and just when he was in the wrong place at the wrong time, someone opened the main induction valve and sucked the Chief, literally, into the ship, actually pulling him through the grid. Death was instantaneous so at least he didn't suffer, but it was a horrible accident and affected everyone on the base. It was a sad and sobering reminder that the Navy can be a dangerous place. Someone's carelessness had cost a good man his life.

* * *

We got a report about a man overboard from a ship that was cruising off the Florida coast. It happened during the night, but the curious thing was, the sea was perfectly calm. Of course it was possible he could have accidently fallen over the rail, but not probable, and I believe that the Navy thought he might have had some help. He was never found and was presumed drowned.

That particular incident frightened the hell out of one of our officers, Ray the engineer. Now, I got along fine with Ray, never had a problem with him, but he had a very abrasive personality. He just could not relate to those who worked for him. In fact, some of his people downright hated him. He must have also mistreated one of our wardroom stewards, because I know of at least one time that his Kool-Aid was either spat in or peed in. It got so bad that when he was out on the main deck, coke cans and a wrench were thrown at him by unseen sailors.

These things began to work on him. The man overboard in a calm sea scared him because he thought the same could happen to him. Thereafter, he would not go out on the main deck after sundown. It was probably a good idea. Then one day I was talking to him in the main passageway outside the wardroom, and he got this strange look on his face, closed his eyes and just slid down the wall into a heap on the floor. I bent down over him and he was conscious but his face had turned an ashen gray. I asked someone in the wardroom to call the doc, who came immediately. I found out later that Ray had had a nervous breakdown right in front of me. It was not such a good thing to see and we all felt sympathy for him. He was MEDEVAC'ed off the ship that afternoon and sent back to the states.

* * *

I almost never argued with my boss, Lt. Norm Davis, for the main reason that he was always right. But there was one time that we got into it in the wardroom in a very serious way.

You must remember that Norm was built like a heavyweight boxer, even better, and no one I knew ever messed with him. Well, he must have pushed my buttons and we got into a real argument. He was sitting in a chair at the table and I was standing next to him.

I really lost my temper and noticed that I had a perfect shot at the side of his head. I said, "Norm, I could knock you out of that chair!" After thinking about it for a moment, he said, "Yes, you could. But then I would be up and get the second hit." In an instant I realized he was right, and that if he hit me I would die. That brought me to my senses and I quickly backed off.

I know that if I had slugged Norm, it never would have gone outside the wardroom, except for the ruckus *my* MEDEVAC helicopter would have caused.

* * *

I have mentioned Don, our Assistant Supply Officer/Disbursing Officer. He had a very droll sense of humor, but not when it came to the Navy or the Herbert J. Thomas. He was very good at what he did, never had any problems, but he couldn't wait to get back to his beloved Maryland. He had left his wife there, pregnant, and during the cruise she gave birth to a little girl. We as a group had a discussion with him as to what he should name his baby, and came up with the moniker "Herbetta," in order to remind him of the ship for his entire life. Now everyone began asking him how Baby Herbetta was doing. I don't think they named her that. Don also asserted that his wife would take care of the baby, that he wouldn't have much to do with it, and he would be free to do his own thing, which was hunting and golf.

Note: After we all had been out of the Navy for a year or so, I visited the family at their apartment in Maryland. And guess what? Guess who was daddy's little girl, and who had him completely wrapped around her little finger? I have never seen a more doting father, who had already bought her a set of baby golf clubs. I did not remind him of his earlier theory of raising a child.

* * *

Rich, the First Lieutenant, was our resident "ring knocker," a graduate of the US Naval Academy. He was very sharp, looked good in uniform, and knew what he was doing. I, like probably everyone else in the wardroom, was a little daunted at first, working alongside an Academy man. But he never pushed it, was a nice and genial-type guy who was well-liked throughout the ship. The conventional wisdom was that after a year at sea (or was it two, or three?), you couldn't tell the difference between an Annapolis grad and an OCS grad. On the Thomas it didn't matter; Rich was a team player.

While overseas the ship held a beard-growing contest. (I have mentioned that our amusements were very few and very basic). Anyway, with his blond hair and beard, Rich looked like a Viking sea captain.

Rich had a wife named Karen. My my my. She was sweet and smart and funny and beautiful, and you couldn't help but fall for her a little bit. She had an infectious laugh. Playboy had been after her to appear in their magazine, but she turned them down. She was in special education for children. Rich and Karen had us over for dinner frequently in San Diego, and I swear that she hoped her guests wouldn't have too much salad, so there would be more for her. She once polished off a rather large, almost-full salad bowl. Amazing. They were a great couple.

* * *

The wealthiest officer on board was undoubtedly Tad, scion of an old Boston family. He was well connected, as his uncle was Elia Kazan, the Hollywood director and producer. Tad used to talk about his visits there, and the people he saw. He walked into his uncle's kitchen once, and Natalie Wood was sitting there having coffee. He seemed to remember that day very well for some reason. My heart would have just stopped.

Besides the Captain and the XO, rounding out the wardroom were Chuck, Bruce, Larry, Dave (Porter), Bob, the other Bruce,

Gary, Mike, Dan, the other Mike, and the other Bob. It was quite a mix of personalities and talents, and the heart of the ship.

* * *

The saltiest sailor on the Thomas was Machinist's Mate First Class (MM1) Ruppell. He had more service than anyone else on board, and had a bunch of tattoos. There were big spider webs on his elbows. There was one other guy who told me he had been at sea for 18 straight years, and when I told him I thought he was married, he said yes, he was, but they preferred it that way. Whatever makes you happy, and maybe the reunions were extra special.

* * *

When I watch the movie *"The Hunt for Red October,"* the character of the brilliant Sonarman "Jonesy," played by Courtney B. Vance, reminds me of a fellow on the Thomas. He was an Electronics Technician First Class (ET1) named Lingenfelter. Not a very big guy, I always thought of him as the little genius. He could fix anything having to do with electronics, mainly the radars, but he sometimes overlapped into other systems, including Radio. I liked the guy and watched him work sometimes---how he could break down the complexities of a downed system and always get it up and running again. He was not staying in the Navy, but was headed straight for a brand name company that made radar systems, where he could earn many times his Navy pay. He was worth his weight in gold in either place. A very gifted technician, and his skills put him on a par with the Jonesys of the world.

* * *

Every division on a ship is a cross-section of society when it comes to the personality of its personnel. For instance, there was usually a "mascot," a guy who just looks too young to be in the Navy. He would take a lot of good natured ribbing from his mates, but they would also sort of look out for him. There were several of these types on the ship. Ours was a Seaman named Chun, a Philippine-American, a handsome kid who looked about 14 years old. He was a little shy, but was certainly not afraid of hard work.

* * *

I was fortunate to have so many good people. There was a young RM (Radioman) who was such a nice guy and so shy, he also was kidded by the guys. It just added fuel to the fire when everyone got up one morning, and he was still asleep with a big erection and holding it firmly with one hand. You can only guess at where he was in his dreams. He never really heard the last of that one, and blushed like hell whenever the subject came up.

* * *

There were two genuinely nice people that come to mind easily when I think about the Thomas. Signalman Second Class (SM2) Nelson was one of my guys. He followed Faust's law regarding the officer-enlisted relationship, as did I, but we got pretty close during many watches on the bridge together, and we could talk to each other on a number of levels. We had a genuine respect and liking for each other. The whole ship knew Bosun's Mate Third Class (BM3) Miller, with his perpetually sunny disposition and crooked-toothed smile. You always had a fellow like Miller on a ship, and thank goodness, because it was never boring with a guy like that around.

I must say that, with a few exceptions, everyone on board had a good sense of humor. It is a trait that sailors have or develop in order to counter the sometimes long and tedious hours at sea. Some were outrageously funny, and some were more dry and subtle, but it was a part of the daily routine. Without that, it would be impossible to maintain ship's morale.

* * *

I mentioned there were some exceptions. One was a guy in my division, who actually worked for the XO, a Quartermaster First Class (QM1) and a very sour man. I'm not sure whether he disliked me, or all officers, or just people in general. He was quite good at his job as a navigator, that wasn't his problem. It was his personality. I remember really losing my temper, I mean totally flying off the handle, only a couple of times on this ship, and he was the cause of one of them.

We both had the bridge watch one day, and I either asked him a question or asked him to do something, and he sneeringly talked back to me, in a very rude tone of voice, within the hearing of other people. I looked at him for a moment, then walked over to the OOD, saluted and said, "Request permission to leave the bridge, sir." I believe he had heard what was going on, and said, "Permission granted." I headed for the ladder at the back of the bridge, and as I passed this guy I said, "Come with me!" We went down the ladder and into the chart room and I said, "Close the door." When he did I just went ballistic, and yelled at him, "Don't you ever do that again! If you've got a problem with me, you ask me to come down here and we'll discuss it, but if you ever talk back to me again, I'll bust your ass!" He didn't apologize, he wasn't the type, but put this blank look on his face and reluctantly said, "Yes, sir." And that was that, except the son of a bitch gave me a killer headache from the exertion. We never did get along, but from then on he was at least correct in his dealings with me.

* * *

As I have said, there was no one quite like my Leading Petty Officer, SM1 Faust. In my division his word was law, as he had demonstrated early on in our relationship. In our group of 35-plus people, we had very little trouble with anyone, for two reasons: first, we had a great bunch of guys. Second, we had Faust.

There was one fellow, though, who had an attitude problem and was becoming a headache to all of us. He happened to be a signalman who had transferred in, and just couldn't get with the program. I knew him well enough, he seemed to be okay, but on the job he was getting progressively more disruptive. One morning after crew call, Faust informed me that he and this man were going to meet on the signal bridge that evening, close the doors, and have a little discussion. He delivered this with his customary poker face, and I said that I understood, and hoped it went well.

The next morning at crew call, my Leading Petty Officer sported a black eye, and a surreptitious look at our problem sailor revealed that he also had a bruise on his face. I asked him how it had gone, and Faust said, again with that poker face, "We had a good talk, sir, and got everything straightened out." And sure enough, they did. The problem disappeared. The direct approach is sometimes the only way to go.

* * *

Everybody has known someone whose name was an exact description of what they did for a living. I knew of a Dr. Dove, for example, who was a veterinarian specializing in birds. Gunner's Mate Chief Sweatt certainly lived up to his name. A small, wiry man with a bird face, the Chief was always all over the ship. His interests went outside of his guns to include everything that happened on board. A nervous kind of guy, he would sweat through his khaki shirt, he was so busy ducking in here, and ducking in there. Outside of the XO, he knew more about the Thomas than anyone else. It was his ship, and he knew his business.

* * *

When we were tied up to a pier, a barge would appear alongside to replenish our fresh water supply. Or if we were being serviced by a Destroyer Tender in Da Nang or Nha Trang, they could fill our storage tanks. In 1969, I don't think we were able to receive water during underway replenishment the way they do now.

Anyway, if you were out for weeks at a time, as we were now, the potable water supply would begin to dwindle. The evaporators were able to make some water, but not enough to keep up with demand. When a certain low point was reached, the use of water was restricted to that needed for drinking, cooking, washing dishes, and wash basins. That was no problem for the toilets, they used salt water anyway. And the engineers used salt water to cool their machinery, so no problem there. The showers were the thing. If you wanted a shower, it was salt water or nothing. So you had to make a decision. Do nothing and begin to decompose in the heat, and begin emitting some foul odors that you could only try to cover up by taking a Marine Shower (the use of a lot of deodorant). Or take a nice, cool, refreshing shower in sea water.

I reached a point where I could no longer stand the heat and my own odoriferous self, and hit the showers. It truly felt great, taking the heat away, and I really felt clean for once. I was happy until I was completely dry and lying in my rack. Then I began to itch all over, particularly on my chest, probably from minute crystals of salt in every pore. It was awful, and it felt as if my skin were drying and cracking and someone was using atomic balm (a particularly caustic heat rub we used after gym class in college) to make it feel better. It was hard to work this way, and impossible to sleep. The minute we were re-supplied with fresh water, I washed the salt off, and vowed that next time we went into water restriction, I would wash my face, brush my teeth, and take a Marine Shower. I remember that 300 men in the same condition could really stink up a ship, but it was best not to shower.

One can only imagine how bad it used to get on the old, cramped diesel submarines on extended patrol. *Whew!*

* * *

The food in the wardroom was generally of good quality. You paid into the officers' mess fund monthly, and the elected mess caterer spent the money and planned the menus with the stewards. Things were okay as long as you had access to a base or supply ship, but during a month-long patrol such as we were on now, sometimes you had to fall back on that staple of Naval gastronomy, chipped corned beef on toast, more commonly known as "shit on a shingle" (SOS). And powdered eggs tasted, well, like powdered eggs. Spam was still around; my step father learned to love it in ships during WWII.

One of the Navy's best kept secrets was whether or not the ship's cooks added saltpeter to our food. Otherwise known as potassium nitrate, it is normally used in fertilizer and gunpowder. Here, if it was used in sailors, it helped keep in check the raging hormones of 300 mostly young men for long periods at sea. We just never knew for sure. No one seemed to be affected when we hit a liberty port, however.

I had never been a big fan of soup at all, never paid much attention to it. That is, until Chief Steward Newburn came aboard. He could take the Navy's roughest ingredients and come out with the most delicate gourmet flavors you can imagine. I can still smell and taste them after all these years. Hopefully, when he retired, he went straight to the Soup Chef's position in a fine restaurant because anything less would have wasted his unusual talent.

Every military entity that ever existed always made fun of the food, and the Thomas was no exception. There was a pretty gross cartoon that made the rounds, that of a big, dumb-looking buzzard with a fat gut, sitting there and burping. The caption was, "She's a feeder!" The Captain didn't think it was so funny, and put a stop to it. But occasionally the cooks held a cookout, or "feeder" (the name stuck) on the fantail, which consisted of hamburgers and hot dogs, or steaks or barbeque, with all the trimmings. It was a nice respite from the routine and everyone enjoyed it. You sat on whatever you could find, and most of the officers, including the Captain, just sat on the deck. Sailors played their guitars and other instruments, and others sang. It may sound a little corny, but these things were actually a lot of fun. And she really was a feeder.

* * *

Probably the best liberty port in the world is Hong Kong. The crew looked forward to our stay there after working so hard for another month on PIRAZ and Plane Guard. Sailors can have fun just about anywhere, case in point—Olongapo (we'll get to that soon), but to them this was paradise.

We had to park out in the harbor, and a carrier had come in with us, so the town was full of Navy men. We of course had motor whaleboats that could take us to the International (boat) Landing, but there were plenty of Chinese small boats just waiting to take "Mellican saila boys" in for a small fee, and over the years that had earned them the nickname, "nickel snatchers." It was a very efficient transportation system, and I caught one once after it had stopped at the carrier, and sat down right next to a guy I had known in high school. Small world still.

The first night ashore Dan and I and a few others went out to eat at a place called "Jimmie's Kitchen." They just piled food in the middle of a round table and we went at it, especially the escargots. It was so delicious! It took a couple of hours for the diarrhea to hit, and it was bad. Real bad. But I'll tell you the truth, that those escargots were so good we went back the next night for more, knowing full well the consequences, and ate our fill. Crazy Americans.

* * *

The Wan Chai district was the place to go. Also called the "Suzy Wong" district after the movie, it was full of bars and bright lights and music and B-girls. The sailors loved it there and those girls loved the sailors. Even though some of the guys who were still fresh off the farm, had seen Japan and Subic Bay by this time, they found out that Hong Kong was the big leagues. I have a picture of one of our crew, he looked too young to be in the Navy, with a girl on each arm in mini skirts up to here, and he has kind of a surprised look on his face, like, "What am I doing here?"

I have another one of those vivid pictures in my mind of one of my signalmen, Thompson, coming toward the landing in a ricksha. It was morning and he had been out doing who-knows-what all night. I caught his eye and he looked over at me with a dreamy look on his face and a big grin spread under his big red moustache and slowly he gave me the peace sign as he went by. I wish that you folks could see that picture, you would be laughing over the years as I have.

In 1969, *the* thing to buy overseas was stereo equipment: amplifiers, speakers, record players and tape decks. Many of the brand names are still around today, but the ones to have were Sansui and Teac. A Teac tape deck was about as good as sound got then. Hong Kong offered every kind in existence, along with myriad Chinese products and souvenirs. A million shops offered these things for sale, but we were able to get into a very exclusive place that sold only the finest merchandise at very low prices, the China Fleet Club. I always loved that name. This was the British Officers' Club overseas, and was well known among WestPac officers. Our group bought boxes and boxes of electronics and other goods back to the ship, and from then on there were elaborate sound systems set up everywhere. My Sansui amplifier never gave out on me, but I upgraded to something better in 1995. And my Garrard record changer still works perfectly even though you can no longer find replacement parts; I have a very innovative electronics guy that keeps it going. I use this "old antique," high quality record player almost daily now, sending all of our LP's and 45's to a CD burner. Speaking of which, another very popular item in Hong Kong was the red plastic LP record album. You could see through it. Pirated, of course, it was only good for one play before it went bad, but that was time enough to copy it onto your reel-to-reel. At only 25 cents a pop, not such a bad deal.

* * *

We crammed a lot of living into 6 days. I was really put out when informed that I had Shore Patrol one night. Junior officers often got that kind of duty. When I reported to the SP building I was informed that I was *the* Shore Patrol Officer for all of Hong Kong, with a carrier and several destroyers in town. Thanks to an experienced staff, though, it became less daunting, and I was able to observe the many ways sailors can get into trouble on liberty. That included the one who was hit by a car and broke his leg, and the one who was found, in a world all his own, wandering down a main thoroughfare completely naked, and carrying a plastic toy hammer.

At the end of my watch, though, our sailors were safely back aboard their ships, with surprisingly few incidents.

* * *

The most efficient communications system in the world, other than the Navy Wives' Club, was the Hong Kong B-girls grapevine. They knew everything. The movements of all US Navy ships was classified Top Secret, but they put signs in the bar windows the day *before* ships arrived, saying "Welcome sailors from USS Thomas, USS Oriskany," etc. As communications officer of the Thomas, I always knew everything having to do with the ship, or thought so until a girl told me she was sorry we were leaving tomorrow, and I didn't know we were leaving tomorrow. When I later saw message traffic saying we were leaving tomorrow, I caught myself admiring these people, and knew for sure from then on that the North Vietnamese, as well as the Chinese, knew our exact movements, even better than we did!

* * *

There was one more fiasco for me, which got me confined to the ship for the rest of our stay, and that is pretty rare for an officer. Four of us decided to get a room at the fabulous Hilton Hotel on Hong Kong Island. After a night out on the town including a terrific Chinese dinner and drinks, and entertainment into the early hours, we all four crashed in our room.

And I mean that I crashed and burned. Out cold. I was dreaming that the telephone was ringing and ringing. When I came to enough to realize it really was ringing, I blearily looked around the room and found that everyone else was gone, and that it was daylight. My mouth tasted like an ashtray. I picked up the phone and it was Bruce saying, "Good morning, were you planning on coming in to the ship today?" My heart froze and I looked out the window and saw the Thomas down there in the harbor about 2 inches long. I asked him what time it was and he said, "Well, you missed officers' call." That's when I knew my life was over. How could I have been so stupid?

I hastily dressed and hurried out to the ship with this great feeling of dread washing over me, all the while silently thanking the other guys so much for waking me up. No one was really that angry, but the XO confined me to the ship, and that was punishment enough, having to watch Hong Kong from the ship's rail.

* * *

And then there were Mary Soo's girls. Mary Soo may have been the most enterprising woman in all of China. Not long after we arrived she had come alongside in her sampan and asked to see the Captain. After a conference with him and the XO, it was agreed that she would take all of our garbage off our hands, and would wash down and paint the hull of the ship! We would supply the paint, she would supply the labor and expertise. What she wanted in return was a small amount of money, but mainly any spare brass, such as spent shell casings, and any old wiring or copper tubing, anything containing "precious" metals. In just a few days, Mary Soo's girls had us surrounded in their sampans with their paint brushes and rollers on long handles. And in no time, there sat the Thomas, as beautiful and fresh as she had looked in 1945, with a perfect paint job.

Mary Soo's coke girl, Josephine, had her sampan alongside every day, providing refreshments for the crew. These people were so nice, and they made you feel welcome in Hong Kong.

Mary Soo became such a legend over the years that I understand that Life Magazine once did a full story on her, and that to the old timers she was known simply as "Hong Kong Mary."

Well, all good things must come to an end, so we had to take leave of our favorite liberty port. In some ways our six days there went by in no time, but we sure did live while we were there.

Note: As a matter of interest, the Hong Kong Hilton was demolished in 1995. What a great hotel. It was replaced by the Cheun Kong Centre, built by the richest man in the city. Also, the ricksha has probably disappeared by now. No new licenses were issued for the human-powered taxi after 1975. In 1999 there were only 15 old men still licensed, and in 2002, only 4. For souvenir photographs only, I'm sure.

* * *

From Hong Kong we now headed for Kaoshiung, a port located in the southwest of the island of Taiwan. The ship needed some upkeep in engineering that was getting a bit critical. Normally any problems I had in Communications were related to the teletypes, which had a bad habit of going down all the time. But if you sailed in, or anywhere near the Straits of Formosa, also known as the Taiwan Straits, the waters between Taiwan and mainland China, you may as well be on the dark side of the moon, because you weren't going to communicate with anybody! The radios just dropped off the air, and it was very disconcerting to be out of touch with the rest of the Navy in such a far-off place. I don't recall whether it was a natural phenomenon, or was induced by China, but it could certainly make the Communications Officer sweat!

Around the same time there was also a period of intense solar flare activity which greatly interfered with long range communications for days at a time. Hardly a message came through that wasn't partly garbled or completely mangled. Most message traffic, both incoming and outgoing, had to be repeated several times before they made any sense. These two situations brought out all of the talents of my Radiomen, and brother, were they good.

* * *

The ancient harbor of Kaoshiung, Taiwan, has a very narrow entrance and treacherous cross-currents. We were scheduled to make only one visit here, but it ended up being two because the first was interrupted by a typhoon and we had to make a run for it.

Anyway, I remember this approach because it made the Captain so nervous. Since we were standing on top of the bridge, and I was relaying his orders down, I was the one nearest him. He was under such stress that he let out these little grunts, like "uh, uh, uh," and had his hands behind his back, working his fingers furiously. I had the thought that if I could drop three ball-bearings into his hand, the picture would be complete.

* * *

In Kaoshiung, the only place to go was Nancy's New Harbor Hotel, best known as New Nancy's. Nancy's "Old" Harbor Hotel had burned down. It wasn't even a hotel, but the best brothel in the Orient. It also included a gigantic bar and a theater. Nancy's was fabled because it was said that she took in only the most beautiful girls from all over Taiwan, and all you had to do was look around to see that it was true.

The reputation of Nancy's was such that even our squadron chaplain came to have a look. He was a very special chaplain and was very popular with the crew. He of course had a drink with us and then left, but we all thought he was a good sport for coming.

I set my sights on one of the Number One girls whose name was Su Su, a Eurasian with long dark hair, great looks and a bodacious body. She wore really tight stretch pants that looked like a zebra. While I was "courting" her, someone came around with a Polaroid camera and took our picture. When I finally got her to take me to her room, the first thing she did was take a pair of scissors and cut me out of the picture. She then proceeded to trim off the parts of herself that she didn't like. That didn't make me feel so good about our relationship. It was evident that she wanted to be the center of attention, and just wanted me to admire her and nothing else, because I never even got to first base with her. Still have the picture, though, or what's left of it.

The other old industry in Kaoshiung was the shipyard, part of which still built and repaired the traditional Chinese Junk, as they had for centuries. In fact, one of their boats used to sail around San Diego harbor. The yard was more limited in our case, as we had a problem with getting some repairs done.

While in Taiwan I had to make a run to the nearest COMMSTA, which was in Tainan, for fresh codes and classified publications. I got a short hop on a Navy plane for the trip up there and back. As I had to travel armed, I strapped on the trusty .45, of course with the chamber empty.

* * *

Near the end of our cruise a poll was taken among the crew regarding a number of things, and for best liberty port, Kaoshiung came in second only to Hong Kong. (The one voted worst was Olongapo). However, the overwhelming choice for the port with the prettiest girls was Kaoshiung.

* * *

In 1969, there were 13 reported typhoons in the Western North Pacific. When a typhoon was coming, you could not be in port because you would bash yourself to pieces against the pier. The best thing to do was run for it, and if you got caught, to head into the wind and sea and ride it out. On this cruise it seemed we were constantly dogged by typhoons. We were ordered to leave Subic Bay once because one was coming, and twice while at sea we had to take evasive action. But the one to remember was Typhoon Elsie in the last week of September.

We had been in Kaoshiung for four days when sudden orders came to clear the port immediately, that a very dangerous storm was headed toward Taiwan. The problem was, we couldn't get underway. We had a main piece of machinery completely torn down for repair. I think it was a generator. The other problem was, we *had* to get underway, and were given only eight hours to put everything back together and get out. So the engineers were feverishly working to get this thing reassembled and up and running, because this was a genuine emergency.

Out of the 13 storms, Elsie is the only one that is classified as a "Super Typhoon" because at her peak she had a wind speed of an unbelievable 175 miles per hour! That's very scary. We got out of the harbor okay and ran in the opposite direction of the storm, but it was of such immense size that we spent the better part of three days riding it out before we could return to port.

The phrase "riding it out" doesn't quite describe what we went through. I had been in the one storm off the Oregon coast in the Bridget, and that had been a bad one. Elsie was a different animal, and her dynamics were different. And the Thomas was a different ship, with her own dynamics. We had already been in some heavy seas on this cruise, but we were about to find out how she handled in extreme weather.

I had a morning watch on the day the sea began to get rough, and had no trouble with the ship's motion because of my own personal theorem that if I could see the horizon, I had a point of reference that my mind could lock on to and give me stability. In my Naval experience up to this point, I had never yet been sick. Oh, there had been some queasiness occasionally, but I was always able to keep it together.

During the day the storm got progressively worse, meaning bad, with high wave action and high winds. The whole ship was battened down and so no one was allowed out on the weather decks. And unfortunately I had the 8 to midnight watch. As I came up onto the bridge, there was a lot of motion, but everyone was quiet and calm in the red glow of the instruments. I relieved the JOOD and was immediately disconcerted by the movement of the ship. Normally in a high sea you will have some amount of rolling and/or some pounding (remember-the up and down movement of the bow). But this sea and high wind were really working us over. Not only were we rolling and pounding, but yawing as well. Yawing is the side-to-side movement of the bow. The combination of all three movements was a gut-wrenching experience, and outside it was pitch black, and I had no horizon to fasten on to. It was going to be a long four hours.

We were taking long, deep rolls, which were accompanied by the usual crashing sounds down below. If you recall my talking about the STOPS system, it put an inordinate amount of weight higher up in the superstructure than the gun mount it had replaced. So when we rolled, we stayed there for awhile instead of popping back to the vertical. You must try this sometime: take a, say, 45 degree roll to starboard and just stay there. You can feel and hear each blade of the propellers digging for all they're worth, to keep you moving forward, and you are wondering when you are going to come upright. We did this a number of times during the watch, and it can be very frightening. Slowly we would come out of it and then roll to port. But it seemed the roll to starboard was the worst; that must have been the leeward side.

There was a simple device on the bridge called the Clinometer (or Inclinometer). It was just a metal pendulum mounted on a base, which was attached to the bulkhead. On the base were numbered 5 degree increments to port and starboard, with individual degrees marked between. When you were upright, the pendulum indicated zero degrees, and when you rolled, it would tell you how many degrees over you were. A simple device, but very effective, and one which now is probably unnecessarily computerized and digitalized. Anyway, the clinometer became the focal point of everyone's attention when we rolled to starboard. We did some 43 and 44 and 45 degree rolls, and it seemed an eternity before we came out of it. The worst one was to 48 degrees and we just lay there. You got the feeling that we could have just rolled on over. It really felt that way. But very slowly, she came out of it.

I had learned at OCS, or heard through the grapevine, I don't remember which, that when a destroyer goes so far over that it might capsize, the gun mounts will fall out and drastically lower the center of gravity and save the ship. It makes great sense; again, simple and effective. We had two dual gun mounts, each weighing about 48 tons, and now that I think about it, had *we* rolled far enough for them to drop out, we would have gone under anyway. Without 96 tons of steel on the main deck, the center of gravity would have shot upward toward those heavy air conditioners and we would have ended up in Davy Jones' Locker for sure. Probably best that we never had to find out.

During the watch I became progressively more miserable. The terrible three-way motion of the ship, and the blackness outside had taken their toll on my stomach, and given me acute dizziness and a headache. But what do you do? There is nowhere to go. You can't be excused from the bridge. I know other people were having problems, too, but I didn't notice or didn't care, I just wanted to finish my watch before I died. And finally, after an agonizing eternity, my relief appeared on the bridge. I was never so glad to see anyone in my life. His name was Mike Rutter, and to this day I am still impressed with that guy.

Mike was slightly built and was perpetually pale, but he had the nerve to come up to the bridge to relieve me, when he should have gone on sick call. He was just as ill, or worse, than I was, and was puffing air the way you do when you are trying not to lose it. But he assumed the watch and I was across the bridge and down the ladder when I threw up on the drinking fountain. There was someone else there but I didn't care, and went down and crawled into my rack and passed out. I think I have never been so sick in my life.

Of course, the storm eventually passed and the sea calmed, and there was one redeeming factor. The entire ship smelled of vomit. When word got around that even our saltiest sailors had gotten sick and thrown up, it made the crew (and me!) feel just a little bit better about the whole thing. We now returned to Kaoshiung and our engineers tore down the generator and picked up where they had left off, before they had been so rudely interrupted by Elsie.

* * *

Upon leaving Kaoshiung, we now headed for Subic Bay to "reload" and prepare for a month on the gun line doing Naval Gunfire Support. When I had first reported on board the Thomas, there was an officer in the wardroom named Duff, and I don't recall his last name. Duff was a handsome guy, looked like everyone's idea of an all-American boy. He was quiet and shy, had a wife and little baby at home, and was the last person you would think of who wanted to become a Navy SEAL. But that was Duff. It was all-consuming, and he couldn't think of anything else but a transfer to SEAL school. It finally came through for him, and he left the ship about the time we went into the shipyard at Long Beach.

A couple of the guys had stayed in touch with him, and found that he was now stationed at Subic Bay. So soon after our second arrival at Subic, three or four of us went looking for him. The SEALS had their own compound within the Naval Base, and were therefore separated from the general population. We were headed toward their main gate, and walked right past this fellow who was just standing there, and we heard, "Hey guys!" We turned around to see who was calling, and it was Duff! No one had recognized him, even those who had known him a lot longer than I had. He was a nut-brown color, had a shaved head, and was wearing fatigues, and his olive drab t-shirt was bulging with muscles. It just wasn't the same guy.

He didn't have a lot of time, so we had a short but nice reunion with him, traded information about the ship in exchange for some of the horror stories about SEAL training. The one thing that stuck in my mind is that they would run from San Diego to Mexico. On the beach, in the soft sand. In combat boots. That's all I wanted to hear, I just blacked out on the rest.

We wished him well and waved as he went back into his compound. The US always needs people like Duff.

* * *

While we were in Subic, my boss, Lt. Norm Davis, was transferred off the Thomas. He was headed back to the states for training in preparation to take command of a ship in the Brown Water Navy in Vietnam. I hated to lose Norm, even though he was a tough and exacting guy to work for, because he was always fair with me and taught me a lot. I had, and still have, the utmost respect for him. His replacement was Lt. Yasuto Tana, who looked sharp, wore the uniform well, and seemed to know what he was doing.

I did my best to help him get acquainted with my division and the ship, and he seemed friendly enough. We talked about our backgrounds, he had come off of a destroyer and had WestPac experience. He made no changes in the Operations Department or in the way I ran the Communications Division, and so I continued to run things as they were and that seemed okay with him. Things appeared to be on an even keel with the new boss.

* * *

Clark Air Force Base, better known as Clark Field, was just across the harbor from the Naval Base. As every Navy officer knows, Air Force "O" Clubs were better than ours because they put a lot more money into them. So at our first opportunity, some of us went over for dinner. And it *was* a nice club. Afterward we went to the informal officers' bar called the "Tailhook Club," signified by the large aviators' tailhook hanging above the bar. This club was known throughout the Far East for the antics of its clientele.

It was quiet this evening, but we could see evidence of what happened to those who lost a bet, or entered the bar covered, or otherwise offended the patrons: it was a small wooden airplane, joy stick and all, with four wheels. It was mounted on a pair of elevated rails that ran downward and through a pair of swinging doors to the outside. The poor sap who got to fly it was put in, given a shove, crashed through the wall doors, and was unceremoniously dumped into a foul, swampy morass which held the byproduct of beer from many, many airmen. Those Air Force guys sure knew how to have fun!

* * *

Once you left the Naval Base through the main gate, you were in the Philippines, and the difference was almost immediate. You began to notice a really foul smell, and as you approached an arched bridge over a small canal or something, it hit you full blast. What a stink! It was called the Shit River, whether by its odor or just by chance, I don't know. The water was the murky color of very dark green jade. And the worst part was that, as you walked over the arch, Filipino boys on the concrete banks would call to you to throw a quarter into the "water," and they would dive into this crap and retrieve it. This sure gave new meaning to the idea of being poor.

Walking down the main street you could see what the town's main industry was: the US Navy. It was all bars, strip joints, night clubs, all of which were filled with B-girls and prostitutes. The street ended in a "T," and if you kept walking, you went right into a club which had a rather unique specialty act. If you took a right, you were headed for the grungiest bar in the world, the East Inn Club. It was so well known, every sailor in WestPac would remember it today. Just ask one! It was so crummy. The only brew they served was San Miguel, a Philippine beer. I think it was also the only Philippine beer. You had to get used to it.

The place was shabby with a rusted corrugated metal exterior, a concrete floor, not so clean, the girls didn't look so good, and everyone of course had to see this legendary club just once. That is why most of the wardroom went one night to have a look-see. There were no rules here, there were a lot of drunks inside, and some of us yokels were a little wide-eyed. You kind of got into the mood of a place like that after a few San Miguels, there were girls hanging on all of us, trying to get business, doing their best to separate us from our dollars. One of our guys would have none of it, so we as a group paid a girl to get all over him and do her best to get him to leave with her. To his credit, he didn't crack, in fact none of us did, and we soon left. We didn't go back.

* * *

Bob was one of our excellent officers and a thoroughly nice guy. He was also happily married, and didn't take part in the more rowdy things that were available in liberty ports. But I think curiosity was just killing him about this place, and he came to me one day and asked if I would go into Olongapo with him and show him a club. He just wanted the experience, and I think he even wanted to describe it to his wife. I said sure, and we headed into town.

I did not want to take him to the East Inn Club, it was just too awful, so we went into the club at the end of the main drag. It was a little more "classy" but had the same action as any other place, girls dancing, girls looking for business, girls asking you to buy them a drink (it was actually tea or a coke) for five dollars. Bob was watching everything, drinking in the whole show, and I told him to let me know when he was ready to go. I think he reached that point when a girl serving drinks nearby, took the guys' money, and made change on the corner of the table with her hoochie-coochie (which gave the club its infamy). I looked at Bob and said, "You ready?"

And he said, "Yeah, that'll about do it." So we went back to the ship and he thanked me. At least he was curious no more.

* * *

A Jeepney is a Willys Jeep left over from WWII, which has been modified to carry passengers. It has a colorful paint job like an LSD trip, and has every type of hood ornament and chrome decoration ever made, stuck all over it. Manila used to be full of them. Anyway, Dan Heck and I were in Olongapo City one day and thought we would take a Jeepney ride. We enjoyed the dusty ride over thoroughly bumpy roads, and got into a hilly area, and came upon a marketplace. We decided to have a look, so the driver stopped at the top of a hill, and the three of us got out. Dan asked how much it was, and the driver gave some outrageous tourist amount, and he said he wouldn't pay. Well, they got into an argument, and I really admired this guy, who topped out at about five feet two, yelling way up at Dan at six two. I think Dan couldn't believe it either, it was so comical. Then the driver shrieked and threw up his arms and ran after his Jeepney, which had begun rolling down the hill. Dan and I looked at each other and laughed like hell and ran as fast as we could in the opposite direction. We were able to lose ourselves in the market and never saw that brave little man again.

* * *

Olongapo was a place where you had to be a little careful. Traveling in groups of two or more was a good idea. Filipinos as a people are very nice, very gentle. I like them very much. But you must remember two things: outside the gates they were very poor, and if you offend them they can be downright ferocious. And a drunken sailor or Marine might on occasion become offensive. Many have ended their lives face-down in the Shit River. Once while we were in port, an officer was knifed to death in an alley, in daylight, his shoes, money and watch gone. You just had to be aware of your surroundings, and not do anything stupid. Like I did.

One night I was out in town partying with the guys, and became separated, or separated myself, and went hunting alone. I found a "house" on a back street somewhere, and went in. From a group of girls in various stages of undress, I chose a slender one, very pretty (at least I think she was), and went upstairs with her. I was shocked when she took off her blouse, because she was almost totally flat and had nipples that were at least an inch long and looked like old pencil erasers or stubbed-out cigarettes.

Well, I stayed for awhile then took a shower and we said our goodbyes. I guess I had lost all sense of the time because when I went downstairs the place was locked up tighter than a drum. The front door had a chain and padlock on it, believe it or not. It must have been past curfew. I knew that I was in trouble now. I was wearing a diamond ring that my mother had given me for graduation, and took it off and put it in my mouth. I then began banging on the door and no one came, so I began kicking it and raising a racket until an old woman who was griping at me came and unlocked the door. The street was totally deserted and I just kept on moving and ran like hell for the base. Anybody that was going to come at me had to catch me first.

Breaking curfew can be serious for a number of reasons, and the Navy was very unforgiving about it. I nearly flew over the Shit River bridge and hauled for the main gate, and the sentry must have seen my face because he just waved me through rather than detaining me, bless his soul. I didn't get into trouble with the Navy, and I didn't get myself knifed, but I learned a lesson that night. Having a bad scare does that to a person.

Soon enough, thank goodness, we left Subic for a month of Naval Gunfire Support.

* * *

One day while we were on the gun line, slowly cruising parallel to the beach waiting for a fire mission, we were hailed on the voice radio by a Swift Boat that had spied us going by. Thanks to more recent politics, Swift Boats are better known now than they were then, and are actually named Fast Patrol Craft (PCF). They are 50 feet long and pretty fast at 28 knots, and carry .50 caliber machine guns and an 81 mm mortar. In 1969 they were still part of Task Force 115, as they had been for years, and were still performing Operation Market Time. Most Navy men from that era are familiar with these two names. Market Time guarded the coastline from enemy supply vessels, from the most humble sampan to some pretty good-sized ships. And now their duties included raids into enemy-held coastal waterways, and the patrol of the Mekong Delta's larger rivers.

Anyway, this guy was calling us at about lunchtime asking if we had any hot chow, that he and his crew had been eating out of cans for awhile. He offered some good company and a boat ride in exchange. This would serve as a break in our routine as well as his. Our CO said sure, and we slowed to where we were just barely making way, and he came around so the deck gang could lash him to our starboard quarter. We then continued on our way while he and his guys enjoyed the hospitality of our wardroom and mess decks.

This kind of encounter was interesting because the conversation was always lively and each side got a chance to exchange information, ideas and stories. We found out about his war, which was a little more risky than ours was, and he learned a lot about us.

After lunch, he announced that it was now time for a boat ride, and several of us got permission to leave the ship. I wanted to see how it felt to be on one of the "small boys" for a change. We got unhitched from the Thomas and broke away toward the beach. The CO asked if I wanted to drive and I said, "Sure!" Sitting down in the pilot's seat and taking the wheel, I took the conn. I put her through some maneuvers and while she had good power, I thought the response to the wheel was a little sluggish, kind of like driving a big old Lincoln with bad shocks. I was surprised at the difference because the Thomas, so much bigger than the Swiftie, could turn on a dime.

The CO took us in close to the beach and headed toward a village that was right on the water. We drifted in close and saw that it appeared to be deserted. Now, what happened next I still don't know if it was a setup by this Swift Boat guy or just a dumb coincidence. We hadn't been sitting there for very long when a plane lazily dropped out of some low-hanging clouds, dropped a bomb, and lazily climbed back into the clouds and disappeared. The bomb went off and just *flattened* the village. I mean everything collapsed in a cloud of dust and smoke. While we destroyer types were staring at all this with our mouth hanging open, or saying, "goddamn," one of the Swifties said, "Wow, that must have been a 500 pounder!" I guess they were used to this kind of thing, but that afternoon we got our first taste of life in-country Vietnam. We also learned to appreciate our brothers in the small boats, and wished them well.

* * *

I will say one thing about Capt. Jack: he could give you a thrill once in awhile. There were several times when we were monitoring radio traffic on the beach, that we would catch a fire fight in progress. The Captain was very aggressive in offering our services, and one day we came across a desperate battle taking place within our gun range. I say desperate because there was heavy firing in the background, and you could hear the stress in the Lieutenant or Captain's voice.

Our Captain got on and told him who we were, and asked, "Do you need assistance?" And he yelled back, "Affirm, affirm, thank you," and handed us off to a spotter. With this, Capt. Jack sounded General Quarters, put the rudder hard over, and ordered, "All ahead full." Now, I am not a big flag-waver, never have been, but he then gave an order that still gives me the chills and goose-bumps, "Break out the Battle Flag!" If you can picture this old destroyer coming about at high speed, and this *huge* American battle flag being hoisted between the stacks, and then we commence rapid firing at the enemy, you may get a small idea of how it made us feel. It was just exhilarating!

Just reading that paragraph gives me the chills all over again. As a matter of curiosity, I went to the internet to find out more about the use of the battle flag in WWII and Korea, and could find very little. My step father could give me a complete history, but he is now deceased. From what I could find, it was supposed to be used to identify a warship's nationality in the smoke and confusion of battle, so as to avoid being hit by friendly fire. I then pulled out three of my books that contain photographs taken during major Naval battles fought by destroyers in WWII. Taking a magnifying glass to photos of destroyers firing, maneuvering, being fired at by enemy ships, and/or avoiding Kamikazes, there is not a battle flag to be seen. Signal flags and normal-size American flags, yes, but not one battle flag.

I have thought about that and have decided that there may be three reasons for this and they all have to do with its huge dimensions: it may have been a fire hazard during battle, or it may have hindered vision from the wings of the bridge, or best yet, it may have made the ship a better target for enemy gunners. For whatever reason, ours may have been the only use of a battle flag on a destroyer in decades. It sure was an exciting moment.

* * *

One night very late and very dark, we got a call to make a high-speed run to a certain point, where we were to provide gunfire support to ground units. We got a course and speed worked out, and began our run. Running fast at night along the coast could be risky except for our good surface radar and a flat sea. I had the conn and of course we ran right through an uncharted fishing field and nearly hit a small fisherman. I had seen a weak yellow light almost straight ahead and just to starboard, and I maneuvered to miss what turned out to be a small one-man dinghy, or sampan, with a kerosene lamp hanging on the stern. The poor fisherman probably still has nightmares about that, assuming he lived. Besides scaring him to death, our wake would have swamped him and his sampan. At the same time, we got some kind of cable wrapped around one of our propeller shafts, but were still able to make good enough speed to our target area.

* * *

I have mentioned that, while on Plane Guard duty with the carriers, we witnessed hundreds of missions, doing what we were supposed to do in the larger scheme of things, but not aware of what damage the pilots and crews were doing on the other end. The same was true on the gun line: we never got narrative reports of what we accomplished on so many fire missions. There were plenty of "bravo zulu's" and "well done's" and "thank you's," but never a true picture. Well, I found a description of a destroyer's gunfire support mission all these years later and it is very gratifying. Just wish all of our destroyer guys could read it. Ironically, it is found in a very good book by a Brown Water sailor, *"Man of the River,"* by Signalman Chief Jimmy R. Bryant, USN:

"An American destroyer off the coast out beyond Can Gio was ready to use its big guns as artillery to saturate a known Viet Cong staging area about 22:00. The ship required a ground spotter to direct its fire. Our patrol (two PBR's, or Patrol Boat, River) received the destroyer's radio frequency and went to a location near the target area at the appointed time. Hoping that the VC wouldn't detect us until this mission was over, we positioned our boats about a half-mile from the target and dropped anchor in a swampy area about a mile off the main river channel. Our boats anchored about thirty feet apart. The destroyer established contact with us, we gave them our location, and they confirmed our knowledge of the target area. Within a couple of minutes the radio said, 'Firing spotting round.' A few seconds later the destroyer's white phosphorus round went off directly over the designated target.

My radio response to them was, 'You are on target. Fire for effect!' Both of our boat crews saw what an American destroyer is capable of. It looked like a two-mile area was totally shredded from the rapid explosions. Several secondary explosions were also heard. After a short pause, the destroyer came back on the radio to ask for an evaluation. It was hard to describe, so I told them the target area was totally saturated, small fires were burning, and several secondary explosions were audible. They thanked us and we said 'Good job! Sure glad you guys are on our side.'"

Thanks, Chief!

*   *   *

Another day on the gun line. We had been shooting for the Marines for a few days, and from the chatter on their radios we could hear that they liked our gunners. It seemed like most of our targets were always truck parks or bunkers or staging areas. While we worked with the Marine spotters, we used one of their outdated PRC-10 (un-affectionately known as the Prick-10) portable radios to communicate with someone on the ground or up in a helicopter. For a portable, it was heavy and cumbersome, and it really wasn't very reliable. It had a habit of crapping out just at the wrong moment. In fact, by 1969, it had been largely replaced by the PRC-25, which was transistorized and much more reliable.

It seemed like everyone we worked with on the beach needed food, and the Marines were no exception. They began bargaining back and forth with the Captain and finally a deal was struck: we would trade a case of 50 frozen chickens for some helicopter rides. Soon we had an incoming chopper and he landed smoothly on our helo deck.

This was the little 4-seater nicknamed the Loach, more formally known as an OH-6 Cayuse or Light Observation Helicopter. It had a teardrop shape, most of which was plexiglass, was fast and agile, and was used as an artillery spotter or as a scout. As a scout it would fly in low over the jungle to attract ground fire, would drop a marker, and then pull away while a Cobra helicopter gunship came in to do its business. The Loach could absorb multiple hits and still protect its crew.

The first group of three included me, BM1 Cobb, and one other sailor. Cobb was well liked on the ship and was one of those real solid, professional sailors that every ship must have. As the officer, I had the dubious honor of sitting in the right front seat, while the other two guys got in the back. I couldn't help but notice that there were no doors on the front.

I looked over and said hello to the pilot. He had a flight helmet on with a large, dark visor pulled down, and was looking straight ahead. He acknowledged my greeting with only a slight nod, and that is when I noticed he had a cigarette butt in his mouth, with the other end stuck into the small black microphone that came down from his helmet. I was beginning to wonder about this guy when he suddenly revved the engine and lifted off.

The pilot had not said anything about seat belts, in fact he had not said anything at all, but I stealthily pulled mine around me and locked it. Thank God! He took us up to an altitude of 500 feet or so, and stopped. He then flipped the copter 90 degrees to the right, on its side, and I was staring at the sea below, no door, only the seatbelt keeping me from tumbling out. The Gulf of Tonkin certainly looked different from that altitude. That's when the obscenities began coming from the back seat. I don't know if they were excited or scared, maybe a little of each, but you could hear them for the entire ride, and there is nobody in the world who can curse like a sailor.

The pilot then abruptly flipped us upright again, and just went up, straight up, for what seemed like a long time. After a while you couldn't see the horizon, so there was no point of reference. Finally he stopped climbing and dipped the nose forward, and there was the Thomas far, far below, and it was only 2 inches long, same as in Hong Kong! He then dove at the ship at full throttle and the guys in the back just went bananas. I don't know how fast we were going, but it took only moments for the ship to loom very large in the windshield. All three of us thought we were going to crash because the pilot had waited so long and never slowed down, but at the last instant he pulled the nose up so the helo's belly was pointed toward the ship, and used his rotor blades as air brakes. I swear to you, folks, I looked up at the rotors, and there was so much stress on them, they were bent upwards. If he had cracked one of those things we'd have all been goners.

Only feet from the ship, or so it seemed, he executed a smooth turn and headed out to sea. He had spotted a Vietnamese fishing boat so he immediately headed toward it and came to a hover directly over the tip of the mast. The poor fisherman had been asleep and all of a sudden had awakened to see this machine from hell right above him. Well, you couldn't hear him but you could see him throw his arms above his head and scream in terror! I'm sorry, but that was the funniest thing I had ever seen, and I looked over at the pilot, who had just a hint of a smile, cigarette butt still jammed into his microphone.

He pulled away, headed for our ship and deposited us on the helo deck. As we got out and three more victims boarded, the three of us just looked at each other, shook our heads and said, "Shit!" That Marine had wanted to scare some sailors, and he sure did.

I need to say something about him. To us on the sea, all pilots were a strange breed, and this guy was certainly no exception. But if there were ever the perfect melding of man and machine, this was it. I have never seen anyone handle a machine of any kind like that, much less become "one" with it. I thought he was crazy, but I also knew that he was a great pilot. I wonder if he ever made it home. Hope so.

* * *

During this month at sea, we had to deal with another typhoon, which meant another bout with heavy weather. An incident occurred during this one, which makes it memorable, and it involved Nuoc Mam. For the uninitiated, I have to explain exactly what that is. Nouc Mam is a fish sauce made by the Vietnamese since ancient times, and I will tell you how it is made, exactly as I was told when I was in-country in 1970. You take a 55-gallon drum and cut one end out and weld on to it a convex metal cone with a hole in the center of it. You then invert the drum, to stand on legs up off the ground. Into this you dump layers of mainly fish heads, tails and innards, alternating with layers of salt. Then put it out in the hot Vietnam sun for 6 to 12 months. What eventually begins to dribble out the bottom is an awful, putrid, fermented fish juice called Nouc Mam. It is a main staple of the Vietnamese diet, and it stinks far worse than you can imagine.

Some Americans actually liked this stuff, but the only one I have ever known personally was my XO, Commander Aydt. Well, he thought he would take some of it home, and bought a case of I think a dozen bottles of it, and stowed it in his stateroom. Now, his stateroom was near the wardroom, and across from the stateroom I shared with three other guys in officers' country. When we hit heavy weather we began rolling quite a bit, as usual. Of course the XO had secured his case of Nouc Mam for foul weather, as we all had to secure everything throughout the ship. I have mentioned the "usual" crashing sounds coming from below during heavy weather, because regardless how well something is lashed down, if there is even a modicum of movement, it will multiply in direct proportion to the length and severity of the rolling. Well, of course the Nouc Mam ended up crashing to the deck, and this foul odor began creeping throughout the superstructure of the ship. It was terrible, and the XO got help cleaning it up, and the deadly gas was contained mainly in officers' country. We could smell it for days, and it made it difficult for me to eat or sleep. I think it even made my eyes water. The XO had it worse, as it must have permeated everything in his stateroom, including bedding and his uniforms, and that would take a while to go away. But, as I have said, he liked it and got a few bottles home after all.

As an example of how our guys remember this stuff, a Riverine sailor, Rod Walker, wrote a story, and I quote from it, "I remember hauling Vietnamese troops out on search and destroy missions. When they came back, they had ducks, pigs, and chickens with them. These animals ran around the well deck where we had to live. What a mess! The smell was almost like Nuoc Mam. Remember that?" Rod Walker's article, as it appeared in the Mobile Riverine Force Association (MRFA) Summer 2008 River Currents newsletter, is entitled, "*My Time on the Rivers.*"

Get the picture? Next time you are in a Vietnamese restaurant, and want to feel like you are going on the local economy, ask for a little authentic Nuoc Mam over rice and see what you think.

* * *

The longer we were at sea, the more concerned I became about my teletypes. These were the high-speed (600 words per minute) machines that printed out the fleet broadcast and all of the rest of our message traffic. They were highly complex things with a million moving parts, and were so mechanically precise that even the smallest adjustment problem would put one out of commission. I had been bothered by them for most of the cruise. The radiomen could make general repairs and do some cleaning, but it took a real expert to do anything beyond that. If you lose your last high-speed teletype, you fall back on the old fashioned, slow as molasses printer at 30 words per minute, or maybe it was 60. Failing that, it's back to the telegraph key. Fortunately I had a couple of guys who were pretty fast on the key.

We finally got some time alongside a Destroyer Tender in Nha Trang. A tender is like a department store and repair facility for your type of ship, destroyer, submarine, etc. Anyway, off the ship came my teletypes, first thing. While they were being repaired, my excellent 1st Class Radioman, Ski, became friendly with the 1st Class who was doing the work. This technician could do anything with these machines, and was worth his weight in gold out in WestPac, not to mention his value to the tender. During his conversations with this guy, Ski began to get the feeling he was not very happy on the tender, that he was bored here and wanted to see some action. Ski's antennae went up (no pun intended), and he asked the guy if he would be interested in going with us. He said, "Sure."

Ski was in front of me in about 2 minutes telling me we had a live one, and after running it by Norm, we were in front of the XO. We relished the idea of "Shanghai-ing" a sailor in the modern Navy. The paperwork guys on both ships did their thing and before you knew it, we had a new 1st Class Radioman with a full set of tools, and our teletype problems were over with. The tender people were howling mad that we had taken such a valuable man, but there was nothing they could do since it was done properly, if maybe a little quickly and surreptitiously. I did have a small twinge of guilt about that, but it passed.

* * *

In the Gulf of Tonkin you were never alone. When operating as plane guard, there were a number of other destroyers around plus a carrier right in the middle of things. And even when operating independently on the gun line, you always had company in the form of "Fleet Skunk Delta." This was an old Russian trawler that was well-known to all WestPac ships. It seemed that he was always on your surface radar.

He was painted a bad pea-green color, and even had fishing nets suspended from booms on either side, making him look like an innocent fisherman who was rather lost. But a look through the binoculars showed a cabin that was bristling with antennae, making him an ELINT (electronics intelligence) spy ship. But this guy took spying to another, low tech level.

In those days all of the ship's garbage was simply thrown over the side. It was a big ocean, right? Some of the food would be eaten by the fish or birds and the rest would just sink eventually. My communications division shredded all of our papers down to $1/32^{nd}$ of an inch, and they came out as big fluffy gobs of paper strips, which went over the side with everything else.

It was eventually determined that Fleet Skunk Delta was picking up all of our garbage, and that of all of our ships, and these guys would go through it for any bits of intelligence they could find. It made sense, really, kind of like a cheap detective going through your garbage can.

Naval Intelligence figured that someone that thorough was going to find a way to read our shredded messages and codes, so we had to begin burning all of our paper waste, and left only empty tin cans and banana peels for the Russians.

* * *

I have described how underway replenishment (UNREP) works, and that is when you have access to other ships for supplies. On the gun line, the majority of supplies were delivered via Vertical Replenishment (VERTREP), that is, by helicopter. Periodically a big helo would come out with a large cargo net suspended underneath, with boxes of food or repair parts or whatever, and always the mailbag. Even if nothing else was coming, the mailbag was flown out fairly regularly. This was one of those few events at sea that was guaranteed to pick up morale. Receiving mail was as about as good as it got. Even if you only got bills, as did Harry Shapiro in the great movie, "*Stalag 17*," it didn't matter. It was still a way to keep touch with reality.

VERTREP was also a way to transfer personnel. Sometimes people were brought in or taken out this way. Two nurses, Judy and Pat, were flown out one day for a tour of the ship. My room mate Gary was assigned as their escort---he was a handsome guy and charmed these nice ladies. They were treated very well and respectfully by the crew and were thrilled, and morale on the Thomas went up a notch or two.

If you were around other ships, personnel transfers could be effected in two other ways which were rooted firmly in Naval history. Our motor whaleboat could be swung out and lowered into the water to be used to transport people. And the other was the use of the Bosun's Chair.

The Bosun's Chair was not in the Navy's supply system, but was fabricated by the guys in the 1st Division. If you can visualize an old-fashioned straight backed chair surrounded by a protective cage, you only have half of the picture. All of the metal surfaces were covered by "fancy work" and then painted a high-gloss white. (Fancy work is the same thing that covers the monkey fist. It is wrapping and finely detailed artwork made from cotton line and rope of various diameters). The chair is constructed with a strong steel top with an eye in the middle. The transferee sits in the chair and, as in an UNREP, is lifted off the deck and hauled across open water by line to the other ship. This requires great coordination of BM's on both sides, to compensate for sea conditions and movement of both ships. The evolution was not without hazard, as the accidental dunking of an unfortunate sailor or officer occurred on occasion.

By mentioning fancy work, I must talk about MacNamara's Lace. It is a very delicate and decorative lace, made from small line, which was used for fancy trimmings and curtains. It requires great skill and patience, as well as dedication, and it is the jealously guarded domain of the Bosun's Mate. As an example of its use, MacNamara's Lace could be found decorating the top of a Bosun's Chair.

* * *

The old maxim held that there was nothing worse than a fire at sea. It is one of the many reasons that we trained so hard to go to general quarters. We had occasion to find out one day when GQ was called. The crew thought that it had something to do with the enemy, but there was a fire burning somewhere below and a fire party was called out. It turned out to be an electrical board gone bad. It was extinguished quickly and did minimal damage, so it turned out to be a realistic drill and good practice for the Damage Control guys.

* * *

While we were out, an earthquake occurred somewhere in the region. It was of sufficient magnitude to trigger an alert to all ships to be on the lookout for a tsunami. All officers of the watch had to read the message and sign off on it. It was rather lengthy, and explained that in deep water such a powerful force may appear as only a 2 inch wave. Ships were advised that if one were spotted, turn directly into it and put on speed as quickly as possible to avoid being affected by subsurface turbulence. Everyone looked for it, keeping binoculars trained in the general direction of its origin. We never saw or felt anything, but there was someone who did.

Another destroyer was steaming independently when the bridge watch spotted a small wave. The decision was made to immediately turn into it and crank it up to "all ahead full," as recommended in the message. The ship gathered speed quickly and closed in on the wave, and *crunch,* it ran up onto an uncharted coral reef. It ripped up their bottom, and we never heard what happened to the ship subsequently, whether it was salvaged or sunk. We were sure sympathetic though; it really could have been any one of us. Better them than the DD-833, though.

* * *

One morning between gunfire missions we were cruising north along the coast and nothing much was going on. I had the watch and the sea was calm, with a perfectly cloudless blue sky. I happened to be looking straight ahead of the ship, when suddenly two black dots appeared just above the horizon. I started to say something to the OOD about it, but never got it out.

The two dots quickly turned into a pair of F-4 Phantoms (fighter-bomber) headed right for us! I have no idea how fast they were going, but it was *very* fast because in just an instant they were flying by the bridge, one on each side, at *our eye level* (maybe 40 feet off the water)! And if you've never heard a Phantom taking off or in flight, you will never understand how loud that was: it was a terrific thundering roar that nearly knocked us off our feet, and the concussion went through the entire ship. Those fighter jockeys had to be Navy or Marines, and they were showing us their stuff.

They were there and gone in a microsecond. It took a little longer than that for us to register what had happened, but by that time, here they came for an encore, this time from the stern: they came blasting down each side of the ship again. Just as they roared past us, they shot straight up into the sky, in perfect harmony, their afterburners flaming. And then they were gone.

It was a hell of a display! All that speed and power and noise. Of course there was no radio contact between us and them, and they were traveling so fast we couldn't read their tail numbers, so they would never get into trouble for hot dogging like that. Besides, it was too much fun for us. There was an interesting discussion later in the wardroom about what would have happened had they been enemy planes coming in to attack. The answer was that we would have been wasted. We were no match for Mach 2 aircraft because we had no missiles. Our 5"38's had anti-aircraft shells but we would have had to ask them to slow down a little.

I'll always be amazed about one thing: when those planes came by the bridge on their first pass, I glanced at the one on the starboard side and actually saw the pilot looking over at us. It should have been just a big blur at his high rate of speed, but there he was, clear as day. I either blinked at just the right time and saw him, or the mind was able to segment time somehow. Whatever, I have that picture in my head as if it had been taken yesterday with the best high-speed camera.

The F-4 Phantom fighter-bomber has been called the workhorse of the Vietnam war. Pilots also called it a "Corvette with wings" because of all that power. During its long career, it was flown by the Navy, Marines and Air Force. These two guys were hot dogs of the first order, but also fine pilots. And as I have said about all of the people we encountered out there, I hope they made it home okay.

* * *

There was a character flying over the Gulf of Tonkin at night whom we got to know but never met personally. Night watches were typically quiet and rather tedious, so we were especially glad when the "Green Dragon" came on the air. He was a black pilot who was very funny and loved to talk, and we think he was visiting with us while waiting for fire missions. He wouldn't say, but we concluded that he was flying either a C-47 Dragon Ship or a Helicopter Gunship. We would chat with him about what was going on in our host country, nothing classified of course, and things that were happening in the Real World. We would all be laughing and he would be, too. Eventually he had to say, "Gotta go," and we would say, "Have a nice day," or "Have a good one, over," and he would sign off with his characteristic, "Ten Fo!" The world needs more Green Dragons, a man of good cheer and probably as deadly as hell.

* * *

I'm not sure why, but the craziest things seemed to happen to us while we were operating by ourselves, cruising slowly, waiting for fire missions. This time, we were under a low, dark cloud ceiling and

I was on watch on the bridge around mid-day. I was looking down, doing a log entry or checking the radar screen or something, when suddenly everyone else on the bridge erupted in expletives or amazement, like, "What the hell was that?" I snapped my head up just in time to see something right out of Buck Rogers: this huge geyser of gray and white water spouting 200 feet high, only about 1,000 yards in front of us.

It looked like Armageddon. No one knew what on earth was happening, and we went to General Quarters just in case. After the sea had calmed somewhat, the radar showed an object in the water, not moving. We couldn't see it well enough with binoculars, so we maneuvered in to get a better look. It was a plane of some kind, and soon enough we could see that it was jet powered and had no pilot. Or cockpit. We had inadvertently seen an unmanned drone crash into the sea.

The Captain wanted to recover it but it was the XO that counseled him to leave it be until we could get instructions. Fearing it would sink first, the CO ordered a recovery, so we swung around so it could be attached to one of the boat davits astern. Meanwhile we put out some message traffic to try to determine who owned this thing, and what should we do with it?

This was a pretty good-sized plane and getting it on board wouldn't be easy. The deck guys were in the water attaching a makeshift sling around the fuselage and attaching it to a davit. When it was ready, they began to slowly pull the plane out of the water. Bad luck, as in the short time it was suspended in mid air, the ship rolled, and the plane crunched against the side, causing considerable damage. To the plane, not the ship. It was finally hauled aboard at an awkward angle across the deck and hanging over the side, and lashed down so it wouldn't move.

Everyone was curious and wanted a closer look, and when I could, I went down to see that it was not clearly marked as US property, but on the belly was a glass rectangle, maybe 8" by 12", with small black lettering around it. What we had here was an unmanned spy plane, or photo reconnaissance plane, with a million dollar payload of cameras. Nasty looking thing. Technical. Expensive. Top Secret.

That last part was right, anyway. We got a message back from someone, one of the "black ops" outfits, I'm sure, saying that the object would float, please stand by for further instructions. Above all, it was *urgent* that we *do not touch* and *do not attempt to recover* the object. Oops!

Well, we had good intentions, anyway.

Note: I now know that this was a UAV (unmanned aerial vehicle) called the Firebee, and was invented by an American named Mr. Norman Sakamoto. The Firebee flew thousands of photo reconnaissance missions over Southeast Asia.

* * *

Now we concluded almost a month of Naval Gunfire Support. If memory serves, we had expended about 1,800 rounds of 5" shells. I read about one destroyer, the USS Bordelon (DD-881) that had fired 5,700 rounds during a 1967-68 tour. She must have spent a little less time on plane guard than we did, and a lot more time on the line. Man, that's a lot of shooting!

I have mentioned what the eye and brain are capable of, in the instance of the F-4 Phantoms that rocketed past our bridge. In the same vein, if you are close enough to 5" guns to feel the concussion whenever they are fired, and if you are there when they are fired so many times, occasionally you could actually see the projectile leave the muzzle. That's a great trick of the eye, because at that point they are traveling 2,500 feet per second, but it happened. Normally, only very fast cameras are able to do that. And once, just by chance, I was able to follow the trajectory of a shell until it disappeared from view. It's a great trick, and very impressive.

The only 5" shell casings I had ever seen were brass, and that indicated we were still expending ammo that was made during WWII. There must have been a lot of it since we were still shooting it 25 years later. The shell casing that is by my front door, now ingloriously serving as an umbrella stand, is marked November 1944. About halfway through our tour we could tell that new shells were being produced because the brass disappeared and was replaced by a metal that looked like tin or zinc.

I have neglected to mention one important factor in the firing of our guns: the urinals. Inevitably, after shooting for awhile you could usually hear some crashing going on down below, and find that some of the urinals had been blown off the bulkhead, and were now lying on the deck. Depending on which guns were firing and when, there was a great deal of torque put on the hull, and the weakest component seemed to be urinals. Sometimes, after a particularly busy day blowing holes in South Vietnam, we would even get a wash basin or two.

Now we headed toward Subic Bay for a final time, for a 3 day stop. There we would make preparations for crossing the Pacific and going home. Everyone was about ready, as the 6 months had seemed much longer. We all looked to our divisions to make sure we had everything we needed, and that done, maybe a last trip into Olongapo. Not for me, though, as I recall. Too busy.

And the time finally came to get underway with an eastern heading. We all believed that we had performed well in the war zone, that we had done what was asked of us and then some. I think a lot of people were changed by the experience; I was, for better or worse. Leaving Subic for San Diego was refreshing, relaxing even, it just felt good. We were going to make the crossing alone this time, or in Navy parlance, unaccompanied. The water was glassy and the skies were clear, and we said goodbye to WestPac.

* * *

There were two things that could have happened on the way back to the states that would have shown the crew our appreciation for all of the hard work during a successful 6-month cruise, in addition to giving them a whopping good time.

The first could have occurred not too long after we left the Philippines, when we found ourselves only 1 degree, or 60 miles, from the equator. There is a ceremony, so traditional that it predates the United States Navy, and is so silly and ridiculous, that every sailor and officer should go through it. It has various names, but "Crossing the Line" is the most common. Those who have been through it are called "Shellbacks," and those who have not are called "Pollywogs." No shellback has ever forgotten the experience.

Those who are to be indoctrinated to the Mysteries of the Deep come before Neptunus Rex and his Royal Court, which normally includes Davy Jones, Her Highness Amphitrite, the Royal Baby, the Royal Judge, and various other royal personalities, such as attorneys, scribes, barbers, etc. These are all portrayed, in full costume, by senior enlisted men who of course are Shellbacks. *No one* is exempt from the ceremony, including the Captain if he is a Pollywog. My step father was XO of his ship when he went through it.

There are hundreds of variations, but in general it goes something like this: Pollywogs are required to entertain the Court by doing things like singing or dancing with your uniform inside-out, whistling Dixie over the PA system, telling stories, reading poetry, the list is endless. Then you are brought before the Court to kneel and accept the charges against you, and the resulting punishment. While there you have to kiss the Baby. This was the big ugly guy with the fattest gut on the ship, on which gut was slathered "monkey shit" grease and you had to kiss it. You might be dunked over the side in a bosun's chair, and then get a really bad chopped up haircut from the Barber, whose clippers might shock the hell out of you. After various other indignities you had to run the gauntlet, a long piece of canvas laid out on the deck and either greased or strewn with yesterday's garbage, or both. You had to crawl through the grease and garbage while being paddled with short pieces of fire hose. There might be a joker at the end with a real fire hose to blast you backwards just when you thought it was over. When you do reach the end of the gauntlet, it really is over, and you are officially designated a Shellback. You earned it, man. This was verified by a certificate from the "Dominion of Neptunus Rex," suitable for framing, and an entry was actually added to your service record.

The original intent of the Crossing Ceremony was for the senior sailors to make sure new recruits could "take it," and therefore become good, tough sailors. Over its long history some deaths and injuries have occurred, and from what I understand it was watered down in the 1980's, to where today it is completely harmless and totally voluntary. One modern sailor's comment on the internet about it was simply that it has become "really lame." But in 1969 it was still for real.

I am still a Pollywog. The Captain had full discretion in the matter, the whole ship wanted the ceremony, and he said, "No." That was really something to remember. Whatever capital he had built up with the crew, went right over the side. The officers just *knew* that he did it in order to save fuel oil and look good to the Pentagon. Or maybe he was a Pollywog and didn't want to go through the ceremony. Or maybe he just wanted to get home to Momma. For whatever reason, he dealt a big blow to the ship's morale.

It gets worse. By implication, not crossing the equator also meant no stop in Sydney, Australia. Word throughout the fleet was that there was nothing like post-cruise liberty in Sydney. It was becoming legendary. Australian girls *loved* American sailors, and when a ship docked it was met by long lines of girls, just waiting to take you home for dinner with the family and a night on the town. We had heard about this phenomenon from too many guys for it not to be true, and they all said you will never believe how great Australian girls are. Many ships had taken the option and gone there, but not the old Herbie J! No sir, we were making a bee-line for San Diego. Damn!

* * *

There were a couple of fuel stops to make on the way back to the states. The first one was at Guam, the second at Midway Island, and the final one at Pearl Harbor. Our call at Guam was uneventful, and nothing out of the ordinary was anticipated for Midway except for the gooney birds. Those are the ones who are very graceful in the water, but on land they are a disaster: each time they come in they crash and roll and tumble. Very clumsy.

On our approach to Midway we noticed that the pier looked brand new. It was concrete and had large wooden timbers running along the side for protection. On these timbers was a fresh coat of thick, black creosote that you could smell a mile away.

Usually there are large bumpers hanging down over these, made of rubber or tightly woven hemp rope. And our guys stand at the ready with our own bumpers in case they are needed. Well, somehow none of these precautions mattered because the guy driving, who shall remain nameless here, came in a little too fast and at too wide an angle, and our beautiful ship with it's seven week old paint job, just smeared down the side of that pier. We didn't hit hard enough to dent anything, so it wasn't serious, but there was a large black creosote skid mark down the port side. Luckily the guys were able to remove it with solvents and a lot of elbow grease, and save Mary Soo's paint job.

Note: In the last chapter of this book you will meet Boatswain's Mate Chief Alcorn Berry. I had recounted this story to the Chief, and he did me one better. He was cruising in the Indian Ocean on a destroyer, in the vicinity of the Arabian Peninsula. But they were way out in the middle of nowhere, when it was decided to put a new coat of paint on the superstructure, that is, everything above the main deck. So all of the 1st Division guys, fondly nicknamed the "deck apes," and others, were out with their chipping hammers and orange primer paint. When all surfaces were prepared, out came the rollers and paint brushes and a new coat of Navy gray was applied. At the exact moment when there was a whole lot of wet paint on the ship, the sky darkened, and the darkness quickly enveloped the ship. It was a large sandstorm! The crew were so flabbergasted at seeing a sandstorm out over open water, that it took a few minutes to sink in that all of that sand was being blown at high velocity onto wet paint! What they ended up with was a ship that looked like high-grade sandpaper. What a mess!

* * *

Last stop, Pearl Harbor, before making the final leg of the cruise to San Diego. Again, it was for fueling only, so no liberty, and that was sort of okay because everyone was anxious now to go home. As we rounded Ford Island and came abreast of the USS Arizona Memorial, I witnessed the strangest scene you can imagine. As I have mentioned, to all Americans and particularly Navy people, this moment is like being in church: it is solemn, quiet, and reverent. But up pipes my boss, Lt. Tana, with a rousing, "Hip, hip, hooray! Hip, hip, hooray!" He then laughed at his own joke. He was trying to inject some humor into the moment, I suppose, being of Japanese descent. His outburst was met with silence, as all of the bridge crew, including the Captain, stared at him as if he were crazy. Really inappropriate, and one of those embarrassing moments you don't forget.

* * *

We were only a few days out of San Diego now. The whole crew were so excited about going home and seeing loved ones. The energy and anticipation made the atmosphere crackle in every part of the ship. I don't recall who had the idea, but the Radiomen were requested to set up a radiotelephone net so that some of our sailors could call home.

First the RM needed to establish contact with some willing amateur radio (HAM) operators ashore. This was not difficult, as ham operators are always willing to help out in a good cause. They needed to be able to patch an R/T call into the local phone system in the San Diego area. Our guys would establish contact at an agreed time, give the ham a telephone number, which he or she would dial. From then on it was just like a normal phone call. (Remember folks, this was high tech then; oh, what changes 40 years hath wrought!)

The sailors signed up to call. The fact that this was for the San Diego area only, that calls were necessarily limited to three minutes, and that an officer (me) and a few Radiomen had to monitor the call, kept the list relatively short. Then, the younger married sailors were given preference. The older guys had done this before, and they knew they would see Mama and the kids in a few days anyway. I sat through the calls and tried not to listen too closely, but that was difficult because the callers used an R/T handset, similar to a telephone, and their wives were broadcast over a speaker in Radio I, where this was set up. The caller needed to say right away that we were at sea, and that she was coming over a speaker with others present. It was very happy at both ends, and the wives just couldn't believe it was possible for hubby to call her from the ship at sea.

One call will always stick with me; I hate to use the words "cute" and "touching," but it was. A young fellow came in and called his wife, and when she answered, he said something like, "Hi, honey, it's me!" There was a brief silence, then she said, "Who is this?"

"It's me, Mike!"

"Mike, where are you?"

"I'm out in the middle of the Pacific."

And she let out a scream and started laughing. And she couldn't stop. Poor Mike would say something, and she would pause and try to say something, then start giggling and laughing again. Unbelievably, she kept this up for the entire three minutes, and he finally had to say, "Honey, I've got to go, I love you," and through her giggling she managed, "Mike, I love you too, I'm sorry," and still unable to stop laughing, hung up. Of course, by the time the call ended, we were all cracking up, including Mike. It was great fun and a nice memory.

* * *

One must never underestimate the resourcefulness and imagination of the American sailor. We were very close to San Diego when the Captain ordered, "All engines stop," and we lost headway and went dead in the water. No one could understand what was going on, particularly since we were so close to US soil. There was no wind, and the sea was calm. By now, we were all in dress uniform and just wanted to go home! But the bridge was silent, and the Captain said nothing. Now we could see several Bosun's Mates in their dress blues go forward on the main deck up to the paint locker hatch near the bow. They popped it open and began bringing out the most wonderful thing you could imagine. We were all completely dumbstruck to see the longest, most colorful Hawaiian lei come out of that hatch.

The BM's, in complete secrecy, had made this thing out of red, white and blue crepe paper. It was maybe 2 feet thick, and when it was laid out on the deck, it was easily 100 feet in circumference. It was just unbelievable. They then draped it over the bow the way they would have draped a flower lei around the neck of a beautiful wahine.

Except for an occasional admiring comment, the whole crew was stunned speechless. It was what you might call a "moment." The Captain then ordered, "All ahead one third," a slow speed, but one that ensured our lei would stay in place rather than blow away.

* * *

I have mentioned Coronado Island, across the harbor form San Diego. There sits the world famous Hotel Del Coronado in all its splendor. Built in the late 1800's, reputedly without the use of one nail, it is a surviving example of Victorian wooden architecture held together with wooden pegs. Occupying two rooms on the top floor, facing the Pacific, were my mother and step father, and my grandmother and step grandfather. Admiral Zim had requested that location so that he could watch for us on approach to the harbor. (Undoubtedly he had brought along his binoculars.) And sure enough, they were all four watching as we slowly came into view, wearing our gigantic lei. They all told me later that it was such a beautiful sight, and took their breath away. Then they hurried, as best they could, downstairs to get their car.

* * *

As we entered the harbor, the order was given to "Man the rails," and our sailors snapped to in their crisp dress blues, one behind each stanchion (5 or 6 feet apart) around the main deck, standing at "parade rest." We must have looked magnificent!

You could tell the minute we came within sight of Pier 6, as a deafening roar went up from the *huge* crowd there. It looked like the entire city had turned out for us! The Navy band was there and started playing, flags and banners were fluttering, women and children were waving and cheering. All in all, it was a great homecoming.

The Captain was going to bring the ship into the pier, and he and I and a few others went topside to the auxiliary conning station on top of the bridge. We had a wonderful view of this mass of happy people. He would give engine and rudder commands and I would relay them over a microphone down to the bridge. As I have said, the Captain was very cautious with his ship, and it took us a long time to maneuver alongside another destroyer in the nest. The crowd was crazy and the band was playing anyway, and it didn't really matter. Our welcomers were on the pier, and on the next destroyer as well.

The Bosun's Mates began to twirl their monkey fists and let go, and they flew through the air toward deck hands on the other end. Well, one of the monkey fists went awry and landed up in the superstructure of the other ship rather than the main deck. But an alert line handler, in the person of Admiral Edwin J. Zimmermann, grabbed it and dropped it to a sailor below. No one knew who he was, as he was in the mufti of a green suit and tie, except the XO who alertly took one look at him and asked, "Is that your step father?" I laughed and said yes. He said he would like to meet him, and I said of course, because I wanted them to meet. Zim looked like an Admiral when he was jogging in a sweat shirt and shorts. He had that certain bearing. He could have easily shown up in uniform, which he wore very well, but he said later that he had not wanted to detract attention from the Thomas and her crew, this was their day. It was a measure of the man's character.

He saw me and we waved at each other, but I had to pay attention until the Captain ordered "All stop," and the lines were secured. With the order, "Now secure from the Sea and Anchor Detail," our six month cruise was over. The crowd surged aboard the ship. It was a happy day for everyone. I spotted my mother and grandparents finally, as they slowly worked their way aboard.

I had a reunion with my family in the crowded wardroom. They were so proud of their "boy," and I introduced them around. Zim and Commander Aydt met. After a while the ship cleared, and liberty was called. I had the duty and had to stay, and spent a quiet day and night aboard.

When I and a few others left for the first time the next day, we found it hard to walk down the pier because it seemed to be moving. We were still on our "sea legs" and our minds were trying to compensate, making us look like a bunch of drunks. It was ridiculous trying to keep our balance on solid concrete, which was not moving. Pretty soon we were able to walk straight, and knew we were home.

San Diego

Once back in San Diego, my tour of duty on the Thomas would last only a few more months, and it would be an anti-climax to the "busyness" and excitement of the WestPac cruise. The same "gang of four" found an apartment again, this time in a brand new complex in La Jolla. The premiere feature of this place was a sunken hot tub in the middle of a large open air bricked patio, which served as a meeting place for night owls, and was used every night until 2 or 3 AM. You were never lonely at these apartments.

A couple of us went with Porter Powell to get his Volvo out of storage. The car looked normal enough, just under a layer of dust, but when he unlocked and opened the door, he let out a yell that got us running to have a look. The formerly pristine red interior of his car was an ugly mess of green and gray and black mold on just about every surface. It took just a moment to figure out what had happened: rather than quietly and mellowly fermenting into a fine vintage, a couple of his gallon wine jugs had exploded and *then* began fermenting on Porter's car. He was really upset because he loved that car so, but believe it or not he was able to scrub it clean again, and the intact jugs yielded up a pretty decent wine.

* * *

Every active destroyer in the fleet was required to make a high speed run once a year to ensure that she still "had what it takes" to do the job. Flank speed is throttles wide open, and is rarely used, even less so for a sustained period because of the strain it puts on the engineering plant. But we have to know if the power is there if needed in an emergency. So here we go, the order is given, "All ahead flank," and you can feel the ship surge and pick up speed. Faster and faster, with 60,000 horsepower driving her, the ship begins to vibrate, almost violently, from the engines and props. When we reach top speed she is really flying, a 390 foot speed boat, and I went out to the fantail to see the most spectacular sight: the 50 foot rooster tail (water jet) shooting almost straight up into the air! When commissioned in 1945, the Thomas was rated at 35 knots. Now, at 25 years old she was still able to make 33 knots. We were so proud of the old girl. They really built those things to last.

* * *

As soon as it could be arranged, I took a short leave and flew back to Omaha to pick up the Corvette. There was a terrific December snowstorm going on at the time, and upon arriving at Quarters 15, there it was, parked out back under a big lump of snow. I could just see a streak of red color down each side. Inside, the Quarters were warm and happy, and it was great to see Zim, Mother, Torres, and Schnapps again.

My visit would be short, as I had to be back on the ship for Officers' Call in just a few days. No problem, I thought, the car was powerful and very fast, and would get me there with time to spare. But, in my rushed trip to bring the car home before the cruise, I had forgotten to add plenty of anti freeze to the cooling system, which is what you *do* against the harsh Omaha winter. As a result, the water froze solid, expanded, and cracked the engine block. My step father had generously paid for a new engine to be installed, and would not let me pay him back for it. The bad news was that the mechanic had told him that the new "327" power plant had to be "broken in," that is, driven at a maximum 50 miles per hour for the first 600 miles! That would slow me down so much that I would be cutting it pretty close now, and had to leave during the night and drive straight through to San Diego. I didn't even have time to scrape off the snow and ice.

I was pretty uncomfortable driving in the dark on icy highways, but the fact that I could only go 50 mph was actually a blessing, in that it kept me from spinning off the road. But it was *excrutiating*, driving so slowly in a Corvette, as it would barely idle at that speed (joke). And people were blinking their lights at me and, I'm sure, shaking their fists or making other gestures, as they went speeding by. *Humiliating* is a good word, also.

Daytime now, crawling westward through Nebraska and into Wyoming. Somewhere between Laramie and Walcott, the magic number clicked over on the odometer (it had seemed like an eternity), and I eased it up to 80, and did that feel good! Now I could cruise and hear and feel that great engine rumble! Up into the Rockies and across the Continental Divide, I couldn't help but notice that the air vent down by the clutch pedal was stuck open and was freezing my left foot, which was encased in an old Acme cowboy boot. No time to stop and try to fix it, there was really nowhere to stop in the mountains anyway. I jammed a towel against the vent and kept going. I was in a real hurry now because the clock was ticking, and if I didn't show up they would list me as AWOL. That would not look so good in the old service record.

At Salt Lake City I hung a left, heading south toward California. It was still icy up there, and I very nearly slid off the road into a reservoir. I have always been a believer in the Posi-traction system on the Corvette; it helps you out of a jam once in awhile. It was still dark when I came down from the higher elevations onto the desert floor. What a change! The road straightened and became flat, there was no traffic and no towns for a while. And this was the most fun I ever had in that car, pushing it up to 100. If there were ever a perfect drive, then that was it. What a beautiful road car. That thing hugged the pavement, and you could feel it through the steering wheel, and you could feel and hear the throbbing of the engine. Some guys, and even some girls, know what I am talking about, there is nothing quite like it.

It became warm enough that I could roll down the window. Never do that at 100 mph. Halfway down, the air pressure differential popped it out of the frame and I had to grab it to keep it from breaking and flying off the car. Decelerating and pulling over, I gently worked it back into the frame and rolled it down, and did the same on the passenger side. Back up to speed, the warmer air felt great, and made the ride complete.

I sped past Las Vegas, longing to stop, but I was now within striking distance of San Diego and pushed on as fast as I could go. It was just after dawn when I finally pulled into the carport at the apartment. Boy, was I grateful! What a hauler that car was. I gave her a pat on the dashboard and said, "Nice job," and really meant it.

I was just able to get cleaned up, get into a fresh uniform and hurry to the ship, to arrive on time to Officers' Call. I wasn't worth a damn to anyone that day, but I was at least present and accounted for. What a great drive that was; I will always remember it, and a great car.

* * *

There was an incident that took place on a weekend, thank goodness, when the full crew were not on board. For some reason, one of the sailors just snapped, went completely crazy, and unhappily grabbed a large knife from the galley. He then went on a rampage, running through the ship swinging that knife. He cut three people until he was cornered in one of the crew berthing areas. One of our Chiefs with a lot of nerve faced off with him, got him calmed down and finally took the knife away from him. No one had been seriously injured; they were surprised, though that a shipmate would attack them like that. The Chief was commended for stopping something that could have gotten a lot more ugly. Just goes to show that a ship can be a dangerous place, even when tied up to a pier.

* * *

I'm not sure exactly why or when the change came over my boss, Lt. Tana. We had gotten along okay, at least I thought so, since he had relieved Lt. Davis out in WestPac. But that came to an abrupt end one afternoon when we were in port. I went by his office/stateroom and asked, "Yas, is it okay if I knock off a little early today, I have some things to do?" Nothing out of the ordinary there, that was the way we spoke with each other: informal and friendly.

But all of a sudden he straightened up in his chair, his eyes turned cold as winter, and he literally barked at me, "*Mr. Cook, that is not the way to address me, and if you want to do something, you request permission in the proper manner!*" I was so surprised at his tone and what he said! I hadn't changed any, I know it, and as we say in Texas, I had no idea what put that burr under his saddle. But I did as he ordered and came to attention, eyes straight ahead, and said, "Sir, request permission to go ashore early today." He said, "Permission granted!" I said, "Thank you, sir," did a proper "left *face*," and bugged out of there. I never called him "Yas" again.

From that point on, our relationship was cold and proper until I left the ship. I don't know, at the time I had in mind that maybe he was trying to emulate some of the great Japanese admirals of WWII. Maybe he thought that being a hardass would get him there. He certainly became a little martinet, at least toward me. It still puzzles me to this day. I must have become a shitty officer since he came aboard, because he gave me a shitty fitness report, and the Captain signed it. Now, Captain Bowen had also signed my fitness report under Norm Davis, which was a pretty good one, so not only did he contradict himself here, he contradicted the opinions of my two succeeding Commanding Officers, both of whom thought I did a good job for them.

Not to belabor a point, but I found out about this report in an interesting way. (Remember, this was pretty heavy stuff way back then). I was in my stateroom and Gary was there, when Bruce came in. He was also a department head, along with Lt. Tana. He, as a good friend, closed the door and leaned back against it. He then told me about the fitness report and I just blew! I headed for the door but he blocked the way and said that I wasn't going anywhere until I calmed down. A very good friend. After cooling off somewhat, and talking with them both, I agreed that that's the way things were going to be, and there was not much to do about it. So I let it go. But I'll tell you folks, it still rankles.

Note: Some time later, as my step father was leaving the Pentagon one afternoon, he was stopped on the steps by none other than Lt. Yasuto Tana. After introducing himself, Lt. Tana abruptly said, "Admiral, I'm sorry I was so hard on Randy." Zim was taken aback, and I am sure made some noncommittal reply, as we kept our Navy business separate. When Zim told me about the encounter, he did say he found the whole thing very odd.

* * *

We gave a great party at the apartment, which ended up, as usual, in the open air hot tub until the wee hours of the morning, with empty wine bottles standing all around. But prior to that part, my former boss, Norm Davis and his beautiful wife Carol, had come to the party. Norm was about to go back to Vietnam, this time in-country, to take command of an LST which operated on the rivers of the Mekong Delta in the south. None of us knew very much about this arm of the Navy, and even though we had a rule against talking business at home, we asked him to tell us about it, which he did. The switch from destroyers to the "Gator Navy," or "Amphibs" (amphibious ships), was a big one, and he had gone to schools to learn how they operate.

Norm was the kind of solid guy who would make a great CO, and we wished him good luck in his first command. He said that after the dust settled a little bit, he would get back to us and tell us what he thought about it.

For me personally, that was a fateful promise because, not so long afterward a phone call came in to the ship from Vietnam, which was an event in itself. It wasn't so easy to do in those days. Anyway, it was Norm calling, and when I got on with him we spoke for quite awhile. When he found that I would be leaving the ship soon, he asked what I was going to do then? As soon as I told him I had no idea, he said, "Well, why don't you come over here? It's *good duty* and I know of an OPS Officer slot opening up soon on another ship in the squadron." Knowing and trusting him the way I did, I simply said, "Okay, Norm, I'll talk to the detailer." And that was it. I never put much thought into it, just called my detailer at BUPERS (Bureau of Naval Personnel), and he quickly arranged for me to report to the USS Monmouth County (LST-1032) in March, as the new Operations Officer. She was home ported in Vung Tau, Vietnam. It may have been a coincidence, but *every time* I volunteered for Vietnam duty, the Navy was happy to oblige.

My step father was supportive of my decision, and I know it frightened my mother, but she never let on that it did. Zim and I had a long talk about it, mainly the difference between the Blue Water and the Brown Water Navy. Besides the equipment, which would be smaller, slower, and less sophisticated, he talked about the officers and crews of the river force. They would not be the spit-and-polish fleet destroyer guys I was used to, rather a little more on the rough side. They were no less Navy, were great sailors, they just looked and acted differently because of where they worked. I later found that what he said was perfectly true, and that I didn't have any problem adapting to the life once I lost my "destroyer" frame of mind.

* * *

George Faust approached me one day and said that he was giving his wife, Rose, a birthday party at his house, and would I please come? I said I would be glad to, and he gave me the day and time. I would be the only officer in the group, so I thought about just making an appearance and leaving early; that they would have a better time without the lieutenant around.

But I was mistaken in thinking that, for one of the nicest reasons in the world. Faust and I had set the boundaries of our relationship long ago, and that had worked very well for us. We had worked side by side for a long time, but had never socialized away from the ship. That went for all of his people as well. However, I was going to leave the Thomas soon, and the day of the party he came up to me and said, "Sir, I have a request to make: just for tonight, in my home, I would like to call you Randy, and for you to call me George." Without hesitation I answered, "I'd like that very much."

On the surface, a simple request. But what it meant to me deep down was that I had the respect and friendship of the finest sailor I have ever known, and that validated my own self-worth as an officer. Lieutenant Tana and Captain Bowen could kiss my ass, I did a good job on that ship, and the people who counted knew it.

I arrived at the party and he opened the door and I said, "Hi, George," he said, "Hi, Randy, welcome." We shook hands and locked eyes for a moment, and a lot passed between us right there. I hugged his wife a Happy Birthday and shook hands all around. The guys took great delight in calling me "Randy," and I felt the same about them. It was all very natural and came easily, and I will never forget the comradeship of those fellows.

* * *

Along the same lines, I felt very complimented when I received an invitation to the wedding of one of the guys in the division. I of course accepted, and upon arrival found that I was again the only officer there. It was an outdoor affair, very nature-oriented, and just a little bit on the hippy side. It was a beautiful, sunny San Diego day, and the couple were married under an arbor of fresh flowers. Very picturesque and done just right. Again, I didn't feel out of place as the lieutenant at a large enlisted mens' affair. Everyone made me feel welcome and comfortable, and I had a great afternoon.

* * *

I met a girl, and boy was she cute! Since returning from WestPac I had not been in contact with Linda, and assumed that she was married and having a beautiful and happy life. Anyway, Joanne was a little Italian girl who looked exactly like the actress Brenda Vaccaro. Boy, was she cute! Oh, I already said that. She had an apartment in Lemon Grove, and after seeing her a few times, she invited me to stay the night rather than go back to my place so late. It was all very proper, as we slept in separate rooms. But we talked like that, lying in separate beds, for a long time, and almost talked ourselves into something, but didn't.

We really liked each other, and she wanted me to meet her family. I thought, fine, meeting her mother and father would be very nice. So we went to their home one evening in a hilly neighborhood in Chula Vista, and I walked into a world that a few years later I would recognize as the Godfather's house in the movie. She had a very big family! There were 30 people there at least, all ages, great Italian food was cooking in the kitchen where the ladies congregated, and the old men sat at a card table playing dominoes. They were all very nice and dinner at a large table was outrageously delicious. Joanne was obviously the darling of the family, and unbeknownst to me, I was being sized up as a prospect for her. This became abundantly clear as we were leaving, when everyone said goodbye, mama gave me a big hug, and papa shook my hand and said, "Come back soon, son."

My natural paranoia kicked in. Oh, it scared the hell out of me, and I'm afraid that I never saw Joanne again. So in retrospect I let another wonderful girl get away. I did a lot of that in those days. Appropriate here is a quote from our buddy *Forrest Gump*, "Stupid is as stupid does!"

* * *

My tour on the Thomas was winding down now. After 16 months here, it was time to move on to something else. What was left was to break in my replacement and turn over all of my keys, safe combinations, registered publications and my .45. I spoke with everyone in my division, thanking them for all their hard work and support. And a number of guys from all parts of the ship would stop me to say goodbye and good luck. Of course, I saw most of the officers every day, so parting from them was gradual and easy. Anyway, sentiment had nothing to do with leaving a Navy ship or station, since sailors transferred in and out all the time. Friendships formed and then dissolved again. Everybody promises to keep in touch, but that rarely happens. And the ship itself? Just a big hunk of metal that would end up as target practice someday, or in the cutting yard.

The last day. I went to crew call with my division, and kept the speech short, thanking them again and telling them that it had been an honor serving with such fine men. I then stepped back, Faust and I exchanged salutes, and I just said, "Goodbye." And then I left.

I had already moved out of the apartment and packed the car, so there was little to do except pick up a few things at the quarterdeck and request permission to leave the ship. Bruce said he would walk with me out to the car. We were just chatting about things and I was about to open the car door, when I looked up to see the USS Herbert J. Thomas tied up to the quay. That's when it hit me; I was completely overcome with emotion, and burst into tears. I laid my head down on the car top and wept. My feelings had run much deeper than I had realized. I was terribly embarrassed doing this in front of Bruce, and I managed to say, "I'm sorry, man," and he said, "It's okay, pal, let it out." Bruce Douglas was a very wise man and a good friend. And the Thomas was a fine ship of the line with a first-rate crew.

Note: The USS Herbert J. Thomas (DD-833) was decommissioned in December 1970, and stricken from the Naval Register in February 1974. In June of that year she was transferred to Taiwan, where she was renamed the Han Yang (D-915).

Decommissioned for the final time in 1999, the old Herbie J. was taken out and sunk as an artificial reef. This venerable old ship received six battle stars for Korea and three battle stars for Vietnam.

.

Brown Water

Early in 1970 I reported to Travis Air Force Base, near San Francisco, for my flight to Vietnam. There I found total chaos, a large and noisy terminal filled with guys who were either calm, excited or terrified. I do know that I was grateful for having gotten my shots ahead of time, as I watched an assembly-line of soldiers being shot with an injection gun, receiving multiple inoculations with one bang. As you couldn't board without them, this was necessary and it made some of the guys sick, particularly as they had to fly out right away. Some of them sweated clear through their shirt after being shot.

All I had with me was the khaki uniform I was wearing, and one bag which was then called a "valpac," a blue foldover which actually held a helluva lot. The bag was tagged and checked and then we were boarded onto probably a World Airways, TWA or Continental Airlines "cattle car," three and three seating as far as you could see. Unluckily I got a middle seat for the first leg of the trip to Honolulu.

Not being a particularly sensitive or introspective person at the time, I had no problem about going in-country Vietnam. Only because I was living in the oblivion of the young and stupid. Not once did I even think that I could be injured in Vietnam or make the return trip in a body bag. I considered myself bulletproof by just never giving it a thought. I was just drifting along with the tide, going wherever events took me, which at the moment happened to be to the west, high up over the Pacific. Our plane was completely full.

During the flight it became abundantly clear that there was to be no alcohol served. This was very disturbing to everyone, knowing that we had a long night ahead and would prefer to be a little numb. On approach to Honolulu we were told that this was only a fuel stop and that we would be on the ground for only forty-five minutes. The crew recommended that we not deplane, but if we felt the need to stretch our legs, be back on board in no later than thirty minutes. In an instant there were a herd of servicemen in all colors of uniforms thundering across the hot tarmac toward the terminal. This was the only open-air terminal anyone had ever seen, and we marveled at it for a micro-second before descending on the hapless and very surprised bartenders, buying anything and everything that contained alcohol. For my part, I drank down two nice cold beers and bought four or five more, cradling them across my chest as I left the terminal, other guys carrying every brand of beer and liquor imaginable.

As we emerged into the sunlight we were all absolutely dumbfounded by what we saw: sitting very bright and white in the sun at the far end of the airport was the biggest airplane anyone had ever seen. It was such a monster! And no markings whatsoever. As we later found out, we had just been treated to a sneak preview of the brand-new Boeing 747.

Lifting off from the Honolulu airport, we had no earthly idea that we had left the last vestige of civilization behind and that our lives would now change forever.

Most people mellowed out pretty quickly from the effects of the alcohol and gradually everyone went to sleep as the skies darkened. When we awoke we would begin to realize that life was going to start going downhill rather quickly and that reality was about to stare us right in the face.

For when we did awake it was to the announcement that we were on approach to Clark Field in the Philippines, sometime in the middle of the night. As we debarked we were told that we would be here for awhile and to get comfortable. That meant a seat in the grass alongside the runway. It was very dark and quiet and for an hour or so we sat in silence with a warm breeze in the face, very peaceful and relaxing after such a long day. I was too groggy to even think about the great times I had had with my destroyer mates and with the Air Force guys at the famous Tailhook Club just down the way. Or of all the time spent at Subic Bay Naval Base, whose lights were twinkling at us across the bay. Or of all the hilarious nights and sometimes dangerous days spent in Olongapo. Not too groggy, though, to notice the roar of several C-130 Hercules aircraft pulling up into a line nearby. We began getting the idea. The Hercules does not resemble in any way the nice sleek commercial airliner on which we had arrived. No, it is a rather squat, muscular plane with four turboprop engines, painted a nice shade of olive drab, and of course with military markings. We were really in the Army now!

After we were seated and comfortable on these new "birds," most everyone was out cold by takeoff time. The next thing we knew, it was getting light and you could just feel that something had changed. Nothing you could put a finger on, just a difference in the atmosphere that we all sensed. And all too soon the announcement came that we were approaching Saigon and would be landing at Tan

Son Nhut air base. Well, I suppose this is it! And now, wheels down, cruising in, and finally the screech of rubber as we touch down in the Republic of Vietnam.

Now here is the young ensign watching out the window as the C-130 taxis to a small, very plain military terminal and is immediately surrounded by ARVN (Army of the Republic of Vietnam) troops carrying automatic weapons. These are small, slender men, very sturdy, with skin-tight pants and the butt of the M-16 resting on the hip. And the young ensign, not for the last time that day, takes in the scene and says to himself, "Aw shit!" For he realizes that he has truly left the Real World far behind and has now entered the twilight zone.

As we make our way off of the aircraft and set foot in Vietnam, most for the first time, we are greeted by a blast furnace of hot tarmac, blazing sun and smothering humidity. On into the little terminal for processing and baggage claim, more of the little guys with weapons all around. And at last we are free to move out toward the bus that is waiting at the curb.

My group of naval officers and enlisted were slated to take the first bus in line, an Air Force-blue one that had been modified with expanded-metal sheets welded over the windows and two American soldiers carefully inspecting the undercarriage. Asked what was going on, the driver said they were checking for bombs before we could board. (Aw shit!) And that the expanded metal kept bombs from being tossed into the bus. (Aw shit!)

As we got underway the driver announced that we would be taken to our billet called the Annapolis Hotel. I thought that sounded pretty cool, sounded comfortable, and that I could relax and unwind after a long trip. Along the way we passed a brand new Buddhist temple, in front of which a large sign proudly proclaimed that the Rockefeller Foundation had donated the funds for it's construction, for the people of Vietnam. Trying to assimilate all of the scenery we could: Shell gas stations, Esso stations, and a number of familiar business names. As we neared our destination we could see that the name Annapolis Hotel was a euphemism for a sort of crummy-looking building of two stories or so, surrounded by barriers made from 55-gallon drums, thousands of sandbags, and barbed wire. (Aw shit!) Suddenly my vision of spending the afternoon in a garden lounge chair sort of evaporated.

Checking in to the "front desk," we were all issued a small green book, the cover of which said, "Welcome To The Republic Of Vietnam and the Annapolis BOQ/BEQ, Saigon's Innkeeper." So it really was named Annapolis but in no way resembled a hotel. We were issued a key to an assigned "bay," given some basic information, and then left to ourselves. I found my bay (room) and sat down in the one chair to go over the little green book and find out what I needed to do over the next three days, along with a schedule of lectures on in-country security, marijuana (drugs are bad), standing alert watches ("You are in a war zone and there is no set time when CHARLIE will strike. Stay awake and alert"). Soon I became very weary and climbed into the rack. Well, more like a wooden bunk bed. I lay there for awhile thinking about all of the things I had experienced in the last 36 hours and trying to sort it all out. I was unable to and for the first time felt very alone. All of a sudden, with a start I realized that on that day I had become a lieutenant, junior grade (LTJG), and felt doubly lonely because such an occasion is normally celebrated with a "frocking" ceremony wherein your commanding officer pins on the new bars, then all of your comrades give a "frocking" party at the officers' club. I didn't even have new silver bars to wear on the collar, so I took the old gold bars off, rolled over to the side of the bunk and rubbed them back and forth on the concrete wall until they shone somewhat silver, "frocked" myself and went to sleep.

Early next morning I was to catch the yellow "B" bus to MACV (Military Assistance Command, Vietnam) headquarters for further briefing and processing. So I boarded the bus and was thrown into the maelstrom that was Saigon. Wide avenues lined with white or stone colonial buildings, thousands of bicycles competing with thousands more of motor scooters which belched both oil smoke and smoke from cheap gasoline, belching buses, beautiful black Citroen automobiles with the hash marks in the grille, and hordes of people everywhere you looked. But the colors and odors and excitement did not bother me, in fact I began enjoying this city of which I had heard so much. The only thing marring the scenery were the olive drab sandbags piled everywhere at major intersections and around major buildings along with barriers and concertina wire. And of course the ever-present little ARVN soldiers manning each barricade and checkpoint. I must say that their appearance was always very sharp and professional-looking.

Over the next three days I had a lot of ground to cover, and also learned a lot. MACV helped me to get into the mood, and also supplied me with the greatest little book ever printed. It was a small 5x7 booklet, I am sure mimeographed and stapled together somewhere within MACV. It was meant to be helpful as an aid to orientation in an alien culture, but it touched so briefly on each important subject that it was really pretty funny. I wish I could find my copy, as it would still be good for some laughs: The South

Vietnamese are our brave friends and allies and should be treated with respect at all times, and no derisive terms are to be used at any time to describe them or when talking to them. The currency here is the dong and the piaster, and when a price is quoted, for instance, as 10P, that means 10 piasters. However, the only currency to be used by service personnel is military scrip, and the U.S. dollar is never to be used on the local market.

It also included a list of simple phrases in Vietnamese such as hello, goodbye, where's the toilet, etc., and the usual warnings about consorting with the local prostitutes and all the diseases they could transmit.

By the way, no one, at least in my circle, ever spoke much Vietnamese because by 1970 there existed a pidgin English language that got everyone by on both sides. What was funny was that as the Vietnamese spoke this pidgin, we spoke the same awful English in return, and everyone got along. To hear a U.S. sailor or soldier in a heated argument with a local vendor was pure fun. An expert in either English or Vietnamese languages would have fainted dead away. The reason that pidgin came into being is illustrated by the following phrases in Vietnamese:

Excuse me, I don't understand   Xin loi ong, toi khong hieu

I'm glad to meet you   Toi han hanh duoc gap ong

Do you speak English?   Ong noi tieng Anh duoc khong?

And that's without all of the numerous accents added. Pidgin English did just fine.

There was another booklet available to us who were now in-country, an older Department of Defense booklet entitled, "A Pocket Guide to Vietnam." While it was much more detailed than the little pamphlet, it was a little less funny.

Under the heading Opportunity Unlimited: "If you are bound for Vietnam, it is for the deeply serious business of helping a brave nation repel Communist invasion. This is your official job and it is a vital one."

"The dangers of ambush and raid will make sightseeing impossible in some places; but, when security restrictions permit, be sure to see something of the lovely country you are visiting and get acquainted with the charming— and tough and courageous—people who call Vietnam home."

And, under the heading Service With Satisfaction: "The Vietnam of today is not the Vietnam of the past nor of the future. As long as there is danger of Communist agents prowling its streets, Saigon necessarily is a tensely guarded 'pearl of the orient,' and until the last Viet Cong sniper has been smoked out of the bamboo thickets, much of the beauty of the provinces will be hidden from visitors."

"But there are compensations. You who help the Vietnamese maintain their freedom will have many fine things to remember about the people and the country. You will have the satisfaction of sharing the experiences of a staunch and dedicated nation in a most critical period of its history. In a broader sense, you will be helping to block the spread of communism through Southeast Asia."

Well, that last didn't quite work out, but that is borne out by later events. At least while I was there we did our part to hold back the Red Tide.

The Annapolis Hotel provided a little tour with a Vietnamese girl as a guide, and I was able to see the palace of President Thieu (and it really was a palace), the Vietnamese parliament building, a number of monuments to heroes, and many beautiful homes. Also traffic, traffic, traffic. I learned that the term "cowboy" had nothing to do with cows, but were the cool young dudes riding their motor scooters with a girl on the back. These guys had pants so tight that their voices must have gone up eight octaves when they zipped. Cool pointy-toed shoes and the most outrageous coiffures of black, long, slicked-back, ducktailed hair this side of Conway Twitty.

I had business in the U.S. Embassy building, the one with the now-famous long white edifice, and found that there were very many pretty girls working there, both American and Vietnamese. And I was walking near MACV headquarters one day when none other than General Creighton Abrams, commander of our forces in Vietnam, came out of a side door heading for his staff car. I nearly popped my neck with my snappy salute, and I must say that he returned my salute and said, "Hello, lieutenant." He probably wouldn't have remembered the episode as well as I do.

The one really fond memory of my first visit to Saigon (Ho Chi Minh City just doesn't do it for me) was the last evening before departing. We had a curfew of 2100 hours (9:00 PM) and were not allowed into Vietnamese bars or "steam baths," so the Navy enlisted went to the Montana Hotel BEQ and the officers to the Idaho Hotel BOQ. Good old Vietnamese-sounding hotels. The top floor of the Idaho was taken up by the most amazing room. I walked back into the twenties in colonial India or Egypt or Africa. This really large room with open-air windows, thousands of ceiling fans turning (well, maybe hundreds), long dark mahogany bar, beautifully polished old-wood tables and chairs, and white linen. Bartenders and waiters all in white jackets, and a crowd of newspapermen and other media types. A few other officers and I enjoyed this time-warp with a number of drinks and a decent dinner, then had to depart soon enough to "cross the white line and be behind the six foot sandbag wall" before 2100. We made it with mere moments to spare.

Just the year before, on July 10, 1969, the Annapolis Hotel was bombed. One of the Riverine guys, Dave Schell, returning from dinner at the Montana on only his second evening in-country, was a witness. As he and a pal, Mike Hamner, sat down in front of the hotel for a smoke, they noticed a man walking a three-wheeled bicycle toward them. They thought he must have a flat tire or something, when he turned the bike into one of the 50-gallon drums filled with sand that lined the front of the hotel. The fellow turned and hopped on to a Honda motorbike that was flying by, and they sped away. Dave then noticed that the bicycle was smoking, and yelled, "*Bomb!* Get Down!" He and his buddy dove behind the sandbag wall. After a few moments a huge explosion rocked the hotel and left total destruction in the street. There were people hanging out of a taxi, and out of a bus that had just turned the corner, and they were bleeding and screaming. As Dave and his friend ran into the hotel they found a dead sailor in the doorway. The Honda had run head-on into the bus, killing the motorbike driver. The bomber was hauled away, missing part of an arm and part of a leg. It turned out that the bomb was a Chinese claymore. EN3 Dave Schell's article, as it appeared in the summer 2006 River Currents newsletter, is entitled, *"The FNG's Were Lucky."*

Reveille came at 0500 hours, which was pretty early in Vietnam. I was up fast because my name had appeared the day before on the flight list out to Vung Tau, where I was to meet my ship. At last! So I was moving fast, ate quickly, and back to stuff the valpac, check out and get transport to Tan Son Nhut. Of course after all the hurrying our small group had to wait awhile for the plane, which finally turned out to be this small, boxy 2-engine gizmo that I had never seen before.

We had to haul our gear out to the plane, and I noticed that the valpac was really heavy! One other thing I noticed was that I was the only one not wearing the standard-issue field green fatigue uniform. Officers and enlisted going aboard a ship retained the normal khaki and dungaree working uniforms of the fleet, while everyone else went native. I did feel a little conspicuous this day, but many times when we ended up in some "mama san" bar in some little hooch in some little backwater village, drinking with guys just out of the bush, we were not exactly their object of affection, rather mostly friendly derision.

At any rate, to the plane, drop the gear and get on board. Web seats, round portholes for windows, and the door to the flight deck was open. We all became a little concerned while the pilot explained to the co-pilot how to fly the plane, really elementary stuff like, "Now this is the steering wheel and this over here is the brake". We just exchanged looks that said what an exciting flight this will be. After the miracle of takeoff the crewman said we could smoke, which we all did. When I was finished I asked him where to put it out and he said to just toss it out the window. What? Then, finding that, indeed, there was no glass in the window I tossed it out. I then stuck my head out and watched Vietnam go by 5,000 feet below.

The flight was not very long, maybe 20 or 30 minutes as, I found out later, Vung Tau was only 45 miles from Saigon but ground transportation was unsafe. So we arrived over the airfield pretty quickly and began to descend. When we were only a couple of hundred feet off the ground, the pilot suddenly gunned the engines and we gained altitude in a hurry and began circling in a lazy pattern, without explanation from the pilot. Finally he came on the horn and said, "Sorry boys, we got a firefight going on right down there on the runway and can't land today, we'll have to try 'er again tomorrow." I shot my head out the window and sure enough, through a swirl of blowing sand and dirt, muzzle flashes near the runway. As the pilot banked the little plane and headed back to Saigon, we all agreed that we weren't in that much of a hurry to get to Vung Tau after all.

And then the rigamarole of doing everything in reverse, undoing all of the good things I had done that day, including getting up so early for nothing. The next morning duplicated the first, except that after a short flight we made a quick approach and came in for a landing at my new hometown.

Vung Tau was the headquarters of Landing Ship Squadron Two (LANSHIPRON TWO in Navy vernacular) and also the homeport of USS Monmouth County, LST-1032 (that's Landing Ship Tank). It was also one of the most beautiful places I have ever seen.

Vung Tau was and is a little pearl of a city situated between good beaches and beautiful green mountains. It has been known as the resort area of Vietnam since the 1870's, when the first large hotel was built. Also known in French as Cap Saint-Jacques or simply Au Cap, it is situated near the tip of an 11-mile long projection into the South China Sea, which angles southwest and partially encloses Ganh Rai Bay. The bay receives the Saigon River on the northeastern Mekong Delta, and serves the ships using the approaches to Saigon port up the Soirap River, as I said about 45 miles away. The name literally means Vung (puddle) Tau (ships).

Upon receiving my gear I was able to get a ride directly to the LANSHIPRON TWO operations office to check in and locate my ship. I enjoyed the cacaphony of voice-radio traffic, that between the squadron HQ and its ships, and began to feel more at home right away. I was told that the ship was on a mission and should return to Vung Tau in a day or two. Arrangements had been made for me to berth at a place named Cat Lo, and that I was to check in (in person) here at operations once each day until the ship arrived. I found that suitable, so the officer on duty located a ride for me to Cat Lo.

The ride turned out to be a good old Willys-type WWII looking jeep driven by a petty officer. He told me that Cat Lo was about five miles up a two-lane road and it wouldn't take long to get there. He then surprised me by saying, "Sir, you might want to get down on the floorboard, this is a real dangerous road and we get shot at all the time. I'm going to go full speed all the way and we should be okay." Well I thought this was pretty funny and told him I'd decline the floorboard and take the scenic route, and sure enough he put the pedal to the metal and we flew to Cat Lo. The scenery sort of blurred as we went by. There were a number of little villages with a lot of chickens, houses with red-tile roofs built right up to the road, naked or near-naked kids everywhere, women bustling about and men squatting in a really unusual position. And finally, safely through the gate of U.S. Naval Combat and Logistics Base, Cat Lo.

It began to dawn on me that this was the Navy I was about to join. It was a far cry from the flashy, fast destroyers and the gigantic carriers with their leading-edge hardware. No, this was the Brown Water Navy, the Navy of the rivers of the Mekong Delta. Since December of 1965, when it was formally constituted, the Brown Water Navy had denied the enemy free access in the delta, both in the interdiction of troops and the smuggling of arms and supplies. Singly, and in cooperation with the Army, the Brown Water Navy fought the Viet Cong and North Vietnamese Army on their own terms. Over time, both tactics and combatant craft evolved and improved greatly, and aircraft were added. At the height of its fighting power, the Navy/Army relationship was formalized as the Mobile Riverine Force (1967-1969). The MRF utilized a number of types of river assault boats and aircraft, which were in turn supported by larger shallow-draft boats and ships, such as the LST's, and barracks/support ships such as the USS Benewah (APB-35). The 2nd Brigade of the 9th Infantry Division and the US Navy formed a formidable and aggressive fighting force that inflicted terrible casualties on the enemy, while itself feeling the wrath of the VC and NVA.

Now, by the time I arrived in-country in 1970, the Mobile Riverine Force, *per se,* no longer existed, because at the end of summer 1969, its river craft had been turned over to the South Vietnamese Navy, and the 6th Infantry guys had been pulled out, all in the name of *"Vietnamization."* So, absent the MRF, I was to find out that I was joining the Brown Water Navy in the capacity of "armed logistical support" to whoever called for our services in the Mekong Delta.

What I saw in front of me at the moment was just a bunch of low Quonset huts set down in a dirt field. Didn't have too much charm. I checked in with the duty officer and got a berth assigned and a little map of the base. All I wanted to know was where was my bunk, where the showers were and the location of the officers' club. My bunk was in (what else?) a Quonset hut and the showers were nearby. I was issued an olive-drab towel that I kept for about twenty years. And the "officers' club" was in another hut, with a five-foot bar and warm beer and I didn't stay long. I had not had the time in the last three or four days for much reflection, but the conversation with my step father now began flooding back to the surface.

Over the next few days I developed a limited but interesting routine: in the morning after breakfast hitch a high-speed run to Vung Tau to check in with operations and be told that the Monmouth County would be back in a day or two, check in tomorrow. Then a high-speed run back to Cat Lo, linger for awhile until lunch, then head for the tennis court that adjoined my "quarters." No, I didn't play tennis, in any case it was too damn hot. But, I found that it was the only place on the whole base where I could be alone. The court was located on the inland side of the base up against the fenced perimeter, beyond which began the emerald green mountains. I scrounged a deck chair of sorts and started on a really good tan. That took care of the afternoon, but after dinner and a warm beer, the day really picked up. I would go back out to the tennis court after dark and watch the most spectacular light show as a UH-1 (HUEY) helicopter opened up on the enemy with M-60 machine guns, firing down onto the mountaintops. Every fifth round was a red "tracer" that enabled the door gunner to see where he was firing, and at the rate of up to 550 rounds per minute, it was a great show. It occurred each night I was there at varying distances from my front row seat.

One night I was treated to the sight of a helicopter gunship firing a "minigun" into the poor enemy. It looked like a meteor shower! The minigun was one of the scariest weapons we had: a high-speed electric Gatling gun that could be set for two or four thousand *rounds per minute!* The word was it could carpet an area the size of a football field, with rounds covering every square foot, with a ten second burst. That's scary, and I can only imagine the terror it caused on the ground. Made my skin crawl a little just watching it, but it was totally fascinating just the same.

I was too far away to hear the guns but had a clear view of the action, and as I lay there on a lounge chair watching the mesmerizing display, I was reminded of lying on a similar lounge chair on the Thomas' signal bridge watching the carrier's night takeoff and landing operations. I thoroughly enjoyed these nighttime light shows.

I was brought out of this reverie one morning when I received word that the Monmouth County would arrive in the bay that afternoon or evening. So after lunch at Cat Lo I packed all of my gear, checked out with the duty officer and left my temporary home forever. After dropping my gear at operations I wandered down to the beach to start looking for the distinctive silhouette of the LST.

All of a sudden I was slammed in the back by something so massive that I almost went down, and it certainly knocked the wind out of me. I quickly turned around and through watery eyes, saw none other than Norm Davis standing there grinning that "welcome to Vietnam" grin. As I struggled to gasp, "Hi Norm", I reflected that normal, mortal men occasionally slapped one another on the back. From Norm, though, it felt like a side of beef, swung with vigor. It was really good to see him, though, as he was one of the best officers I knew, and a friend. Even though it was his fault I was standing here with him on a beach in a war zone. We had time to visit about the Thomas and about his command, the USS Clarke County (LST-601). His was a busy ship, working the rivers of the Delta doing any number of types of missions, the same as I would be performing, as we were in the same squadron. With one exception: Norm told me in a low voice that he had run a mission deep into the Delta and across the border into Cambodia, but he wouldn't say what the mission had been or who he had been working with, but that it had been very hairy and he was most happy to be out of there. After this brief reunion, we said so long and I went back down to the beach, and lo and behold, there she was: the ungainly and even homely silhouette of my LST. Gone were the days of the sleek ships, and here was the day of the big ugly boat.

At any rate, operations got me a ride out to the ship at about twilight on a calm sea, and I climbed the ladder and set foot on the Monmouth County and my new life. Not only was I now part of the Brown Water Navy, I had just joined the Amphibious, or Gator Navy.

The World War II-type LST was a real piece of work. If you remember your old John Wayne movies, it was the one that steamed up onto the beach and opened gigantic doors on the bow to disgorge men and tanks and armored personnel carriers (APC's) and supplies. It had a good-sized main deck with many tie downs onto which any manner of supplies or vehicles could be lifted with its own old-fashioned steam shovel-looking crane. The spacious well deck, or tank deck, from which the big doors opened, carried everything else. Along each side of the tank deck ran long, straight passageways which contained most of the living spaces for the officers and crew. Due to its nature of being run aground on purpose, the ship could be ballasted up and down in the water as well as any submarine. Because of this feature, and the numerous watertight compartments it entailed, it was virtually unsinkable, a big floating cork. (In fact, during WWII in the Pacific, LST-750, mortally wounded by a Japanese aerial torpedo, was ordered sunk. After two torpedoes missed due to her shallow draft, it took almost 150 5-inch shells fired by destroyer USS Edwards to finally send her to the deep.) Add to that a perfectly flat bottom and a rounded bow, and you have a ship that rides very well on smooth water but was absolutely awful in a sea (anything other than smooth water).

This ship displaced 2,366 tons of water, was 328 feet long and had a beam (width) of 50 feet. Flank (top) speed when new was 11.6 knots and that subject will be discussed in the ensuing paragraph. The World War II complement of men was 119, now down to about 100. The original eight 40 millimeter cannon were down to two twin mounts on the stern, and of the original twelve 20 millimeter cannon, there were now two twin mounts on the bow. Add four .50 caliber machine guns and on the bridge an M-79 grenade launcher and some M-16's, and you have sort of a workhorse freighter with an attitude. As I have said, officially it was called armed logistics support.

The speed was the thing: it was really slow! By the time we got the ship, flank speed was a maximum 11 knots, or a blinding 12.6 miles per hour, that is with a good following wind. And long-range cruising speed was a blistering 7.5 knots, or 8.6 MPH. Well, you get the idea. But with two massive General Motors 12-cylinder, 2900 horsepower diesel engines driving you, the cruising range was unbelievable. Try 5,000 miles on one load of fuel!

The Monmouth County began life in June of 1944 when her keel was laid at the Boston Navy Yard, and she was commissioned on August 1 of that year, Lieutenant J. M. Medina commanding. After a shakedown cruise and transfer to the west coast, she embarked troops in Hawaii and sailed on January 23, 1945 for the assault on Iwo Jima. While debarking Marines there, she was hit in the bow by an enemy shell, killing one Marine and wounding nine others. Despite a withering fire and rough seas, she completed debarking her troops and supplies and proceeded to Saipan. There she loaded troops and supplies and sailed into the invasion of Okinawa. She then ferried troops and supplies among the Philippines and made two additional runs to Okinawa until the Japanese surrender. After ferrying occupation troops to Japan until November of that year, she finally sailed for the states.

After various fleet duties and an interim six years in mothballs she was brought back to full commission in 1965 and took part in the Dominican Republic crisis, and in 1966 sailed for Vietnam and combat duty so late in her life. Her new homeport was to be Vung Tau. So what I ended up boarding that day was an enigma: a ship out of the past that was so simple, yet was so superbly adapted to a modern war, and a riverine war at that!

After introducing myself to the quarterdeck watch I was escorted to the Captain's cabin and shown in to meet Lieutenant Commander William F. Story, my new commanding officer. He was tall, dark-complected and quiet-spoken, and after a brief chat he took me around to meet the other officers, including the Operations Officer I was replacing, LTJG Fish. Everyone was very polite and seemed glad to have me on board, then the Captain explained that they had been out for over a week and would I mind taking the ship while everyone bailed out on liberty? I said of course not and immediately most of the officers and crew went ashore. I was left with "my" ship so I made sure of the watch and then spent the evening getting familiar with the ship and meeting some of the people. I had a short meeting with my leading radioman, petty officer 2nd class Morin, who was a very large guy, a full-blooded Cherokee Indian and a very nice fellow.

Several hours later I was to get my first taste of life aboard the Monmouth County. As I was peacefully sitting in the wardroom over a cup of coffee and the ship's logs, learning about the most recent missions, one of the enlisted guys on watch suddenly burst through the door, out of breath, and shouted, "Sir, there's a big fight on the mess deck," and ran out to lead the way. As I dropped the logs and said to myself something like, "Oh darn, and on my first watch, too," I hauled after my guide and came to the top of the wide ladder leading down to the mess deck, a large area where the crew took their meals and relaxed. All I could see were a half dozen guys going at each other, fists flying. This was really unacceptable and so without thinking, I mean *really* without thinking, I went straight down the ladder and waded into this bar fight to what seemed to be the center of the problem, yelled as loud as I could, and pulled a guy around by the shoulder and he pulled back on me to throw a punch with a fist about the size of a ham, when he realized he was about to cold-cock his new boss. I told Morin that he really didn't want to do that and he dropped his fist and looked extremely embarrassed. There was almost immediate silence and I told everyone to have a seat, that we were going to have a little meeting. In essence they were told that I didn't know them and they didn't know me, but that I did not allow any fighting on "my" ship, that there were other ways to settle differences, and that if it ever happened again every goddamn one of them would go to Captain's Mast. I didn't know it at the time, but no one really wanted to be around the Captain when he was angry, and so I was very pleased with myself that my words had such an impact. So, after a bunch of yessirs and nossirs we adjourned the meeting and I retired to my spacious stateroom to end the first half-day of my new adventure.

For the next few days we remained at anchor and I was able to get to know my people in the communications and signals divisions, along with the rest of the officers in the wardroom: Wayne the engineer, Jim the weapons officer, Larry the supply officer, Useless the communications officer, Useless the XO, and Captain Story. LTJG Fish was very helpful in getting me settled in, and the fact that he had recently been wounded by shrapnel while running to general quarters made me pay a little closer attention. After a time, he turned the Operations Department over to me and prepared to leave for home.

An officer in a new situation tries to identify those people who can be counted on and those who are just along for the ride. Morin the radioman was solid, as was my signalman 2nd class, even though my leading petty officer was a signalman 1st class. And I could tell that the wardroom was a good one except for the two uselesses.

Captain Story was in a class by himself. An Annapolis graduate, he would prove to be the best commanding officer I ever had at sea. My advantage over the other officers was that I was destroyer-trained, as was he, and that put me in good stead with him right away. As I have mentioned, he was soft-spoken but I came to see him as a very tough guy whose hobby was cooking gourmet along with his sister. The enigmas of this place were just piling up everywhere I turned. As an example of his talents, I learned that, in the middle of a war zone, aboard this old ship, the officers and crew had "surf and turf" (steak and lobster) every Thursday night and, unbelievably, Eggs Benedict on Sunday mornings, depending of course on the availability of the necessary ingredients. Now, this ship was too small to have an officer's galley so all meals were prepared on the mess deck and the whole crew ate the same thing. The captain decided that everyone should eat well so he taught the cooks what foods to scrounge for and then taught them how to cook with real finesse. You would be hard-pressed to find better Eggs Benedict in any fine restaurant.

In a few more days we moved into a docking area to begin taking on a load of supplies. I noticed that a group of guys were forming into a shore party, busily loading a truck with boxes of food and carpentry tools. Being curious about it, I asked one of them where they were headed. Turns out that whenever they had some spare time they would go to the orphanage that the ship had "adopted" to take food, money and clothes and do what they could to repair the shelters there. The crew had started this when they were approached by a nun in the area who asked for help. Upon finding the camp in poor condition and the children barely clothed and fed, by general consensus they were all adopted by this very tough Navy crew. By the time the truck left I had found a few pair of socks and some t-shirts and a little money and sent it along to the orphans.

While out on the main deck I was finally able to meet the senior enlisted man on board, Chief Boatswain's Mate Johnson. He was a hardy-looking guy with a bone-crusher handshake, a square jaw, and the top half of one ear missing. As surreptitiously as I could, I asked a nearby sailor if he knew what had happened to the chief's ear, and he replied, "Oh yes sir, he got it bit off in a bar fight last year."

I was now getting the idea about how it was to be in Vietnam: nothing was normal. Everything was twisted, upside down, tragic, funny, bizarre. My Naval career up to this tour had been normal, or as normal as life can be where sailors and the Navy were concerned, but now everything was coming unraveled and I had to make the conscious decision to loosen up, at least a little, and try to adapt to this strange environment. So I decided to try and go with the flow, and thought I would now go for a cup of coffee in the wardroom. As

I was on the main deck forward, I went down a ladder and stepped into the long passageway leading aft and noticed a large pile of something lying on the deck at the far end. I couldn't tell what it was, but as I got about halfway down the passageway this thing began a low, deep, very threatening growl in my general direction. I then stopped and focused on possibly the biggest German Shepherd that I had ever seen! He took me so aback that I didn't move for awhile, and then began backing slowly all the way back to the ladder, since there was no other way out. The dog had stopped growling and just lay there, watching.

As I reached the ladder a sailor was coming down. I pointed down the passageway.

"What the hell is that?"

"It's a dog, sir."

"Let's try this again. What the hell is that?"

"Oh, that's Otto, the ship's mascot."

"Why did he growl at me?"

"Well, he hates officers, sir."

And it was true. Otto hated the sight of an officer so much that everyone avoided him by either going back the way they came or finding a way to go around without getting near him. This included the Captain. After much thought and argument the officers had concluded long ago that Otto didn't like khaki uniforms and that made any officer his enemy. There was some suspicion that one of the crew had somehow taught this trick to Otto, but this was never proven. The Captain thought that all of this was pretty funny except when he was avoiding the dog, but he knew that in Otto he had a secret weapon. For, as not many people know, the primary duty of a ship's captain is crew morale, and the crew loved Otto, especially when he was harassing the officers. A guaranteed morale booster every single day. The same as when the chiefs' bowling team used to beat the shit out of the officers' team on the Thomas. There are some things that money just can't buy. God bless Otto.

I had heard a number of people use the expression, "Well, it's just another day in the 'Nam." I found myself beginning to use it to myself more and more. It really helped make things seem normal. I tried not to mutter.

Since LTJG Fish was about to depart for the USA, he suggested that we go into Vung Tau for a farewell beer. So we found a "taxi," a cross between a motor scooter and a troop transport, and took a dusty and noisy ride into the city. During this and subsequent trips into Vung Tau, it became apparent to me that the vagaries of this place could be applied over the entire map of Vietnam and no one who ever served there would even bat an eye. To begin with, it was truly a divided city. Remember, it had been a popular resort city for many years, and was used by the U.S. and other allied forces as an in-country Rest and Recreation (R & R) area. Well folks, Vung Tau was also used by the Viet Cong and North Vietnamese Army for the same thing! How, you may ask, would this be possible, for two deadly enemies to vacation in the same spot? Somehow it just happened. There was a part of town we never went to at all (spelled suicide, particularly at night), and by day the enemy, in civilian clothes, of course, certainly mingled all around us in the crowded streets. But there was never any trouble, and the guys on the ship said they had never heard of any problems. Just keep to your part of town and don't think too much.

What a wonderful place! You could walk down the street and find an astonishing array of goods for sale by sidewalk vendors: car parts, scooter parts, weapons and ammunition from the USA and China, Zippos, watches, fans, everything you need including cigarettes. I smoked Marlboros at the time and bought a few packs off the street for a dollar apiece. None of these packs had a tax stamp on them, nor did any of those sold by the peddlers; they had all been heisted from the PX (post exchange) system for resale to the stupid Americans (including me!). At twice the PX price! You gotta love it!

Speaking of Zippos, they were in great demand by everyone in Vietnam. They, along with the HUEY helicopter could be called the icons of this war. Every insignia of every outfit that served there appeared on a Zippo. Including a handsome lighter from the Monmouth County that sits on my desk as I write this. Anyway, everyone carried a Zippo and it didn't take too long for the enemy to use their fertile imagination in turning it into a weapon. Many American and allied servicemen lost hands and/or faces when the lighter they found left in the "pisser" by some inebriated soldier or sailor, exploded when they tried to use it. So the rule was, never pick up a "lost" Zippo.

Besides adopting an orphanage, the crew of the Monmouth County had adopted a whorehouse. Although they weren't called whorehouses in Vung Tau, but barbershops. I suppose this was to "fool" the local gendarmes except that when you walked down the streets of this neighborhood full of barbershops it was hard to miss what the main trade was. At any rate, it was Barbershop #39 that the crew called its own, and many of them spent a lot of shore leave there. A few of the guys took me once to see the sights. I did some window shopping along the street, perhaps for too long, because I was called a "butterfly" by the ladies since I couldn't make a choice. Finally I chose a small, very beautiful girl who took me home nearby and we spent a really nice afternoon admiring her most prized possession, a new electric fan. It had blue plastic blades that you could see through.

LTJG Fish took me to the Grand Hotel, all the way arguing with the driver whether I was a "number 1" officer (according to the taxi driver), or a "number 10" officer (according to Fish). "Number 1" in pidgin English was the very best, the greatest, while "number 10" was the very worst. Every American and every city Vietnamese used these expressions every day. A lexicon of this war. I think I remember the taxi driver won the argument. He say I numbah 1 officah. Fish say no, no, he numbah 10.

The Grand Hotel had a large gray edifice and portico, and looked very grand indeed! The lobby and lobby bar were cool and spacious with very high ceilings, having a colonial feel. Fish had some things to do so after having a beer he departed. I was at the long mahogany bar and fell into conversation with some Australian soldiers, enlisted guys. They seemed very happy to talk and kept refilling my glass with beer. After a while I was getting a little wasted but the beer seemed to have no affect on these soldiers. There was now a small group of Aussies animatedly talking with me when one of them blurted out, "Sir, how come you're talking to us?" I was caught off guard and said I thought they were a good bunch of blokes who were buying me beer, what's so strange about that? He explained that their officers never talked to them at all, least of all on a social level, and they were most surprised that I did. I tried to explain that, in my Navy, sailors were people and were to be treated as such and with respect. They were amazed! I never had to pay for a beer at the Grand Hotel again, for there were usually Aussies there. A tough bunch, and could they ever put away the beer!

In addition to Australia, New Zealand, the Philippines, the Republic of South Korea (ROK) and Thailand participated as part of the Free World Force effort in Vietnam. This brings home the fact that it was not a purely American action, and that in our grief and confusion over this war, we must not forget the numbers of our allies who were killed or wounded for our cause. There were stories about the ROK troops of the Tiger Division who were truly feared by the Viet Cong and North Vietnamese. Perhaps they were able to fight untethered by the rules and politics that governed our military policy. For whatever reason, they struck terror in the hearts of the enemy, and that was always nice to hear.

Since we were making ready to put out to sea, or out to river in this case, I worked hard to finish my familiarization with the ship, the men and the job at hand. As a department head I finally had my own stateroom, a fairly large affair with its own sink, porthole and working area, and the officers' head was nearby. It was a palace when compared with officers' country on the Thomas, where I bunked with several others. The wardroom was also nearby and was comfortable enough with its dining table and chairs and a sitting area. I do remember some pretty bad fake wood paneling and a kind of rumpled red carpet, but with a certain fondness.

The radio shack was the biggest surprise/culture shock of all. It was not very roomy but was adequate unless more than two people were there. I had just come off a ship that had the latest in high-speed communications and printer equipment for sending and receiving message traffic and for receiving the fleet broadcast. And now I discover that the speed of communications was determined by whoever was operating the telegrapher's key! In 1970! The same as in World War II! Oh well, just another day in the 'Nam I guess. I soon found out it was sufficient for our operations, and it was most interesting to watch the telegraphers. I remember that Morin was the fastest with the key, and he said that all of the operators who regularly talked could recognize each other from the telegrapher's signature, or how they handled the key. Totally amazing, and these guys could copy an entire (long) fleet broadcast at one sitting, in front of an old-fashioned upper-case typewriter, wearing earphones, and selecting the messages to be copied from the call signs broadcast. It was broadcast at the comparatively slow speed of 18 words per minute, but the guys talked to each other at a much faster rate. The modern phrase "time warp" comes to mind.

On the second or third visit to the radio shack I sat at a built-in desk and idly opened the middle drawer to discover a pile of old dog-eared cheap girly magazines. Hardly Navy regs but acceptable to pass the time. I thought an inspection was in order so as to make sure they were okay for the men, so I picked one up, flipped to the centerfold and there in all her glory was the girl I had been seeing in Los Angeles the year before, the one who wouldn't let me into her harem pants because she was "too shy." I could now see just how shy she was. I told the guys I knew her, that her name was so-and-so instead of so-and-so, and they tried to act as if they believed it. I don't think they did. But I know a naked shy girl when I see one.

As I was to learn, the bridge and signal bridge of the ship were where I felt most comfortable, and was where I spent much of my time. The bridge was a wide expanse on the fourth level above the main deck, with an ample open walking area from wing to wing, and an enclosed wheelhouse located just aft. For protection, some genius had designed the perfect armor to protect the bridge crew while underway in hostile territory. The shells for our 40 millimeter guns came in heavy gauge metal cans that were about two feet tall and ten inches square. Filled with sand, they were welded one on top of the other to make a can about four feet tall and then the sides were welded together to make a wall that stretched from wing to wing of the bridge. Then welded to the metal stanchions at the front of the bridge, you had the very best in armored protection. Another example of the ingenuity available in any Navy crew anywhere. Nothing but an armor-piercing shell could get through that thing and it gave us a very secure feeling that when under fire we could hit the deck without fear of injury.

The signal bridge was just aft of the wheelhouse and consisted of a small deck area with a shack on it, a couple of flag bags (flag storage boxes) and signal lamps. The most important ingredients here were the signalmen and a large TEAC tape deck that entertained everyone in the bridge area with tunes for cruising a war zone, not a lot of Wagner's "The Valkyrie," as used in another story, but more like Three Dog Night. This was also the domicile of a character called "The Mad Midget of the Mediterranean," actually my 2nd class signalman. Prior to coming to Vietnam he had become quite well known in the Mediterranean (in the 6th Fleet) when doing his act. He would climb on top of his shack, sit on his knees, turn his ballcap backwards (very prophetic fellow), put his olive-drab foul-weather jacket on backwards to make his arms appear to be very short, and talk to other ships with his miniature semaphores (signal flags). Maybe you had to be there, but the effect was very clever and funny, and cracked up entire crews on other ships. The sometimes boring Navy life was always dependent on guys like this to keep things lively and interesting. Necessity was truly the mother of invention back then.

And so with this wonderful crew and venerable old ship it is time to head into the hostile environment of the Mekong Delta. After observing my familiarity with the ship and instructing me on the bridge, Captain Story qualified me as an OODU (Officer of the Deck–Underway), meaning that while he was off the bridge the ship was mine. I enjoyed the moment very much, first being fully trusted by my Captain and second, operating this big piece of machinery in a war zone. The Captain's confidence rubbed off on me and soon enough I felt that I could handle any situation. And in this way I never faltered.

I found that the rivers of the Delta differed as much as the landscape did. For the most part they were narrow, shallow and had a swift current although any of these factors could change from time to time. At some times the riverbank would be only a few feet from the sides of the ship, which was a little scary when there was dense undergrowth. The ship's flat bottom kept us from running aground, and her long slender profile made for easy navigation (most of the time) in this tangle of waterways.

The river towns all looked alike: tightly-clustered buildings on stilts with either corrugated tin or thatched roofs, boats of all descriptions tied to one another and to the riverbank, trash and debris and detritus everywhere, people swarming like ants, and a certain smell that still permeates my memory. This rather ugly polyglot could suddenly drop off to some of the most stunning countryside imaginable. It is, after all, a beautiful place, or was before all of the fighting. Many areas showed the scars of ground combat or shelling or bombing, with bare ground, craters, blasted trees, and the most eerie of all, the effects of Agent Orange.

Agent Orange is the defoliant ordered into use by Admiral Elmo Zumwalt in order to deny the enemy his most effective weapon: concealment. The jungle was so dense and the enemy so adept at using it, the Admiral determined that this was a way to reduce our casualties. We are now all aware of the long-term effects Agent Orange has had on our soldiers, sailors and airmen, and in fact I know people who are very ill from exposure to it. Regrettably Admiral Zumwalt eventually lost his own son to cancer caused by Agent Orange. This fine man later went to his grave with the sadness of the world on his shoulders.

The first time I saw an area that had been defoliated I was both repulsed and fascinated at the same time. There was nothing living from the river back to about 100 yards. There was only brown earth and the ghostly, twisted trunks of what had formerly been trees. It looked like a moonscape. But this was a very hot area of enemy activity and let me tell you, there was nowhere he could hide. Had there still been dense cover down to the riverbank we could have been shot to pieces very easily, and please believe me when I tell you, we were grateful for Agent Orange. It has caused so much pain and suffering since, but we loved it then because it saved countless lives, not to mention boats and ships. It is another irony of the Vietnam war that it is still claiming victims and affecting families so many years later.

The first stop we made was nothing but a muddy clearing on a riverbank to unload supplies to a firebase. The river was sluggish here so we were run up onto the bank bow first with a couple of stern anchors out. The only features of this "port of call" were a rickety wooden tree house off the port side and several CONEX boxes dead ahead in the clearing. CONEX boxes were very large metal shipping containers for explosives that you saw everywhere.

I was idling on the main deck near the bow shortly after we arrived and watched a Vietnamese boy climb the steps into this precariously perched tree house out over the river. At the top he turned around, pulled down his shorts, sat down and took a shit right into the river. So much for a tree house. This is the same water people used for bathing and cooking and everything else, and I noticed that women were washing clothes in it, thankfully upriver.

I learned something new every day in Vietnam. Some days, two or three things. For instance, the CONEX boxes in front of the ship turned out to be little houses, complete with windows and doors cut into the metal. Some of the guys were going ashore, I assumed maybe to find a hooch bar somewhere, but found out they were going on what they called "CONEX box liberty," which meant a forty foot walk to the nearest CONEX box whorehouse. I had then, and still have, a big soft spot for sailors. They are never, *ever* boring.

One day I and my leading petty officer held a thorough inspection of all of "my" spaces: the radio shack, bridge area, signal bridge, crew quarters and storage areas. We found that everything was really pretty clean and in good condition until we got to a small, out-of-the-way flag storage locker located off the tank deck. Opening it up, we got a blast of stale, moist air and the smell of moldy cotton flags. Sure enough, there were a number of large foreign flags (used when entering a port of that country, to show respect), all deteriorating from the humidity, and several cases of Miller High Life, the Champagne of Bottled Beers, all in excellent shape. The last of my fleet destroyer's rule-book mentality disappearing out the nearest porthole, I asked my 1st class if he saw anything wrong here.

He said, "No sir, I don't." I agreed and we battened the hatch and finished our inspection.

Navigating the river one day I was introduced to one of the more famous landmarks of the riverine war, the "sunken tug." This was a Navy tug that had been attacked and sunk a couple of years before, with loss of life. It was spoken of almost with reverence by the sailors, and besides being a hazard to navigation, was now on the charts as a navigational aid since part of the mast and crow's nest were sticking out of the water near the river's edge. It is probably still there as a reminder of the ferocity of attacks on American ships.

While we're on the subject of naval lore on the rivers, I was told a story that was so incredible I still don't know whether it's true or just Navy baloney. Supposedly, a year or two before, on the *Monmouth County*, a chief was getting dressed, pulling up his pants standing spread-legged, when an enemy rocket slammed through the side of the ship, flew right between his legs and slammed again through his bulkhead to land in the tank deck. Two things about this story: the rather surprised chief was badly singed but remained intact and was evacuated for treatment. Plus, the rocket failed to detonate, and the tank deck was empty because a large amount of ammunition had just been offloaded. *Whew!* Fact or fiction? I had been told the same story by several people who all swore it was true.

Days began turning into weeks, and weeks into months, and as we progressed on our missions deeper into the Delta I became more and more impressed with how well this ship was suited to riverine service. Normally loading cargo at a larger port such as Vung Tau or Saigon, we ended up delivering to spots that varied from a pier of sorts that we could tie up to alongside, to nothing more than a mud hole as already described. In most cases we simply ran up onto the shore. If the current was sluggish we dropped the stern anchors to stabilize the ship. In a medium current we ran one inch-thick wire cables from both sides of the stern, hooked them to trees or driven stakes, and winched them taut until we were hard up on the beach. (This was a dangerous evolution: if a cable ever parted under such a strain it became a lethal widow maker). If the river was swift, cables and anchors were put out and then we had to "steam to the beach." This meant that the ship was actually underway, with the props turning, keeping us up on the beach with the engines. This also meant that a qualified OOD had to maintain a bridge watch as long as we were under power. This ship could adapt to any situation, could make a landing anywhere. Then the giant bow doors were opened, a large ramp was dropped, and the unloading began.

I was amazed and amused one day at how resourceful Captain Story could be in a difficult situation. We were run up onto a beach and had pulled up the ramp and closed the bow doors and were trying to back off but the ship wouldn't budge. All engines back full wouldn't do it either. A high tide during the night had probably put us hard aground. So doors open, ramp down and the Captain goes ashore and grabs a Seabee (a member of a Navy Construction Battalion, or C.B.) driving a large bulldozer and asks if he can help us shove off. With agreement, he drove down to the ship. Our crewmen assisted in getting the ramp raised enough so that the Seabee could get the 'dozer's blade safely aligned with it, and with our engines back full, he gave it full power and with a mighty shove slid us back off the beach. Ramp up, doors closed, a wave of thanks to the Seabees, and we were underway.

Each type of ship in the Navy, since the first sailors boarded the first wooden ships, has always been given an affectionate nickname by her crew. Destroyers are "tin cans" or "little boys," carriers are "flat tops" or "chicken farms," submarines are "sewer pipes," etc. The LST had the ominous nickname of "large slow target." The first time I heard that, I cracked up because it was so clever. But after thinking about it for a minute, I figured, "Hey, they're *right*." I had always thought one of our crew came up with this perfect description, but I now know that it came right out of World War II when these wonderful ships were introduced. In very rough water another nickname was "the floating brick," but that is another story.

Along our routes were two different types of "zones" that determined what action we could take in the face of the enemy. A "free-fire" zone meant definite enemy activity, no civilians were present, and you shot at anything that moved. In this case all guns were manned and ready and everyone expected some action. A "restricted-fire" zone was different. This area was not quite as hot and was questionable as to the collateral damage that might occur, to friendlies, civilians and/or structures. That did not mean it was necessarily less dangerous to *us*, it wasn't. As a large slow target we were just as vulnerable here as anywhere, but politically speaking the enemy was less so. For we were required to request permission to fire on the enemy or to return fire. Really. We had to radio the squadron, who would in turn radio whoever had purview in this area. "They" would make a decision, relay it to squadron, squadron would relay it to us, I would relay it to the Captain, etc., etc., etc.

One day we took automatic weapons fire from a tree line that ran parallel to the river, 60 or 70 yards distant. As we were in a restricted zone I began the cumbersome chore of calling in for permission to return fire. As the situation began to get hot very quickly, during the rather lengthy interval between my call and a call back, the Captain was forced to open fire, and with a terrific noise four cannon and two .50 caliber machine guns made shredded wheat of the tree line and of whoever was shooting. In the loud silence that followed the Captain's "Cease fire, cease fire," came the answer over the voice radio, "Permission granted."

Our restricted-fire zones were a constant source of irritation, and came under what is known as "Rules of Engagement." You might say that what we were doing in Vietnam was something less than all-out war.

There was a quote attributed to President Johnson, which he never denied having made, and I must paraphrase, "They can't even go to the outhouse over there without me knowing about it." Thus his fondness for micromanagement of the war was revealed. It was, and is, generally acknowledged that the war in Vietnam was run from Washington, and that it was so politicized, by extension, politicians were running the war.

Note: As an example that the war was run from Washington rather than Saigon, I give you this story: I had a friend after the war named Phil, a tall handsome black fellow living in Northern Virginia. Genial, cheerful and smart, everyone who knows him is crazy about the guy. Phil had been a Marine enlisted man working under some kind of top secret operation when he was captured by the North Vietnamese. On his back was a radio over which he had been talking to his controller in the *basement of the Pentagon!* Halfway around the world! Phil's interrogators suspected a secret mission owing to this sophisticated equipment, and began torturing him for information. But he wouldn't give. They made incisions and pulled major blood vessels from the full length of both arms, but he never gave them what they wanted.

On the open bridge, to starboard, stood the Captain's chair. Every Navy ship has one. It is the exclusive domain of the CO while on the bridge, and it meant certain death for anyone else who sat there. It was large and leather-comfortable (I was told) and was so elevated that the he sat well above our "armor" and was able to use the top rail as a footrest. And as he usually wore shorts he would sit up there and air out on our normally hot and airless days. He also made a great target for a sniper or anyone else.

Captain Story had a habit of sitting up there even in the hottest free-fire zones and the officers had come to the conclusion that he wanted a purple heart out of this tour. Sure enough, one day we were navigating through a very hostile area. As usual, the Captain was up in his chair, enjoying the day. I remember recommending that he come down from there, that this was a really hot area and he made a tempting target. He said something like, "Oh, those bastards can't hit the side of a barn." And *blam blam blam*, someone was shooting and we were all hugging the deck. Problem is, you can't say, "I told you so" to your CO.

We made a stop at a remote town located up one of the rivers, I don't remember its name. This place made us a little nervous because it was a known hot spot with no American or ARVN presence in the town proper. And Americans had been attacked here before. Nonetheless some of us decided to play tourist and walked around for awhile taking pictures. It was a typical river town as described earlier, with a "main street" of dirt and mud puddles, and pigs running loose. The danger to us here was palpable so we didn't wander far, and although the people were openly hostile there was no incident.

We decided to have a beer before returning to the ship so we stopped at a bar near the river, that had a view of all the live-aboard boats tied together in the mud-brown water along with the attendant trash and junk clogging the water and the riverbank. The bar was open to the street and we sat with our back to the wall, as we knew that Americans had died in this spot not too long before; a scooter had sped past with a "dragon lady" on the back and she had hurled a satchel bomb into the bar with deadly results. That was why our back was to the wall and we could see everything. After an uncomfortable hour out of the sun we went back to the ship.

As most of our landings were at or near our firebases, there was usually a little hooch bar nearby run by a "mama san." Many times it was nothing more than a thatch-roofed hut and served warm beer but when in Rome..... And invariably, since we wore our working khaki uniforms we stood out like a sore thumb from the guys just in from the bush in their green jungle fatigues: hot, dirty and often heavily armed. We always got the same basic line, "Oh look boys, the Navy's here, we're saved!" There were a number of variations on this line and we heard them all. And it was delivered in sort of a joking tone, but with an edge of challenge to it. There was never an incident, though.

One landing was near a compound which consisted of a house trailer and some storage buildings and garages, surrounded by an eight-foot hurricane fence. Even as we were coming in we noticed that the trailer had a couple of air conditioning units in the windows.

Air conditioning! As soon as we could, and trying not to seem too eager, a few of us walked over to pay a courtesy call on our new "neighbor." A sign on the fence announced it was the property of a Houston-based construction company, and that no trespassing was allowed.

The guy was very friendly and not stupid, he knew why we were there, and invited us in for lunch. We had one hour of absolute pleasure. The trailer was ice-cold and so was the beer, and even though we ate well on the ship, everything he had was fresh! When you are deprived of things, even the smallest things you take for granted back in the real world, you can derive the greatest pleasure from even a moment's exposure. This guy lived in an oasis in the middle of a desert, was paid very well for what he did, and even though we were a little jealous then, he probably earned every penny and every "luxury" he was afforded.

On one occasion we were parked bow to the beach with the guy wires rigged because of a steady current. In this particular area large clumps of grass and weeds would float past us, carried from far away upriver. Heavy rains would cause erosion of the riverbanks and they would cave into the water making these floating clumps. Well, here was another example of a cunning enemy, for we were warned that the Vietnamese would hang mines, no less, from these things and release them downriver. A perfect floating delivery system. So the Captain ordered a sentry on watch to carry an M-16, patrol the deck regularly, and fire into any clumps that got too near the ship.

There was a lot of firing during the night and no one could sleep but considering the alternative, no one complained. Except the Army guys. From their tug. What a weird war this was. I *still* haven't figured out why the U.S. Army needed a tugboat but there it was, in all it's olive-drab glory, tied up to a small pier perpendicular to our bow, on our starboard side. Well, the Army was having a party on their boat, complete with booze and prostitutes, and our firing was disturbing their good time. And instead of sending someone over to talk to us, or even yelling across to us, whoever was in charge thought it would be funny to shoot at the Monmouth County. The grenade, fired from a launcher, landed close to my porthole and exploded with a loud bang and blinding flash and just plain woke me up! The reason that Army crew is still living is that they did not hit the ship. For Captain Story was absolutely livid. I had never yet seen him angry although I had heard about his temper. He was over on that boat within two seconds and the party was over right away. I can only imagine him exploding all over those guys, and the boat went dark and quiet and there wasn't so much as a peep out of the Army before we got underway the next morning.

Along about this time I had a real problem with one of my people, caused by the XO who was unfortunately the officer directly over me. The ship put out a newsletter and he did a piece in each one which included a "quote of the day." One day the newsletter came out, I picked it up, read the "quote" and was horrified! This brilliant guy had inserted "The only good Indian is a dead Indian," a worn-out saying from the days of Custer. Everyone froze when they read it and I headed straight for the radio shack hoping that Morin (remember, full-blooded Cherokee) had not seen it. He had, and he was deeply hurt and *very* angry. This big guy could take out half the crew but all he could do was stand there with his fists clenched and cry in frustration.

I did my best to calm him down because I really was fond of the guy. And the Captain called him in and they had a long talk. We both persuaded him that the XO didn't really mean it or believe it, but was just trying to be funny and wasn't thinking about what he was doing (brother, that was an understatement).

Periodic gunnery exercises are required to keep up the gunners' proficiency, so if they're not shooting at the Viet Cong or NVA, they shoot at a floating target made up by the engineers. I always enjoyed this evolution because of the great noise that it made. Twenty and forty millimeter cannon, .50 caliber machine guns, M-16's, the Captain shooting the M-79 grenade launcher, and me popping away on a .30 caliber M1 carbine, all add up to a thrilling wall of sound. Plus I enjoyed watching the gunners who were so good and so fast without the aid of computers or sophisticated optics. They could rapid-fire those shells anywhere you wanted. I recorded one of those missions and whenever I need a thrill, I pull out the tape, put it on the big speakers and enjoy the big noise again.

Note: With the mention of our .50 caliber machine guns, I have to say something about the legendary sniper, Carlos Hathcock (*"Marine Sniper,"* by Charles Henderson). Sergeant Hathcock is one of those awesome people I have spoken about. There are many parts to this man, but his most enduring feat was to kill an enemy soldier at the incredible range of 2,500 yards, or about 1.4 miles. He had rigged a sniper's scope atop a .50 caliber, and by letting loose a single shot with the heavy slug, sent it home. The victim never heard the report from the big gun. That was in 1967. His record stood for 36 years when, in 2003, a Canadian soldier in Afghanistan, using a .50 caliber rifle, killed an enemy fighter at 2,430 meters, or 1.5 miles. We're talking professionals here, folks!

In those months that I had been in-country I had seen and learned many things about this war. Some doubt had begun to creep into my consciousness about what we were doing there in the first place, whereas before I had just kept volunteering for Vietnam because it was there. I suppose that at the age of 25 I was showing the first vestiges of a thinking person. There was a single incident that occurred one afternoon that changed me forever, and taught me that we had no business being here. This event is etched into my memory and I can call it up anytime and it appears with the clarity of a digital photograph.

The ship was moored bow to the beach, with steel cables out and we were steaming hard to the beach, unloading supplies to a firebase that was located directly in front of the ship. There was a helicopter pad about 200 feet straight ahead and a volleyball court closer to the ship on the port side. I had the noon to four watch and was on the bridge with nothing much to do and so was spying on people with the binoculars.

Playing a vigorous game of volleyball were a bunch of ARVN soldiers in their white t-shirts, and nothing else was going on. All of a sudden from behind a row of hills to our starboard came a stream of HUEY helicopters bearing hard and fast for the helo pad. As they appeared there was a flurry of activity at the pad, medics, nurses, doctors and American troopers turning out to help. Because within 30 seconds this peaceful scene turned into the carnage from hell! As soon as the first chopper landed and unloaded its really bloody cargo, I started to get a sick feeling in my stomach because the stream of choppers was a long one, reaching back to the line of hills and beyond. All full of American soldiers, chopped to pieces in some nearby firefight. They kept coming and coming, unloading countless numbers of these poor boys. And as I watched this scene of horror, I panned my binoculars over to the left and watched as the South Vietnamese soldiers calmly played their volleyball game. The little sons of bitches never turned their heads or batted an eye toward our troops.

In total fascination I watched this scene for a long time. Panning from this scene of pain and death and destruction over to this pastoral volleyball game. And as my anger grew, so did my doubts about the validity of the war and our role there. This was the day I felt betrayed, let down, and finally asked myself what the hell we were doing here? I changed, no longer wanting to be here, and began seeing the war in the context of that one scene.

To be fair to those ARVN troops, for them this was just another day in the 'Nam. But the picture remains, the image was still there, and the air went out of the balloon for LTJG Cook. I would always do my best for the ship, but I now wanted to just finish my tour and go home and never come back, even if ordered to do so.

* * *

I have mentioned before that the Captain had somewhat of a temper, and this was never more evident than when we had sailed up to Da Nang to take on a load of supplies. Getting to this dock was a long and laborious process because it involved coming into the bay then navigating down a long waterway to the pier. The pier was at a dead-end, and off to our right was a bridge that crossed the waterway and led immediately into the bush. By mid-afternoon the loading process was going well and we were about halfway through it when the CO got an urgent message that the port master needed to speak with him. We had a phone hookup and so the two were connected and he was informed that we were being kicked out of port *now* because an enemy rocket attack was expected at 1730 hours (5:30 PM) from the other side of the bridge.

The Captain's temperature began to rise as he explained that we were not through loading yet and that we couldn't leave and there would be an unnecessary delay in our schedule if we did. We would have to secure everything in place, get underway and move back down the waterway and anchor out in the bay until the next day. And then repeat the whole evolution. This port master's stubborn attitude rubbed him the wrong way and he really began to lose his temper.

He asked this guy why he was so certain of an attack at 1730, and he replied that they attacked every day at that time. (What a war!) That's when the he went ballistic and actually his face turned purple. That's the first time I had ever seen anyone do that. The Captain was furious, demanding of him why we weren't informed of this, that we could have gotten an earlier start and been out of there. But this guy was playing deaf and dumb, in the manner that dense people with a little power often do, and couldn't be dealt with. And unfortunately he had the authority to kick us out. Which he did. We were ordered to get out and could do nothing but comply.

Probably the most fun I ever had in Vietnam was when we steamed upriver to the Port of Saigon to pick up another load of supplies. We had a couple of days here so we could have ourselves a little R&R in the big city. As we were tied up near the PX I went right over to stock up on cigarettes and other necessities. Out in the yard was more beer than I have ever seen, and haven't since. Rows and rows of Miller High Life and Falstaff and others, in large shipping boxes about four feet square, stacked three high as far as the eye could see. Twelve feet of beer to the horizon!

Anyway I bought some socks that were so well-made that I can still wear some of them today. And I also bought a little GE transistor radio that stopped working as soon as we got underway, giving me no chance for a refund! When you click the "off" button, the sound goes off but not the battery. I have kept the little radio ever since to remind me of this ridiculous place.

That night I felt the need for female companionship and somehow made a connection to go to an address in downtown Saigon. Since I had been in-country for a while now, the Plan of the Day was "*no sex in Vietnam.*" The rumor mill had it that if you caught what was called the Black Death, a venereal disease that was totally resistant to penicillin, you would not be able to return to the USA because of its virulence, but would join a group in quarantine somewhere in the Philippines. Forever. And the black teeth of the older Vietnamese women (from chewing betelnuts) served to remind you of this scourge every day. Now that I think about it, those rumors could have been fostered by MACV as an extension of the old WWII Army films about cankers and shankers that we slept through at OCS. Nevertheless, many of us had the ability to shift our brains to the south after dark, so warnings and even good sense had no effect on us.

The next day was our last in Saigon so we decided to make it good. Three of us, me, Jim the weapons officer and Larry the supply officer, somehow talked the Captain out of the Dodge Power Wagon. The Dodge Power Wagon was this behemoth of a truck that we kept in the tank deck. With its massive size and massive winch, it could push and pull the ship under any conditions, and was only occasionally used for transportation. Produced beginning in 1945 for WW II veterans wanting trucks like those they used in the army, this venerable vehicle weighed almost 5 tons, stood 7 feet off the ground and had a grille and bumper that looked like the front end of a locomotive. This was one of the most perfectly-named trucks ever built.

To put this joyride into perspective and to show just how much fun it was, you need to recall two things: the wide avenues of Saigon choked with people, cars, scooters, bicycles and smoke and flying dust. Add to that our growing distaste for anything Vietnamese. In fact, we were getting damn sick of the whole place. And I will add a third ingredient to the pot: the Vietnamese had begun faking injury by "accidently" being knocked down by American vehicles or having their scooter or fruit cart or fishing boat or whatever, "damaged" by Americans, and filing claims against the U.S. government. They had discovered the word "reparations." Of course, these suits were by and large settled in favor of the complainants, and in quick time, so as not to upset the political applecart. And so a new cottage industry was born. In fact, in March of 1969 an Army sergeant was driving my future wife around Saigon (don't ask!) in a jeep when a Vietnamese man threw himself across the hood and screamed. The sergeant, who had been around the block a few times in-country, just laughed out loud, yelled, "Fuck you" and kept on driving.

While we're on the subject, another little industry was born called "extortion" and was much more simple. A crowd would just surround an isolated car or jeep or truck and threaten a beating to the passengers unless they paid up. They took everything of value before releasing the vehicle. Sometimes the unfortunate Americans were beaten anyway.

So this was the climate we had in mind as we climbed up into our Power Wagon. Maybe our pilots were restricted from going "downtown" Hanoi, but the Navy was about to go "downtown" Saigon!

You should have seen them scatter. The truck wasn't very fast but it was so big it didn't matter. It was like Moses parting the sea, as all of these people looked around to see what the loud noise was, got a load of us, eyes like silver dollars, and ran for their lives! When it first started we began to get tickled, and then we started laughing and then we started howling! It was so infectious that we couldn't stop laughing, it was so comical, and that only made us go faster and try to terrify everyone in Saigon. We were on a power trip. I still believe that it was one of the funniest things I have ever seen. After laughing and yelling and "speeding" for awhile we finally had to pull over to catch our breath and calm down. Everything after that was anti-climactic, as nothing before or since could touch the fun we had that day.

As it happens we had stopped near our destination, and Larry and I got out and left Jim with the truck and our three cameras, which were on the seat next to him. Man, it wasn't five seconds before some guy was at the driver's window asking a question and another guy was through the passenger window and back out with three expensive cameras and *gone* into the crowd. As we returned Jim was out of the truck and headed into the crowd with murder in his eye (and I'm not kidding). Larry and I had to wrestle him back to the truck because he had completely lost it and was going to kill someone. Anyone. He was getting a little scary so we stuffed him into the floorboards and hauled back to the ship. As I write about that day, so long ago, just one modern phrase comes to mind, so appropriate: "Paybacks are hell!"

Before leaving Saigon an errand took me out to Tan Son Nhut air base for the last time. I ran into a group of Aussie troops, some of whom I had known from the Grand Hotel bar in Vung Tau. As we were catching up on things I noticed two or three old DC-3's parked nearby, with very spiffy paint jobs and the words "Air America" down the side. Also an American flag was painted on the tail of each. I am an admirer of the DC-3 and asked around about this airline I had never heard of, and got almost a universal answer, "Oh yeah, mate, that's the CIA's own private airline."

Damn! That took the cake. What the hell is a civilian spy agency doing running its own airline in a war zone? Folks, I really don't think we want to know *what* they were doing there. The records are probably still sealed and that's good, because I am sure they rained unimaginable mischief on Vietnam and other countries, and it is just another example of civilian meddling and presence in this war. I think I shook my head all the way back to the Monmouth County, as I still do sometimes.

We continued with our missions in the Delta without major incident until one day out of the blue we got orders from the squadron to return to Vung Tau and prepare to depart for the USA. Under the Vietnamization program, our duties were to be assumed by the VN Navy and we were no longer needed here. Our orders were to prepare the ship for crossing the Pacific, take on a load of excess war materiel and, accompanied by three other ships in the squadron, sail for San Francisco. Upon arrival we were to act as the decommissioning crew for the good old Monmouth County.

Personally, I had not served my full year in-country, but I really didn't care by then. It was okay by me. And the crew were happy. From then on all they played on the PA system was the song, *"San Francisco (wear some flowers in your hair)"* by Scott McKenzie. In fact they played it so often that I can still sing it backward and forward in my dreams.

The Vietnamization of the Vietnam war sounds funny just in the saying. As we were back in Vung Tau making preparations for sea, we were able to observe just how well this was going to work, at least in our sphere of operations. Parked near us were a number of LST's that looked as if they were just off the showroom floor. These beauties had recently been turned over to their Navy and were supposed to take over where we left off. They had been pulled out of mothballs or from active duty and completely refurbished for the turnover, and were so clean and shiny that you couldn't tell they were WWII vintage except for the "stove in" steel plating along the sides.

We naturally were envious because their ships looked better than ours, but we slowly began to realize why: they never seemed to get underway. We never observed them doing so. They washed them down a lot, though. Two of us were at the rail watching one of them one day, and saw this guy out on the main deck trying to plug something into an electrical outlet. But instead of a two or three-prong plug, he had a bare wire in each hand and was sticking them into the outlet while standing on one foot. For real. Neither of us said anything for a moment, then I asked what the hell he was doing. The guy with me explained that when they don't have a plug they use bare wires, and by standing on one foot they believed that the circuit can't be completed, and they won't be electrocuted. I just thought, okay, yeah that sounds logical, and I'm so glad we gave them such low-tech ships that they can't hurt themselves or the ships too badly.

But the moment came when we knew that they were really going to lose the war, and that moment came at 1700 (5:00 PM) every Friday when they all *went home!* For the weekend! In the middle of a war! The commanding officers couldn't prevent it, it just happened. They couldn't have gotten underway for love nor money! This was the crowning glory of the whole Vietnam experience and was probably the moment when many of us began muttering, "We gotta get the hell outta here." And really meant it.

Getting ready for an ocean crossing in an old LST is a piece of cake. I remember the Captain asking the XO if we needed to "top off" with fuel before departure, and the answer was negative, that we were about ¾ full. (You will remember the incredible cruising range of these things—we could refuel somewhere along the way). Also, the Captain had a diver inspect the ship's bottom and it was found that we had a total of 39 holes there. A discussion ensued whether we were fit to cross the Pacific, or should we go to the Philippines for repairs first? It was decided that we were seaworthy even with 39 holes and that no repairs would be necessary. Remember all of the watertight compartments. The nickname I have mentioned, the "floating brick," was never so true. The old Monmouth County rode in the water like a brick and was built tough. As you may be able to tell, I am an unabashed fan of the vintage LST's.

There was one piece of business to be done before we left, and that concerned Otto, the ship's mascot. We couldn't take him with us across the Pacific as the Navy had rules about that kind of thing. Neither the crew, nor the officers, believe it or not, wanted to leave him, but there was nothing to be done. Luckily enough, an American civilian based in Vung Tau said he would gladly take Otto and make sure he was happy. Hopefully this magnificent beast made it out of Vietnam with his new friend before 1975, and lived to be a grouchy old man in the USA.

Our cargo for the return voyage was to be for the Marines. On the main deck was a large load of bridging material, all the steel and aluminum girders and supports you would need to throw a bridge across a river on short notice. In the tank deck we carried a capacity load of APC's, or Armored Personnel Carriers. The skinny was that these things had a reputation for incinerating when they were hit in the gas tanks, and that out in the bush the guys rode on top rather than down inside. Guess I would, too.

Now we come to the most important cargo of all, a brand-new Datsun convertible, white with a black soft-top. This car was the darling of a four-stripe captain. This fellow came aboard just before we were to leave. Tall, graying hair, handsome, Tarzan physique, he was the poster boy for obnoxious Navy officers. Pushy, liked to throw his weight around. He was here to inform Captain Story that he had a car he wanted transported back to the states. When Story informed him that it was against regs to transport personal vehicles, this guy got all bent out of shape. He didn't care about the regulations and told him to bring the car aboard. We could do nothing but comply, but the Captain told him that the tank deck was full of APC's and we only had room on the main deck. So the brand new little car was hoisted on board and was secured to the deck just in front of the bridge, out in the weather, where we could keep an eye on it. We all grinned to ourselves about this location, and the reason for that will be evident later in the voyage. But as the four-striper left the ship we all seemed to be thinking, "What an asshole!"

It takes a destroyer about 8 days to make a crossing of the Pacific, depending on her cruising speed. It can be done more quickly if necessary. But on an LST with a cruising speed of 7.5 knots, it takes somewhat longer, like 45 days. It's true, we were the turtles of the fleet.

We left Vung Tau in company with three other ships, all heavily loaded, headed for our only stop along the way, the island of Guam. One of the other ships, Norm Davis' Clarke County, was smoking badly as he had burned out a piston, but it was no problem, she would make the crossing without incident. Good old LST's.

Note: The Monmouth County and the other LST's had the capability, while underway on the rivers, to purify the brown water for drinking and washing. And while in Vung Tau we took on fresh water from barges. In 2006 the Department of Veterans Affairs in Australia announced that, for their ships that took on desalinated water in Vung Tau harbor between 1965-1972 (the same as we did), definite linkage had been made between four distinct cancers found in a number of their sailors, and the fact that the water was contaminated with Agent Orange. Very fortunately, I have had no problems with Agent Orange, but I know people who do. There are so many of them.

The Voyage Home

It was to be a 17-day trip to Guam. After four or five days at sea the crew began to settle into the routine of making an ocean crossing, an unusual undertaking for this ship which had been home ported in Vung Tau for five years.

In order to commemorate our successful tour in Vietnam, the CO called for a Mess Night. Mess Night is the almost-forgotten Navy tradition of having the officers to a formal dinner at sea hosted by the Captain. Uniform is dress whites (without sword). Yes, even going to a war zone the tradition-bound Navy requires you to pack a dress uniform. And after all the rust stains and spots were removed, we were a pretty spiffy-looking group.

So here we are at sea in our old WWII bucket, sitting around a perfectly-set table, young and handsome in our full-dress uniforms, having a truly gourmet dinner with cigars and brandy (did I say that?) after. And thinking about the tradition and of the moment, I do not believe that I have ever spent a more elegant evening in my life.

And then reality intruded and I had to excuse myself to go and stand my bridge watch in dress whites, which amused the crew no end. I had to be really careful not to touch or lean on anything!

We had a smooth crossing to Guam. The sky was clear with only a few clouds, and the sea was calm and a very deep blue. These beautiful waters contrasted sharply with the polluted, dirty brown waters of the Mekong Delta. It was very comforting to be topside and to watch the four old warhorses slowly head for home after performing so well in Vietnam.

Every sailor is proud of his individual ribbons and campaign stars, best exemplified on film by actor Lee Marvin during the trial of "*The Caine Mutiny*." Landing Ship Squadron Two received the Meritorious Unit Commendation for "providing armed logistic support to the Free World Forces' effort throughout Southeast Asia and, especially, in the hostile environment of the Mekong Delta region of the Republic of Vietnam. In the face of frequent enemy attacks, the personnel of Landing Ship Squadron Two demonstrated outstanding alertness and exemplary navigational and piloting ability on the rivers of the Mekong Delta and its contiguous waters. Their professional skill, diligence, etc., etc., etc." Every man in the squadron and each of the old ships were able to add this ribbon to the many others each one already wore.

We were all looking forward to our short stay in Guam, for the sole reason that we would see some "round-eyes" after such a long time. As a reminder, a "round-eye" is an occidental woman, as opposed to being oriental. We all attached great importance in just seeing one. I suppose it was a sure sign that we were actually back in the "real world" again.

Well, we landed in late afternoon, tying up alongside the Navy piers, and everyone slicked up for liberty. Since we only had the evening there, no one went into the city of Agana which was some distance away, but stuck to the dock area, which offered a small selection of bars. Four shiploads of sailors debarked in eager search of a round-eye and refreshment. All of the officers ashore gravitated toward one place which turned out to be *empty*. No women anywhere, just a big empty place with a bored barkeep and a jukebox for company. The disappointment was very real, so we did what all good sailors do after 17 days at sea, we got wasted. The jukebox was loud and the beer flowed, and the entertainment for the evening was a lieutenant who could dance with a full bottle of beer sticking out of his face, no hands! Pretty amazing stuff! We killed the evening there and wobbled back to our ships at some early hour, still unfulfilled.

The bosun's pipe blew reveille *very* early and *very* shrill as the pink of dawn glowed through my porthole. I reluctantly rolled out of my bunk and went straight to the sink and threw up, knowing that I had to be somewhat sober because I was getting the ship underway this morning. I felt really lousy and sick, but after a good breakfast, felt a little better and went to officer's call then up to the bridge to prepare to get underway.

I loved this evolution. Four ships came to life as people came up on deck and to the bridge, and all the noises so familiar now as we get up steam (or diesel in this case). Then the four behemoths begin moving out to sea, and I take great pride in the fact that I did not once hit the pier or another ship or anything else.

It took almost thirty days to transit Guam to San Francisco. It could have been boring but Scott McKenzie kept on singing, the Mad Midget of the Mediterranean kept on signaling, Norm's ship kept on smoking, the signal guys played good music, we did some target practice, we dreamed of California women, and the funniest thing of all, we did "tic tacs." If you will remember, these are the high- speed maneuvers used by tin cans to protect ships in formation.

With a group of destroyers it is really something to behold. Flags snap up the halyard and are yanked down just as quickly. Ships turn together as on a dime, wakes foaming white. Very exciting and very "old Navy."

With a group of ancient LST's it is really something to behold. The signaling is always excellent. But instead of turning on a dime, our herd of turtles took 10 minutes to complete a turn that destroyers did in seconds. But it was fun and picturesque, even though some of the OOD's were rusty and turned the wrong way. But instead of a collision all they suffered were off-color remarks from the other ships. There were enough of us from the destroyer force to enjoy the difference.

The days passed and then the weeks passed, and soon we were beginning to close in on San Francisco. The sea had been almost dead calm, with some gentle swells from time to time, so we had a good crossing. That is, until about five days out. The ship began to ride differently, subtly changing its motion, as the sea began to pick up. We noticed the change and discussed it at the evening meal, and by reveille the ship was really beginning to ride rough. Earlier in this narrative I mentioned the heavy seas we encountered within sight of the Oregon coast. Now we were hitting the relatively shallow water off the California coast in the midst of a building storm, with the same effect.

As I came up on deck to see what was going on, I could see that our course took us directly into the rather high sea, which was being whipped up by a strong wind. And it was getting worse. As you have read, a destroyer heading into a sea such as this could use a good bit of speed to slice through the wave with its knife-like prow, with steady movement forward. An LST has a lot of "sail area" and is very susceptible to strong winds. But the blunt, rounded bow is the killer. Heading into a sea, it tends to pound the wave directly, then floats up and *over* the top, just in time to pound the next wave. During this motion you could actually feel the bite of each of the propeller blades because of the constantly changing depth of the water around them.

The Captain had already issued the order to secure the ship for foul weather, which was being done, and over breakfast discussed the day. Weather reports indicated that this was going to be a bad one, and the deck crew were to see that all cargo, including our Datsun, was still secured good and tight. He would be on the bridge all day. He then took me aside and said that when it gets real bad he wanted me on the bridge as OOD (destroyermen always stick together), which still pleases me to this day.

Well, it didn't take too long before it got real bad. I went through my spaces to make sure everything was lashed down. The ship was beginning to ride very badly and was really pounding. And over the PA I got the call to report to the bridge. Muttering, "Oh shit, here goes," I threw on my foul-weather gear and reported to Captain Story. I had no way of knowing that this was going to be the most exciting day of my life, before or since.

I emerged onto the bridge to a scene straight out of Armageddon. The sky was dark gray, the wind was blowing, and the sea state was six (sea state one is calm to one-foot waves, six is consistent waves of thirteen to twenty feet). My first sight was the bow pounding and banging head-on into a heavy sea. The noise level was so high, the Captain had to yell into my ear that we were trying to maintain our course and speed, and to stay in company with the other three ships, but it was becoming more difficult. He told me to go ahead and take the conn.

I yelled at the OOD that I was ready to relieve him, and he yelled the course and speed and the fact that the surface radar repeater was becoming "snowy." And rather than trying to further explain, he put his arms out, palms up, and presented me with this mess.

"I relieve you, sir."

"I stand relieved."

"I have the deck and the conn."

And so I took the ship, with the CO on the bridge, during one of the three worst storms I had endured in the Navy. You might recall that in the first one I had been a green ensign on my first bridge watch with an unconscious OOD. In this one I was a two-time Vietnam veteran and the OOD with the confidence of my Captain. And this time I was up to the job.

The radar set was useless because of the height of the waves and since the wind was whipping whitecaps off their top. It made the screen look like a snowfall in Minnesota, and it could no longer be used to maintain station on the other ships. They were still visible by binoculars but the formation was breaking up as each one found it more difficult to keep a constant speed and bearing on the others.

We continued banging into the sea and trying to maintain station with the others, until finally one by one, we began to lose sight of them. The sky was darker gray now and the sea the color of slate, and we could now only see the one ship that was about 45 degrees off our starboard bow at about 2,000 yards. That at least gave us some small comfort. This was now a classic battle of men against the sea: it was trying to tear us apart and sink us, and we were fighting hard to stay in one piece. We could have been in an eighteenth-century man-o'-war in the middle of a North Atlantic storm because the sea was the same, and the sailors were just as good and just as brave. That's what made it so exciting.

For some hours we on the bridge operated as a perfect team. All of our training and experience with the sea and ships kicked in, and a finer bunch of sailors never existed. The Captain and I were in for the long haul, but the stress on the rest of the bridge watch, particularly on the helmsman, was so wearing that he was relieved every two hours rather than standing a normal four-hour watch. They would have had to drag me off the bridge because I was having the time of my life! It was a pure adrenaline and testosterone-driven fight and I wouldn't have been able to stop for anything.

Captain Story was so calm and cool, his demeanor rubbed off on the rest of us and gave us confidence. He knew exactly what he was doing but conferred with me from time to time as OOD, on the state of the ship or our course and speed or any of the myriad factors that make up such a day. We were holding our own against a very bad sea when the worst thing that could happen, happened: the cargo began to shift.

The constant banging of the ship had done a number on the main deck cargo, which had been so thoroughly secured before we left Vietnam. The chains and wire rope had been checked and adjusted regularly and had been double-checked for heavy weather the night before. But the force of Mother Nature had caused movement of the girders and other equipment on the port side about a third of the way from the bridge to the bow.

As strange as it may sound, when cargo begins to shift it can change the ship's center of gravity. That can be very dangerous, particularly in a heavy sea because it affects the way the ship rides. For instance a ship could become top-heavy and simply roll over. Or, it could ride with a list, take on water and roll over. There are many factors involved. The other danger is cargo breaking loose, banging into other cargo and doing severe damage to the ship and hurting people.

We had a real problem. The port lookout and the Captain noticed the movement at the same time and yelled, "Cargo shifting, port side!" The Captain immediately yelled at me, "Find a trough! Get me into a trough *now!*" As he passed orders to the deck crew I executed a left full rudder, making a hard turn to port to find a trough for the ship to lay in. A trough is the "valley" between waves, and so a turn of approximately 90 degrees put us into one and the constant banging of the bow stopped but the rolling began. The rolling motion was more gentle than the pounding but we were taking water over the starboard side and the cargo was moving but not as much. This ride gave a better footing for the deck crew (everything is relative), who now had to go out and secure several tons of bridging material.

The movement came from a section of material that was secured from port to starboard, perpendicular to our position on the bridge. While the sailors prepared to go out on deck, the Captain eyed the movement and told me to just keep it in the trough and to make rudder corrections for the smoothest ride possible. It was very tense. I had to keep the deck as steady as I could in the middle of a terrible sea, for what seemed like an eternity, because our guys were going out in this stuff.

The ship was riding as easily as I could get it while a half-dozen men worked their way out onto the deck and toward the problem. There was still plenty of motion and we were still taking significant water over the starboard side, but it was away from the men. They began to crawl onto the long bridge support beams and to use wrenches to tighten down the turnbuckles attached to the chain and wire-rope tie-downs. Everything was seemingly under control: I was able to gauge the rhythm of the waves enough to keep the ship's movement constant, and the deck guys were finding and tightening loose turnbuckles, when our worst nightmare occurred.

The wave was a big one, bigger than the rest, and it came out of nowhere to slam the starboard side, catching us all by surprise, and hitting hard enough to break away a beam the men were on and sending it sliding out over the port side with sailors on top, hanging on for their lives! It was an awful sight because anyone falling into this sea was a dead man. Our ship did not have enough power to maneuver for rescue in this storm, and help was too far away.

I could do nothing except to keep the ship as steady as possible while the crew worked frantically to get those men in off the beam and to winch it back in. It took a scary and heart-stopping few minutes but finally they were able to scramble back on deck and go below while their mates finished lashing down. That was as close as anyone wanted to get to a real disaster.

Once everything was secured we were able to turn into the sea again and continue our journey. We were now on our own, as the other three ships were scattered over a large area. When I was finally able to leave the bridge, I was wet and very tired, grateful that this storm was letting up a little, grateful that we had no loss of life or injuries and the ship was safe, and feeling very much fulfilled as a U.S. Naval Officer.

It took several days more until we reached the west coast and civilization again. It seemed strange to be coming home after all of our adventures in such a strange and alien place, but there it was. We offloaded all of our cargo at the huge Naval Construction Battalion (Seabee) base at Port Hueneme (pronounced wyneemee) located northwest of Los Angeles, including the little white Datsun that now had a bleached white top and that had been thoroughly drenched with salt water and salt air. We laid bets that it would be a total rust-bucket basket case within a year or two. Served that posturing captain right. My step father had a great saying, "Time wounds all heels." It certainly applied in this case. We then struck north for San Francisco.

We all had a real thrill approaching the Golden Gate Bridge just as the sun was coming up, the main deck glistening wet from the scrubbing it had gotten the day before. The day was fresh and the ship was fresh and the view was magnificent! Sailing under this great beast that symbolized the end of our journey brought the whole crew out on deck. We were home again.

Vallejo

There is a long-standing tradition in the Navy that all ships returning from war are accorded a hero's welcome. I had had this experience when the Herbert J. Thomas returned to San Diego from Vietnam in 1969. There is always a band, plenty of Navy brass, banners, and great joy and excitement. And when a ship returns to its home port, you have family and friends also to cheer and cry for you. Since we had been homeported in a war zone, our families were scattered across the country and so the crew weren't looking for anyone familiar, just our Navy brothers and sisters and maybe a politician or two, to give us a big welcome home. We were all high as a kite, having just passed under the Golden Gate Bridge into beautiful San Francisco Bay after a serious 45-day crossing, and we were now ready to receive our laurels from a grateful country.

And as this wonderful old ship, manned by as good and brave a crew as ever put to sea, approached the pier, we were greeted with, *nothing*. Silence. No one. A completely empty pier. No, not completely empty, there were two sailors in dungarees as line handlers.

This was the meanest and cruelest thing I have ever seen. The disbelief, the anger and the heartbreak of the crew were almost palpable. I remember that in the deafening silence the captain, barely controlling his anger, shouting, "What the fuck is this?" His voice echoed off of the empty pier.

So this was the way it was to be. Nobody gave a damn, not even the Navy. We were on our own, and had to swallow the disappointment. This was to be our first lesson, the lesson that all Vietnam veterans learned: keep quiet, turn it inward, don't think or talk about it. Crew morale dropped like a rock, from exuberance and excitement to a dull, silent hurt. The same as one might feel after being hit in the head with a baseball bat.

We tied up in total silence and began offloading ammunition and most of our fuel. Once that was finished, we got underway and quietly made our last trip on the Monmouth County, across San Francisco Bay to the ship's graveyard, or mothball fleet, at Mare Island Naval Facility, Vallejo, California.

We pulled into a berth next to a large pier, surrounded by what seemed to be hundreds of old ships. It was quite a scene, but we were really anxious to go on liberty and paid scant attention to anything but getting into San Francisco. Down the gangway and the first step onto the USA in a long time. Jim, Larry, Wayne and I, still in working uniform and not bothering to clean up very much, rushed into the city straight for the Mark Hopkins Hotel and straight up to it's world-famous bar. If no one else was glad to see us, we were at least going to have a "welcome home" bottle of champagne at the Top O' The Mark!

Riding up the elevator we looked at each other and realized that we did look a bit shabby to be going to such an elegant place but we didn't care much. It didn't help matters, though, that Jim, in his carnival barker's voice, tried to collect tickets from hotel guests at each stop: "Tickets please, tickets please, nobody gets on without a ticket." Well-dressed people (including our first round-eye women) stared at us in the elevator and in the bar as if we were a band of barbarians, but we held a solemn toast to each other, Vietnam veterans, brothers, "Welcome Home."

* * *

Now it was time to get busy, as we had a ship to decommission. The guidelines for this were promulgated by the Board of Inspection and Survey (INSURV), and its president, Admiral John "PT" Bulkeley, one of the true heroes of WWII, and a man both feared and respected throughout the Navy. (He was also a beloved friend and mentor to my step father). As we stripped down and cleaned the ship, the INSURV boys would inspect our work microscopically and do a final survey, at which time the ship would be released from active service. The job ahead of us was long and hard, but everyone pitched in to give the old Monmouth County a clean bill of health.

Life went on as normally as possible while your home was being stripped. We began transferring people out here and there, and as work continued we settled into life in Vallejo, California.

* * *

At first chance, I went into the city to take the Corvette out of storage. As I hadn't driven anything but a large ship in quite a long time, I was a little rusty just driving down the street. The steering on the car was very sensitive, so even a little movement of the wheel would really move the car around on the road. Running up onto one of the elevated bridge approaches, I let her out a little and we began to roar until I heard a siren and saw a California Highway Patrol car in the mirror. Red Corvettes attract the CHP like flies. But when he stopped me he asked if I had been drinking because I was swerving all over the road. I said no, that I just hadn't driven for a long time. He took in my uniform and asked if I had been in Vietnam. When I said yes he just said, "Be careful, and have a nice day." Nice guy, and I did exactly as he said.

We also discovered the Buena Vista, a café/bar just across the street from the streetcar turnaround by the Cannery. It is still there, still serving the best Irish Coffee there is, the best "black bottom" pecan pie, and the mysterious drink we called the "aqua blue." The aqua blue was *so good* and *so intoxicating* that you could drink several before you began to feel the effects. And when you got to the point that your teeth and tongue turned the same color as the drink, it was too late, because by then you were genuinely wasted. We had many a good time there, sitting at the big round table by the window, meeting people from all over the world and watching the colorful society of San Francisco parade by on the sidewalk. The Buena Vista became our "Officers' Club" in the city.

Speaking of which, we never wore our uniforms when we were in town on liberty, however even in "civvies" it wasn't difficult to guess what we did for a living. But not once, not once, did anyone give us any trouble for being in the military; quite the contrary, everyone was very friendly toward us.

* * *

Back out at the ship our days were very hard. Besides removing equipment and cleaning the ship, everyone was working on his next duty station. I had started to nose around, knowing I wasn't going to request a return to Vietnam. One day I happened to call Gary, my fellow officer from the Thomas, now a civilian in Seattle, and he asked why I didn't come up there, that the Navy was reactivating an old Naval Air Station. He said it sounded like good duty and besides he needed a roommate on his houseboat. That sounded pretty good so I said, "Okay," and again called my detailer at BUPERS in Washington. He said that there was an opening for base security officer at the newly opened Naval Support Activity at Sand Point in Seattle. I asked him how it would look on my career path if I decided to stay in the Navy beyond my obligation, he said it would look fine, so I asked him to put in for it and he said he would get back to me.

I got the duty to act as proctor (or monitor) to administer advancement testing for all of the ratings on the ship. These were all of the enlisted guys, young and old, going for more seniority in their ratings, and a better pay grade. Such advancement involved a combination of intensive study and training by their petty officers on the job. Testing was done on the mess decks of the ship, which was filled with sailors trying to better themselves. I did not mind this duty at all, as I was very proud of these guys, and one standout in my memory was a young Seaman Apprentice (SA) going for Seaman (SN). He was a tall, handsome, clean-cut kid, every mother's ideal son. He was well liked by everyone because he was such a nice guy and a good sailor, and was willing to learn everything. He will also figure later in this story.

Since the ship was still in commission, regular quarterdeck watches had to be stood, even when the crew began to move out of crew's quarters and onto a barracks ship that was parked down the pier. The officers were eventually moved into the local Bachelor Officer Quarters, not very fancy but adequate. At any rate, the ship got very quiet after the working day was done, with only a few watch standers on board.

When it got dark, the ship's graveyard became very spooky, and I'm not trying to be funny. It was completely silent, except for an occasional creaking noise or a metallic groan. Around us were hundreds of old gray ghosts who had done their fighting in other wars, their guns now silent. Men had fought and died in these ships. Battles had been won and lost in these ships. And now they were entombed here, most never to get underway again, their stories forgotten except for those who sailed in them, but also remembered in Naval history and Naval lore.

Sailors are known to be superstitious but even that doesn't explain the feeling we had in this place. The night noises, the loneliness, the histories of these valiant ships, and maybe the spirits of the men who manned them, combined to create an almost physical sensation or presence, that gave everyone the creeps. We all thought it was haunted. Many of the guys did their best to trade watches so they wouldn't have to be there at night, particularly on the mid watch between midnight and 4:00 AM. That was when it was the worst.

Occasionally I would rotate into one of the night watches, and even though I still get goose bumps thinking about it, I didn't mind so much because I loved these old ships. I had read my step father's books about the Navy in WWII, particularly the excellent series by Samuel Eliot Morrison of Harvard, and I was familiar with the names of some of the ships involved in the important Atlantic and Pacific actions.

One night I had the mid watch and it was so quiet and so boring that I told the guys to watch things and to give me a shout if anything came up, that I was going to take a walk. The yard was so quiet you could hear a sneeze from far away. So I took a flashlight and had a nice stroll. Actually I left my post, which under normal circumstances would never happen.

Walking among the quiet hulks I shined the light across some of them. The names on the stern had been painted out long ago, but they were welded, letter by letter, there, and so you could still make out what ship you were looking at.

During my meanderings in the daytime I had read the names of destroyers and destroyer escorts that had rung a bell in my memory, but now on my nocturnal walk, half-dreaming of the actions of so long ago, I shone my light across the stern of an old destroyer and was electrified when the name *O'Bannon* jumped out at me. It still makes my heart beat faster remembering that I was in the presence of this great warship: the USS O'Bannon, DD-450, the most decorated destroyer in WWII with *seventeen* battle stars and the coveted *Presidential Unit Citation.* This was the same ship that took on the monster Japanese battleship Heie at close range during the battle of Guadalcanal in November 1942, rapid-firing 5-inch shells into her superstructure, while so close-in that the behemoth's massive 14-inch guns couldn't depress far enough to return fire. The legends abound: in October 1943, during a desperate gun and torpedo battle against three Japanese destroyers and motor torpedo boats, O'Bannon accidentally rammed the mortally wounded USS Chevalier in the dense smoke, ripping up her bow, but surviving to rescue Chevalier crew and officers from the sea. (*ref: United States*

Destroyer Operations in World War II, by Theodore Roscoe, 1953, and other sources).

And suffice it to say that O'Bannon is the only known destroyer to sink a Japanese submarine after a pitched battle with good Maine potatoes. As the ship was killing the sub with 5" gunfire and depth charges, the Captain brought her almost alongside to deliver the coup de grace. As the enemy came pouring out of what was left of the sub's conning tower, American sailors grabbed a bin of potatoes and some spare parts from nearby, and began pelting them with potatoes, large nuts and bolts, and machine gun parts. A large, heavy steel nut caught an officer "square" in the head, and he tumbled into the water. (*ref: Action Tonight,* by James D. Horan, 1945). When it comes to US sailors, truth *always* beats out fiction.

This ship was involved in so many actions that she seemed to taunt fate along with the Japanese, who were unable to defeat her. And by the way, O'Bannon was not yet finished: she won three battle stars in Korea and saw service in the Gulf of Tonkin in Vietnam.

As a matter of interest, while refreshing myself on the O'Bannon's history, I pulled out a photograph I took of some of our "yard mates" at Vallejo, a row of two LST's and five destroyer escorts, with hull numbers very clearly shown. Please bear with me as I give a thumbnail history of war service for each of these heroes:

LST-1123, USS Sedgwick County- toward the end of WWII, duty in Okinawa and other islands of the Ryukyus, and in the Marshalls and Marianas. Six battle stars in Korea, six battle stars in Vietnam

LST-901, USS Litchfield County- missions to Saipan and other of the Marianas, Ryukyus, Iwo Jima in WWII. Two battle stars in Korea, service in Vietnam.

DE-642, USS Paul G. Baker- escort duty, western Pacific. Escort for Okinawa invasion. On patrol off Okinawa, fought off heavy and frequent suicide plane attacks on herself and others including battleship New Mexico (BB-40), splashing several and damaging others. One battle star.

DE-386, USS Savage- manned by US Coast Guard crew. Convoy duty, North Atlantic and Mediterranean, 18 crossings without loss of a ship. Fought off German submarine and bomber attack in the Med. One battle star.

DE-586, USS Lough- battle of Leyte Gulf. Fought off air attacks. Fought off 25-30 fifteen-foot suicide boats, sinking six. Unfortunately participated in sinking two US PT boats which approached without proper identification. Three battle stars.

DE-683, USS Henry R. Kenyon- convoy duty, Atlantic and Caribbean, 5 crossings. Escort duty, Philippines, New Guinea, Okinawa.

DE-414, USS LeRay Wilson- battle of Leyte Gulf. Lingayen Gulf landings. Facing a twin-engine Japanese suicide bomber, gunners held their ground, steady fire knocked it off course, still hit the ship killing six gunners. Invasion of Okinawa. Four battle stars.

These are all echoes of long ago, but you may now be able to understand the emotional attachment that can form between a sailor and his ship, now an inanimate hunk of cold iron tied up to a pier, but once a vibrant, throbbing, swift, fire-throwing vessel that became one with its crew, the perfect fighting machine.

* * *

Back to the Buena Vista, we continued our good times there and began to get to know some of the "regulars." San Francisco in the 1970's was a very colorful town, full of all sorts of characters in all manner of costume, basically having their harmless fun. It was always a carnival atmosphere, day or night. (Not that it has changed that much over the years). One day I got word that one of my oldest friends, Dick Caplinger, was coming to SanFran along with a buddy of his, Marty, to ship out of Travis Air Force Base to Vietnam. Dick and Marty were "HUEY" pilots headed for the Big Show.

And I knew immediately what I was going to do to them, unsuspecting young Army officers that they were. I simply requested that they meet me at the Buena Vista the afternoon of their arrival/departure, and I would give them a ride out to Travis in the evening. Remembering my own experience of not too long ago, I decided that these two would be so drunk by the time they got to Travis they wouldn't know whether they were coming or going. After all, it was for their own good.

So I formed a small party of ship's officers and we went down to the Buena Vista to do our duty. We took one of the big round tables and soon enough here came Dick and Marty, in uniform, each with a duffel bag (sea bag in Navy parlance) and introductions were made all around. The Navy guys knew what Dick and Marty had in the back of their mind, they had been there, so they were really nice about it and were going to show them a good time. We ordered aqua blues for the table, explaining to them it was a new drink they should try. They liked it and so we ordered some more and pretty soon we were loosened up, and a few people joined our table, people from all over the world including the cutest Australian girl you've ever seen: small, about our age, dark hair, pretty figure, beautiful face, cute, cute, cute, and with an accent that would melt the coldest heart. Well, she and the other new arrivals ordered aqua blues and pretty soon we had a real party going on. My diabolical plan was working perfectly. It was really fun, and of course the Army and the Navy all fell for this little Aussie.

And then came the magical moment: Dick and Marty's teeth and tongue turned blue, and they were wasted. Unfortunately so were we, so we had to stop for a while. My guys stumbled out toward the ship, so I and the Army were left with this little doll who, though happily married, knew exactly what she was doing: I was just back from Vietnam and they were going over tonight, and she liked us. And she was also aware of the effect she had on us, and wanted Dick and Marty to leave with a smile on their face. We ended up in her hotel room nearby for a farewell drink, nothing more, three guys who were eight sheets to the wind, and a very nice and lovely Australian person.

When it came time to go, we each said a reluctant goodbye to her, receiving a very memorable hug and kiss in return, and headed for my car. Only then did we realize that we had three grown men and two large duffel bags to transport in a two-seater Corvette. El Problemo! But soon solved, as Dick and I stuffed Marty and his

duffel bag down behind the seats into the "trunk," Dick sat in the
passenger seat and I stuffed his duffel bag onto his lap and down to
the floor. He couldn't move or see where we were going. We were
full. It felt as if you stuck a pin into the car it would explode. I doubt
that any Corvette has ever transported so much livestock and cargo,
before or since.

When we somehow got out to Travis, we pulled into a parking
lot and unloaded. Marty went on ahead and Dick and I talked for a
minute. When the time came we shook hands, gave each other a hug,
and I said, "So long, Bub, keep your head down," or something to
that effect, and he was gone. My intent was to pour them onto that
flight and that's what happened, and bless Australia for her. (Both
guys had a rough tour but came back in one piece).

* * *

The Monmouth County had a personnel problem: our young
seaman (he had done very well on his advancement test) failed to
muster with his division one morning and was listed as AWOL. This
was very unusual because he just wasn't the type to go over the hill,
he was too good a sailor. None of his friends knew where he was, he
had just disappeared. We were all concerned but there was nothing to
do about it but to wait to see if he would contact the ship.

One afternoon some days later, a sailor came to the ship in a
rather excited state and asked if the Captain was there, and I told him
that no, he and the XO were elsewhere on business, but I was the
senior officer present, could I help him?

"Could you come with me, sir, we've found a body in the water
and we think we know who it is but we need an officer to identify

him." With a real dread I walked slowly down the pier to where a Navy ambulance was parked and on the far side was a wheeled gurney jacked up about two feet off the pavement. I remember moaning, "Oh, no," for there lay our young sailor, still recognizable after being in the water for a week, dripping fluids of all kinds, his youthful face a terrible color.

His death upset the entire crew. The Captain wrote a very heartfelt letter to his parents. Found among his effects was the classic "Dear John" letter from his girlfriend, ending their relationship long-distance. As we pieced together the story, our sailor read the letter, went ashore to the Enlisted Men's Club and started drinking. While at the club he got into a pretty serious fistfight with someone, which was totally out of character for him, and left the club. He was very drunk, could hardly walk, and apparently accidentally fell off the pier and drowned. He was found face-down under the pier by an inspector in a small boat. So it goes sometime for the young and innocent. What a dirty shame.

The clock was ticking for the old Monmouth County. We had to do fitness reports on our crew, and that can be either easy or difficult, but it did have a direct impact on advancement so it was very important. Most of mine were easy, but one was a problem, and it was my leading petty officer. He had no leadership skills and was a goldbricker. He had let his 2nd class shoulder most of the work he should have been doing. Trouble was that I liked the guy well enough. But I wrote a very negative report on him, which for a 1st class petty officer was likely going to stop his ever making Chief. Officers were required to review and discuss each report with its recipient. I didn't relish doing this one; having had one done on me, I knew how it felt. But he and I sat down on the barracks ship and I read it to him. He was visibly shocked and got very angry and as we stood up he made a fist and pulled back on me (second time for me this tour) and I said that if he hit me it would only prove what was in his report. He backed off and left. Personally I really felt for him but professionally it was the only report I could write on him.

My detailer called one afternoon and said that I was confirmed as Base Security Officer for Naval Support Activity, Seattle, gave me the reporting date and said my written orders would follow. I informed Captain Story, and called Gary in Seattle and told him he just got a new roommate. I was happy about the assignment, as I had liked Seattle during my brief tour in 1969. And I always got along well with Gary.

That taken care of, I got to work in my spare time doing some amateur bodywork repairing cracked fiberglass on the Corvette. We were all projecting ahead to the day we would leave the ship. Larry the supply officer bought a shiny new, bright yellow MGB, a real looker, to drive home to the East Coast, as he was separating from the Navy.

The mothballing process was nearing its end now, our beautiful brass and mahogany ship's wheel was sent away for storage at the Washington Navy Yard. Everything else had already been stripped down and stored or sent away, that is, everything but a few items that were not covered by paperwork. Like the chrome quarterdeck clock and the old-fashioned brass looking glass (about the size and shape of a Louisville Slugger). Which I got to first. Ahead of the XO, who coveted them mightily. I have never gotten a look as dirty and as hateful from anyone as I did from him when he found out. There was nothing he could do, as I had simply stolen them before he could steal them, but that look shouted volumes! Too bad.

Finally, Admiral Bulkeley's boys from INSURV certified the ship ready for survey, or taken out of service and commission, and the date was set and plans were made for the decommissioning ceremony.

In early August the captain officiated over a very solemn ceremony, ending the career of our beloved old workhorse and ending our days as her crew. We were in full dress whites and the officers had swords, and we tried a little sword drill which was well-meant but not very good. But the moment was not lost on any of us. There is a phrase that comes to mind when I think of the Monmouth County, so truly appropriate to this moment: that I lived here among brave men. And then we all went our separate ways.

LST-1032 was awarded two battle stars for WWII and three battle stars for Vietnam. She was stricken from the Naval Register on August 12, 1970.

Note: The last we heard, she was to be sold for scrap. The crew's affectionate parting joke to each other was, if you bought a pack of Gilette razor blades and they had rust on them, you would know they were from the Monmouth County.

Seattle

Because of some close timing, I delayed taking a well-earned leave and headed straight for Seattle, as I had to report for duty on Monday of the following week. That still left a couple of days for travel and a weekend to settle into my new surroundings.

I adapted quickly to living on dry land again, wearing civilian clothes and taking one of those memorable drives, this one up Interstate 5, San Francisco to Seattle, in my bright red rumbling Corvette and feeling good! Normally interstates block out views of the countryside, but not this time. It was thoroughly scenic almost all the way and I remember the magnificence of Northern California and Oregon. So many beautiful forests, and my first glimpse of a river full of logs.

Along the way I checked in with Gary, told him my approximate arrival time, and he said to come on, and gave directions to the houseboat.

I arrived in Seattle on a Friday and was able to find my new home with ease. It looked kind of industrial as I pulled off the street into a parking area through which ran a pair of railroad tracks. On the other side of the tracks (there was a clue there somewhere), was the sign: "Scull's Boat Landing, Boat Sales" which marked the entrance to the dock I was seeking. Down sort of a rickety wooden dock made up of a series of floating sections in all shapes and sizes, and lined with a hodgepodge of wooden buildings. Also my first look, at the far end, at Lake Union, supposedly at the time "the most polluted body of water in Seattle." Fourth house down on the left, at no. 6, and I step from the dock onto the deck of my new home.

My first reaction was, "Oh man, this can't be right, this place is a dump!" A floating wooden platform held a dilapidated shack. A number of boards on the deck were loose and lay at odd angles and elevations, the shack had boards that had simply fallen off the sides so you could see the insulation, and the whole thing sort of leaned to one side under a brown tar-paper roof and an ancient paint job of something like Caribbean Aqua Paradise with white trim.

As I am wont to do, I had pictured in my mind a modern houseboat made of fiberglass and featuring a large comfortable living area, lounging decks at the stern and on top (for sunbathing), and a couple of bedrooms with their own heads. You know, something like Travis McGee (by John D. MacDonald) would be living on. Well, wrong again. There was one of these on the dock, but all the rest were merely variations on no. 6.

I knocked but Gary wasn't home and had left the door unlocked. Going in, I found that, thankfully, it looked better inside than it did outside, in fact it was downright homey and comfortable, with a small kitchen, one bedroom, dining area, living room with a fireplace and bay window overlooking a back porch and across Lake Union to a boathouse and a large "Mother's Cookies" sign. Gary was set up to live in that room so I emptied the Corvette into the bedroom and settled on the couch with a beer and enjoyed the view. Eventually Gary did come home and we had a good reunion, catching up on the adventures we had both had in the last year or so. He was now a graduate student at the University of Washington, and had also adapted quickly to civilian life, letting his hair and moustache grow far beyond "regulation" length and eschewing his khaki uniform for jeans and a lumberjack shirt. He said that the people on the dock were really amazing and that I would begin to meet them on the weekend. I was glad to be there and had no earthly idea how much fun was in store for me both on the dock and at my new Navy base.

On Saturday I was able to find my way over to Sand Point to have a look-see at the base, and to my surprise the main gate was chained and padlocked shut! I had been told that this was a startup operation, but nobody had started yet! At least I could see down a wide avenue that led from the gate out to the old runways and taxiways, with Lake Washington beyond, and on the right was a white building with a control tower that had obviously been the flight operations center. After having seen all I could with my nose poked through the gate, I explored Seattle for awhile then headed back to the dock on Lake Union.

On Monday I arrived early and went directly to the Administration Building to report to the XO, Commander Atkin, and to meet Captain David Scott, my new CO. In a meeting with them and my immediate superior, Lt. Jim Beesley, the Operations Officer, I found that no security apparatus existed and that, at the end of my 365-day tour here, there would be one.

With that in mind, I located my offices to the right of the main gate, and entered my new world. The building was good-sized and included the gatehouse, a front counter area, large office area for the staff, a break room, four holding cells and my ample, comfortable office. Some groundwork had been done after all, as I already had a

21-man Civil Service police force that had been put together from other area Navy installations. This force was administered by Sergeant Raines, a very tall, fit, handsome guy with an impeccable uniform and moustache. Raines was a dead-ringer for every Sergeant-Major in every British war movie ever made. He certainly made a good impression on me!

In the back office I met my new Chief of Police, Jim McCann. Chief McCann was sort of the opposite of Sgt. Raines, at least in appearance and first impression. Here was an old Irishman with fuzzy red hair going to gray, round red face, somewhat overweight and with a rumpled uniform shirt that had caught some of the tobacco juice before it got to the spittoon. He made a terrible impression to look at him, and my heart sank a little, that is until he smiled. Rather, he beamed. That is when his personality came out, right onto that old Irish face. And he cackled like an old crone. With McCann, however, I learned the lesson of not judging a book by its cover, as within about ten minutes I could recognize the consummate professional who sat across from me. The original Old Pro, lucky for me.

On the Navy side my right hand man was Chief Boatswain's Mate Alcorn Berry, a tall, rangy black guy with a quick smile, long sea service and long shore patrol service. He had a firm grip and looked you straight in the eye when he spoke. He was intolerant of anyone who broke the rules, and whoever did, even the slightest infraction, to him was a Crook! It was easy to see that Chief Berry was my type of Navy, totally reliable, experienced and efficient. We got along from the first moment we met.

Police Chief McCann had already rounded up some new and not-so-new Navy gray pickup trucks for use as patrol vehicles, and had somehow come up with my truck (which I ended up sharing with him and Chief Berry), a brand-new Chevy Carryall panel job, completely outfitted as a command vehicle and ambulance, and equipped with police lighting, siren, gun racks and 2-way radios. There might not have been much of a security setup here yet, but by God we had ourselves a truck! It was a real piece of work and I don't think I ever asked McCann where or how he got hold of this thing. Probably best not to.

As there was no security procedures manual for this base, it was our job to write one. I ordered some Navy publications to cover the major areas of security on a base, such as lighting, alarms, weapons,etc., which could be integrated into a manual. But local procedures covering virtually every category needed inclusion also. McCann, Berry and I decided to "rule by memo." That is, to make our decisions on the best way to handle each situation and promulgate them by memo to the staff. The situations we could not anticipate, we covered as they occurred, and wrote a memo. Each memo was placed in a master book by Sgt. Raines, who kept the police force informed and trained on a daily basis.

Of course, I had "borrowed" manuals from other bases, for form and some content. But the bulk of our security manual came from those memos, and I was able to present the finished product to Captain Scott before my year was up. I attribute the success of this methodology to the fact that McCann, Berry and I ended up working so well together. My Navy luck was still holding---that through pure providence I was given such a superb team. Of the thousands of decisions we made, not yet covered by official procedures, every single one was correct with the exception of my one big blooper, which I will get to later.

We were given another building to use as an armory, as we had to have safe storage for an unusually large number of rifles, shotguns (riot guns), side arms, and riot-control gear. This building was down toward the water from the main gate and on the right. It had evidently also been an armory in its previous life, as I found inside a long wooden crate. And in this crate lay the most beautiful, brand-new .50 caliber machine gun you have ever seen. Still in its coat of grease from the factory, and completely not covered by paperwork, entirely forgotten by the Navy. A fleeting thought flashed through my brain, but then I began hearing the words, "Leavenworth, Leavenworth, Leavenworth," in my ear and quickly forgot about it. We re-covered the gun with Navy paper and sent it back into the system.

"My" base was over 400 acres in size and was kind of a fat peninsula jutting out into Lake Washington, with about a mile of shoreline. You can imagine how much the developers and just about everyone else in Seattle wanted to get their hands on that property. It had been a Naval Air Base from 1926 to 1970, so it consisted of a complete air operations complex of airstrip, taxiways, aprons, hangars and bunkers, as well as administration and living quarters, a PX and bottle shop. And of course an officers' club, chiefs' club and enlisted mens' club. In effect we had a small city and society to protect and serve.

The mission of Naval Support Activity, Seattle was to provide logistics support for Naval operations throughout Puget Sound and a good-size chunk of the Pacific. I and my police force were now ready to do our part in this effort.

* * *

Back on the houseboat dock, I was beginning to meet the cast of characters who lived there and who would make this year so much fun. There was of course Gary, who was doing quite well as a grad student, and was getting back into the outdoors. He used the extraordinarily beautiful waters and mountains surrounding Seattle for hiking, camping and skiing.

Ben was Gary's brother, and was frequently over to visit. If Gary was an outdoorsman, then Ben was doubly so. Blond, stocky and athletic, he was very outgoing and ready for adventure at any time.

Greg, Rick and Bill lived in a rather large houseboat across the dock from us and to the right. Greg was a tall, handsome guy, so totally fit and athletic that he had once been the great tennis champion Stan Smith's practice partner. No small deal. At first I thought that Greg, like me, was a little too straight for this dock crowd, but later learned that he was just as crazy as the rest of them.

Rick was a dark Italian guy, not so tall, mild-mannered, funny, whose main mission in life was to "turn on" the whole world to marijuana. He found it so comforting and peaceful, he wanted everyone else to feel that way, too. He just gave the stuff away, and was a very happy guy in his quest. Rick was also a licensed pilot and was always offering to take people for a ride, but for some reason no one really ever wanted to go up with him.

And then there was Bill. Bill was good time Charlie. *He* was crazy. Crazy fun. Always looking for mischief and a laugh. A tall guy with long flyaway hair, sometimes a Fu Manchu moustache, sometimes not. If there were ever any noise on the dock, it usually emanated from him. He worked for Shell Oil, going around inspecting all of their gas stations in the area. A profession totally mundane for such an active mind, but the job market was pretty tight at the time. But even Shell Oil was no match for Bill, as he was able to wring some laughs out of it, sometimes not without consequences.

Mystery Guest lived across the dock and to the left. No one ever saw this person, hence the name. Someone did live there, though, because everything was well tended, plants, etc., and the mail and paper were taken in every day. Later in the year I was up late one night and finally saw someone come out of the house, a rather overweight woman who turned out to be a man, who entertained as a female impersonator at some local club. Now, I was just an innocent boy from Texas and had never seen or heard of anything like that in my life!

And finally, Bruce, who lived two doors down toward the street. He was a small, skinny guy with a large intellect, and had been an engineer at Boeing. He was on unemployment, having been part of the massive layoff of 60,000 people resulting from cancellation of the SST (supersonic transport) project by congress. For a "company town" like Seattle this was a real disaster. But Bruce was getting along just fine. He was a nice guy and was always pleasantly stoned.

Absolutely everything in his house was covered with fake fur. Everything. Also everything in his car.

As a whole, a very esoteric crowd, very bright, laid back, fun and funny. I got a taste of this right away: as most everyone on the dock was rather hippy-ish, I sort of stood out with my "white sidewalls" haircut and khaki uniform. I was still a lieutenant, junior grade, or LTJG, and from the first day that's how I was greeted when I came home: "Hey, LTJG!" From the houseboats, from a boat, from anywhere, whoever was around, it was "LTJG!" From there they

came up with variations, the two most popular being "Officer" and
"Officer Groovy." When I made full lieutenant I was properly
recognized as "LT!"

* * *

As mentioned, I went to and from work in uniform. Not too
long after I arrived in Seattle there occurred a very beautiful day, so I
popped the top off of the Corvette and took off for work. I was trying
different routes to the base on occasion, and on this day I had a few
extra minutes and decided to drive through part of the University of
Washington campus. If looks could kill I would have been dead
meat. Just a guy in uniform in a convertible going to work. I can still
see the sheer *hatred* on those faces, and learned my lesson that
Seattle was a very liberal town and UW was the center of that
radicalism. These people didn't scare me but I was so shocked at
their vehemence! I thought we were all supposed to be on the same
side! On arrival at work I mentioned to McCann that I had just
driven through the campus. He said, "Oh shit, sir, I wouldn't do that
anymore, hee hee hee!" I didn't.

Pretty soon I began to collect my collateral duties along with the
other junior officers. These were all important assignments not
covered by officers as a primary duty, and I never minded the extra
assignments except for the one where I had to inventory the Enlisted
Mens' Club every quarter. Just because it was so boring.

The Navy had a brig in Seattle that handled prisoners for a
good-sized area of the West Coast and was therefore a large
operation. This was run by a senior lieutenant, a heavy-set guy with

dark Mediterranean looks, who, by his demeanor, had been around the block a number of times. He was a genuine tough guy who knew his business, and the longer I knew him the better I liked him because he was an extremely well-rounded and grounded individual.

The XO assigned me to inspect the brig twice a month. This included sighting each prisoner in his cell, speaking with the guards about any problems, and having lunch, eating the same food as did the prisoners. These visits were such a rich experience for me that I began looking forward to them. I also learned why the lieutenant always carried a gun in a shoulder holster: there were some truly bad guys in this prison, and he had received enough death threats to make it necessary.

The last two collateral duties I was assigned were not happy ones, but I took them very seriously and with great solemnity. I was directed to form a detail that would perform the duty of burial with honors for active duty and veteran Navy and Marine personnel in the area. We got together a team with a very sharp Petty Officer, equipped them properly, and trained and drilled them to perform the coffin and flag-handling rituals by the book, and had them ready in fairly short order. These guys were good, and really cared about giving our Navy and Marine brothers and sisters the respect they deserved. We thought about forming a rifle team but there were only so many people to go around, so we decided against it unless full military honors were ordered. At that time we could form a team fairly quickly. The burial detail was called out more often than we had expected. I attended the first few in order to observe the team and to pay my respects. Our guys were very impressive and our bugler blew the most beautiful and haunting "Taps" that one could hope for. I would have no worries about this detail.

The last collateral duty still bothers me. I was assigned to join a group of three or four officers in the sad performance of Death Notification. On a rotating basis, an officer, along with a Navy chaplain, would have to go to the home of a Navy/Marine member to break the news to his loved ones that he had been killed in action or had died of other causes. There were no volunteers for this duty, everyone avoided it like the plague. The lieutenant who ran the brig also "ran" this program and up to that point had been the only one doing notifications. He needed some help.

He called a meeting to give instruction on procedure, which was fairly simple and straightforward, and lots of advice stemming from the many visits he had already made. The most incongruous thing he said was that when you tell the family the bad news, try to leave six feet or so between yourself and them, and prepare to defend yourself. People had come at him swinging fists, and, in particular, women had attacked him with their fingernails. Not everyone reacted in this way, of course, but it had happened. It was a very primeval reaction to terrible news, and the messenger became the focal point of the rage. Even if attacked, you were to be understanding for this reason.

After breaking the news, the officer becomes the liaison between the family and the Navy, to make sure they have to worry about as little as possible concerning the transportation of the service member, burial arrangements, and any paperwork and benefits due them. The warning here was to learn to grow a thick skin and not get too involved with the family, keep a certain distance. It was easy to become so sympathetic and caring that you slip into the role of family member and are sucked in emotionally to this tragedy. You lose your objectivity and it ruins your efficiency. This was maybe the hardest part, as you looked into the sad and wanting eyes of these people.

During my year at NSA Seattle I did three of these Death Notifications, experiences I will never forget. Two service members died while on active duty and a Chief had a skydiving accident. I was never attacked physically but certainly was emotionally.

During the myriad meetings with Capt. Scott and/or his staff, or while scrambling all over the base "putting out fires" while getting situated, I kept running across this Chief Petty Officer, a journalist who was the captain's PAO, or Public Affairs Officer. You could hardly miss him, he was as big as a house, had a very deep, mellifluous "FM" radio voice, and a personality that always engulfed everyone in the room. I never saw Senior Chief Journalist (JOCS) Ron Walker as being black, in fact I never thought about it at all. We just hit it off, as slowly and naturally as something inevitable always is, and became friends. He was very intelligent, articulate, funny, and had that mischievous look in his eye at all times. He was Roosevelt Grier in a Navy uniform, in fact they had met once and agreed that they were about the same size. I don't think Chief Walker could do needlework, however.

Ron Walker would become one of the closest friends I will ever have in this life. We came to love each other as the closest of brothers, something that neither of us gave a second thought to, it just happened. We made kind of funny looking brothers, this huge black guy and a skinny white guy, but there you are, truth being stranger than fiction.

It was Ron who got me into yet another collateral duty. He got wind of a request for a few volunteers for a prisoner escort program, in connection with the brig. This entailed going just about anywhere in the country to collect prisoners and escort them back to Seattle, or taking them from the brig back to their ship or homeport. Ron had already volunteered because it was a chance for travel to new places and new adventures. Of course, because of his imposing size, he would never have a problem with a prisoner. He urged me to jump on it and I did, for the same reasons.

* * *

I was beginning to become more comfortable with my life on the houseboat, as I got into the rhythm of dock life, and found that after the stress and pressures of the day at Sand Point (and there were many), I could go home, get out of the uniform, and become a civilian for awhile. It was very relaxing. The pace was so slow and everyone so mellow. You could go onto the back porch and feed the Canadian Honker geese, our perpetual neighbors always swimming by. Or just sit in the living room with a fire and a glass of Red Mountain wine and stare at the "Mother's Cookies" sign and the boathouse across the lake. One night I was doing just that, when the boathouse just blew up! A terrific explosion and fire, a real light show reflected in the water.

Turns out one of the boats had collected gasoline fumes in its bilge and when the automatic bilge pump came on, the spark blew it apart along with two other boats and part of the boathouse.

Some days I might get home to find that someone has been out diving and speared a nice big salmon. We would clean it, wrap it in foil along with lemon and butter, and slap it on a sort of community barbecue pit on the dock, and let it bake for awhile. Someone would fix up a salad, and you had a most tender and delicious fish dinner with whoever happened to be home. Life was good on the dock.

Lake Union was so polluted that you couldn't swim in it. There was kind of a sickly dark green cast to it and even in the brightest sun you could only see six inches down. Early in the century Seattle's air was foul and black from the coal that was used primarily for cooking and heat. Its use was eventually banned, and was replaced by cleaner-burning fuels shortly after World War I. As such, the air had begun to clear and by 1970 was quite clean and fresh. The sewers were leaking all over town because the wooden staves that had been used for main pipes 80 years before were beginning to give out. The city was busy replacing these with more modern materials. And now there was a movement afoot to clean up Lake Union.

Believe it or not, we and all of the other boats and houseboats around the lake were flushing our waste directly into the water. The city finally ran a sewage line to the dock and invited everyone to pay the hookup fee or else. We all grumbled at the cost but paid because we all felt guilty over fouling the lake every day. And I'll be damned if you couldn't see down three or four feet in less than a year. It was a good start.

As I have said, part of the recreation on the dock involved marijuana. Not that it was a way of life particularly, but just part of it. As "Officer Groovy" I wasn't having any part of it, not only because I was on active duty, but also I saw no need for it and was probably a little jittery about it. Several of those on the dock were gently urging me to try it, telling me about how good it feels and how great music sounds and how funny everyone is and how it enhanced just about everything. I was listening but kept politely refusing, and I wasn't going to crack. Not yet, anyway.

* * *

Somewhere in those first few weeks Captain Scott found time to host a reception at the "O" Club for his staff officers and families or girlfriends. It was a good idea because it gave every officer the chance to meet the whole staff and get acquainted over drinks, and to meet the families or best girls (these days called significant other). Being new in town, I did not have a date, so was free to admire some lovely women. And it was a crying shame that the two who made my pulse beat a little faster were both married, and to guys I really liked! Two strikes and I'm out! But I did get to know both of these ladies well and remember them very fondly today.

There was a LTJG named Tim who assisted in running the brig, whose wife was so pretty, a blonde with a nice figure, a quick wit and brains. We became friends over the next year, and if it hadn't been for Tim I would most certainly have made a run on her.

And then there was Commander Crawford. This guy was so cool. Everyone liked him. I remember going to his office and seeing him sitting there, bald as a newborn baby and smoking his pipe. Well, here he comes through the door, almost unrecognizable in a full wig, looking like a 22 year-old full commander, on his arm one of the most dazzlingly beautiful women I have ever seen. Ever "hear" a room go silent when someone walks in? The room went silent. She was one of those whom I call Nature's Perfect Creature. Black black hair framed electric blue eyes and a face more beautiful than Elizabeth Taylor on her best day, and the chiffon she floated in on couldn't hide her superb figure. A really gorgeous dame. She and I hit it off right away and became fast friends. This was a great couple, good-looking and fun, who gave a great lift to the somewhat staid Officers Club. The girl who followed them into the room was a 16 year-old carbon copy of her mother (maybe that's why Cdr. Crawford had lost all of his hair). She looked like an exquisite angel. The rest of the time we knew each other, her mother was hard at work trying to figure out how to make me a little younger, or how to make her daughter a little older, as we would make the perfect couple. I have always regarded this as one of the nicest compliments I have ever received, coming from such a nice woman who was also one of the World's True Beauties.

I would digress here to talk a little about my CO, Captain David A. Scott. These days the word "hero" has been bandied about so much that it has lost its true meaning. But Capt. Scott was a hero in the old fashioned, WWII sense of the word. He had been a fighter pilot, flying against the Japanese in 1943 and 1944, operating throughout the Solomon Islands. Flying the F4F Wildcat with squadron VSG-11, and the F6F Hellcat with VF-33, the then LTJG Scott became an ace by downing six enemy aircraft in aerial combat. He was also shot down over Rabaul in 1943 and spent Christmas and New Years, 10 days altogether, in a one-man life raft before being rescued. This feat of survival received considerable media coverage back home. For these and other actions, he received the Distinguished Flying Cross (given for heroism or extraordinary achievement in aerial flight), Purple Heart, Air Medal and the Navy Unit Citation.

By the time we "got" him at NSA Sand Point, Capt. Scott had had a distinguished career which included carrier squadrons, several shipboard assignments, two Pentagon tours, Command at Sea on USS Manatee(AO-58) and the Amphibious Assault Carrier USS Iwo Jima(LPH-2) during Vietnam Operations, then Chief of Staff at Naval Air Reserve Training, Glenview, Illinois.

I liked Captain Scott very much. He was a fine leader and a fine man and I was really lucky to have him as a CO. That made two great CO's in a row and for me that was a personal record.

* * *

As I have mentioned, living on the dock was a great way to relieve my tensions and stress of the day, and to help this along I bought what is called a body bag. This is the heavy bag you see boxers hitting, imagining at the time that they are pummeling the enemy in the ring. Well I thought it would be a good way to stay in shape and to clear my head at the same time, and it worked; the tension just melted as I belted. The only place to hang this thing was on the back porch, and so a few evenings a week would find me "out back" pounding away. Pretty soon I found I had acquired a coach, for as I was flailing away one evening, someone yelled, "Uppercut, uppercut, give him an uppercut!" I thought, what the hell was that, and looked around but could see no one. Finally I spotted Bruce---he had a green lap strake rowboat that sat on a floating platform behind his house, and he was lying in it watching me, only his head visible. His favorite punch seemed to be the uppercut and he had great fun yelling it at me from time to time. I never had the heart to tell him that an uppercut was not possible because this bag didn't have much of a chin, which is where you put the well-aimed uppercut.

Bruce spent many afternoons sitting in his boat feeding the Canadian Honkers swimming by, yelling "uppercut" at me, or just lying there contemplating things.

The geese stayed year-round, as they enjoyed the weather and had found a good food source (us). And so they also bred there. One afternoon we found an egg just sitting on the back porch, and did our best to incubate it with a light bulb in a box, but it just sat there doing nothing until we decided it was not fertilized and it began to decompose. So we had to give it a burial at sea. But one day we heard this peeping noise out back, "peep, peep, peep, peep," well, you get the idea. There was a small yellow baby honker paddling around by itself looking lost, no adults in sight. Normally you would leave things alone and hope this chick would be found, but there were large rats lurking along the bank, under the dock and other structures. So Bruce and I formed a Search and Rescue party, and armed with a net, launched his rowboat and gave chase to this chick. And chased. And chased. He, or she, was very fast and was not going to be caught, as we chased all over our end of the lake. After an hour of this, near collapse, we limped back to base, agreeing that that chick wasn't going to be caught by us *or* the rats, and would live a long and healthy life.

Greg and Bill were serving their country in the Air Force Reserve, and were assigned to the same unit. One weekend a month they both dressed in their blue uniforms and walked up to the head of the dock, where an Air Force blue bus would actually pick them up. Now, Greg looked the part, tall and fit in his neat and tidy uniform, while you knew Bill was just faking it---he just didn't look right in a uniform and had no military demeanor whatsoever. Besides, to avoid cutting his longish hair, he managed to wear a short-haired wig with his own tucked under, with a hat on top. The effect wasn't too bad except that during an inspection the wig came askew and Bill caught hell from his CO. He had to cut his hair somewhat but was soon back using his wig. From listening to their "weekend warrior" stories it was apparent that the Air Force wasn't getting much in return for their investment.

As a real jock, Greg had his own ideas on physical fitness. And whenever talk turned to women, which it frequently did, we had a running discussion as to which tummy style was most preferable, "hard belly" or "soft belly." Hard belly was of course the tight, lean, muscular belly of the very fit woman, while soft belly was the more feminine, soft, warm belly with just a slight roll to it. Listen folks, this was serious stuff! And we all spent many hours espousing the attributes of both styles! I think that no one ever really won the argument, it was simply a matter of preference. Greg had a really beautiful girlfriend at the time, and as he pretty much tried to keep her away from the rest of us I don't remember her name, but I do remember that all of us, including Greg, called her "Hard belly."

The group on the dock were very inventive and were interested in games of the mind. There was something called the "book trick" where a hardcover book was simply placed on the floor in the middle of a room. Total quiet was required regardless how many people were there, and the "victim" was asked to take off his or her shoes, stand on the book and close their eyes. After a moment of quiet, one person would ask the victim to clear everything from the mind, relax, and concentrate on the fact that this was not a book but a small platform atop a 50-foot flagpole, and even though the flagpole was beginning to move a little in the wind, you must concentrate on not falling off of the platform. Many people were down below and were watching you. Now the flagpole was beginning to sway a little bit, but you must keep your balance or you will fall. Swaying more and more, people watching, wind blowing. At this point, the person stopped talking completely, and in the silence you could tell who was really concentrating and had this whole picture in their mind because they would begin swaying trying to keep their balance, finally flail their arms and fall off the book. I fell off the book. Sounds stupid doesn't it? But if you are truly able to concentrate, you will fall off the book, which is maybe 2 inches high. (Caution: Please do not try this at home. Falling down 2 inches may be hazardous to your health).

* * *

One Monday morning I walked up the dock toward the parking lot, ready to go to work. Strolling toward the spot where I thought I had parked the car, I vaguely registered that it wasn't there. Not thinking too much of it, I looked around, and in a disbelieving fog,

couldn't find it anywhere. And in slow motion my brain began to
wake up to the fact that the Corvette had been stolen. Shouting a few
obscenities at no one in particular, I went back down to the house.
Needing to get to work and knowing Gary had no classes that day, I
woke him up and told him my car was gone, stolen. He mumbled,
"Oh, shitty Monday mornings," turned over and went back to sleep. I
woke him again to ask if I could use Betty for the day, he said yes,
tossed me the keys and I was gone. Betty was his 60's, faded blue
VW Beetle. She was not quite as elegant as the white Jaguar XK150
roadster (that Gary had owned in San Diego) had been, but she was
far more reliable and somewhat cheaper to run. Anyway, I drove
Betty over to the base and went right in to see McCann.

When I told him what had happened he became all business,
asked me the year and plate number, and picked up the phone to call
someone at the police department. It could have been the Chief of
Police for all I know because within 45 minutes McCann got a call
that the car had been located. I was very impressed. Seattle was a
very large city. Having not expected to see my car again, here it was
found in less than an hour.

Though he tried to cover it, Chief McCann was pleased with all
the praise he got from me and everyone else in the office. He got all
red in the face and I asked him whom he had called and he said, "Oh,
just a friend," and gave a big Irish smile.

The car was not driveable so the police had it towed to a good
garage, where the guy told me a real amateur or amateurs had taken
the car and tried to get the transmission out. Trouble is they didn't
know that the engine has to come out before the trans will. They had
dropped the drive shaft and tried to remove the trans with a 10 lb.
sledgehammer and had pretty well beat things up. Frustrated, they

had left it on the roadside and thankfully had not taken it out on the fiberglass with that sledge. The garage kept it for two weeks and got it back to me in perfect running (and shifting) shape, plus a nice shiny new red paint job.

As previously mentioned, anti-war and thus anti-military feelings were running pretty high in Seattle in those days. In fact, prior to my arrival, 1970 saw some pretty heavy riots and demonstrations, particularly in and around the month of May. This was always of concern to the FBI and they kept their antennae tuned to any hint of problems concerning the military installations in town. Of course I was directly affected and was ordered to raise and train a riot control team. We had heard of a riot control course being taught down at Fort Lewis, Washington, and I was able to get a slot and went down for this one-day course. It was chock full of information given by professional MP's, including how to make jelly-gas (crude napalm) from soap flakes and gasoline, and more than we ever wanted to know about CS, or tear gas. In order to drive home the effect that tear gas can have on a crowd, and why it was important for us to always have a gas mask handy in riot situations, the Army gassed all of us.

There were a dozen or so of us "students," all men except for one woman, an Army WAC, who was wearing a skirt (this is important). We became familiar with the gas mask, how it works and how to use it properly. An instructor then led us into a sealed room and explained what was going to happen next. They were going to pop some CS canisters and, on command, we would put on our gas mask. After checking each of us for a proper seal and that we could breathe easily, he would call us up, one at a time, to stand facing him, exactly 12 inches away. On his signal we had to rip off our mask and stare at his eyes without blinking. Immediately the most painful burning engulfed our eyes and nose, like they were on fire. The problem was that we had to keep staring at him until he had made his point: CS really hurts! Only on his signal could we bolt out through a side door into the fresh air and hose down our eyes and face. There was much foul language because everyone was hurting, especially the WAC, who had double trouble. She was burning at both ends because someone had "forgotten" to tell her to either wear pants or to apply a coat of Vaseline to her private parts, which were as sensitive to CS as were her eyes and nose. She was really mad, rightfully so, and I am sure this was a little private running joke among the Army instructors.

Other than that it was a pretty good class, and the printed materials they provided gave me the basics I needed to form a force. We put together a 25-man team using a mix of my civil service policemen and sailors, and headed up by Sergeant Raines. They were outfitted in blue jumpsuits with white combat helmets, yard-long riot batons, gas masks and a web belt for side arms. They were drilled and drilled and drilled in moving formation tactics and the effective use of the baton, in order to repel rioters. Our jurisdiction was just to the inside of our gates and fence, and the outside belonged to the Seattle Police Department.

There were some rumblings that an "event " was about to take place, and one day my "ace in the hole" came in to see me. This guy was a veteran FBI agent (of course, an old friend of McCann's) who could have just stepped out of a Humphrey Bogart film noir or a Mickey Spillane paperback. He was roughly handsome, steel gray hair in a crew cut, a long scar ran north to south on the left side of his face, and of course his name was Sam Patton. Had to be. He talked tough and he *was* tough, and he had my full attention. Sam turned out to be a great guy, very savvy, who could give us a lot of advice and would be our liaison with the Bureau until the troubles passed.

The expected troubles took the form of the Mayor of Seattle. Hizzoner was not the kind of mayor I was used to in Texas, you know, where they wear a suit and tie. No, my lingering impression is of a guy in a cutoff sweatshirt who wore a beard or at least didn't shave much. Wes was okay, though.

To give a little background to this story, we had stored on the base a large supply of surplus government butter and cheese, which were bought up in the form of subsidies from the butter and cheese farmers in order to reduce a flood on the market and keep prices stable.

The mayor was to address a large rally or demonstration or some such thing and the FBI sensed that there could be some trouble coming our way. Sam Patton had stopped by to see us and to say that we should be ready to protect the base. He said he would have an operative in the crowd with a radio so we would always know what the "temperature" was, minute-to-minute.

McCann talked to the Seattle Police and made arrangements with them to respond if we called. All of our ducks were now in order to cover most anything that could happen.

Well, Hizzoner didn't disappoint. On the big day, he got up in front of this crowd and began talking about the fact that many people didn't have enough to eat, etc., etc., etc. Eventually he got to the part about all of that butter and cheese stored at Sand Point, and *why don't we just go down there and get it!* Well, my phones lit up like a

Christmas tree and we sprang into action, closing and locking the main gates and doing a general lockdown of the base. The police arrived in force and blocked the gates with men and cars. Our riot team was suited up and it was decided to station them inside the armory (less visibility might mean less provocation), as a surprise force to "repel boarders" if necessary.

Alas, sort of, we got all dressed up and had nowhere to go. It was all very exciting and we were ready for action, but all it turned out to be was hot air and the crowd never made it to the base. So the Great Butter and Cheese Raid never took place, thank goodness. But everyone involved on our side took great satisfaction in a well-planned and -executed evolution.

My division was sort of a catch-all for sailors in transit, in trouble, or awaiting orders. Sometimes we had to "make work" for these guys but for the most part there was something for them to do. Once I had a sailor who was awaiting separation due to his chronic drinking problem. He had been told that there would be no drinking while he was with us and he had given his word. But there was just something about him and we wanted him out of there as quickly as possible.

The armory was nearing completion. Four large fabricated steel containers in which to store our firearms and ammunition, with three locks and an alarm system in front of them. A working party was to be formed to transfer by hand all of these weapons from their temporary home in my holding cells to the armory. Each guy was to carry one weapon, checking it out of the holding cell and checking it back in to the armory. All weapons were *of course* not loaded, having been thoroughly inspected before storage.

Well, I wheel into work the next day and walk through the front door to see Sgt. Raines behind the counter, rigid as a fencepost with eyes as big as silver dollars. Like he had just seen a ghost. I was about to ask him what was wrong when I smelled spent gunpowder and saw all of the white smoke in the back office. Raines managed to tell me that a shotgun had just gone off but no one was hurt. Leaping through the door I saw Chief Berry towering like the Angel of Death over the same cowering sailor trying very hard to make himself small on the couch. There was a hole the size of a dinner plate in the wall, smoke everywhere, several sailors and police frozen in place, and McCann making sure there were no more shells in the gun.

There had been a line of men carrying weapons to the armory and this sailor, whom we determined had been drinking again, somehow chambered a shell into a 12-gauge shotgun, lowered it and pulled the trigger, making a deafening BOOM and scaring the shit out of everyone, and barely missing a sailor who had just walked past the line of fire. The blast would have caught him about waist-high.

After putting a stop to the transfer and notifying my boss and the XO of what had happened, Chief Berry, McCann and I took this hapless guy into my office for questioning about his near-fatal action. We needed to know how a supposedly empty weapon came to be loaded, cocked and fired. He was no help whatsoever, was only confused and very scared.

This could have been a lot uglier had someone been hit. It is still a great relief to me that no one was. After an investigation it was determined to be an unexplainable accident, but we triple-checked each remaining weapon before it was transferred. The hole was patched, the transfer was completed without further incident, and that miserable little guy was out of the Navy so fast his head may still be spinning.

During my year at Sand Point I was called to serve on two Courts Martial. While preparing to serve on the first one I recalled my step father's story about his first time serving on a Court Martial where the sailor involved was convicted and given a dishonorable discharge. When admonished by the President of the Court on the fact that the dishonorable discharge was very serious and would follow him the rest of his life, the sailor replied, "Well sir, it don't make no difference to the back end of a mule." Whereupon I guess he went back to the farm, hitched up the mule and plowed his fields. In this case he was probably right.

The first panel I served on involved the sale and use of drugs on Navy property, was pretty cut-and-dry, and resulted in a dishonorable discharge. That was helped along by the lousy service record of the accused and his really bad attitude.

The other one was not so easy. The sailor was just a kid, a nice guy and very respectful to the court. He and another Navy man had been caught in "the act" and charges were brought. (In those days "Don't ask, Don't tell" was de facto Navy policy and actually worked quite well. Just don't get caught!) The problem was he loved the Navy and was an exemplary sailor. He had homosexual tendencies, though, and was really ashamed of them, but he just couldn't help himself. During questioning he wept on the stand while giving some very honest and heartfelt testimony. During deliberations the whole court was sympathetic to the plight of this sailor, and voted to separate him from the service with a general discharge, which would stand him in better stead than something worse. And I will never forget the compassion with which the President of the Court, a full Captain, delivered the verdict and remarks to this sailor.

* * *

Three Dog Night was my music of choice (oh, heck, throw in some Joe Cocker and Creedence Clearwater, too), and there was a commercial-free, very hip radio station that played mostly them and Janis Joplin, and there were many cold evenings when we would light a fire, stare out across the lake at the Mother's Cookies sign, sip our Red Mountain or Red Ripple wine, and listen. It was good times, all right. The station really was the sound of Seattle.

They were so cool and laid back, that I remember two incidents that just bent them out of shape: one when the deejay announced that Janis Joplin had died of an overdose of heroin, he was so angry that he could barely talk. His rage was so great, he tried to talk through clenched teeth, and I wondered with whom he was so upset. Seemed he was blaming the Establishment, certainly not Janis herself.

And I know it was the same guy whom I happened to hear one day, grimly announcing that the station could no longer afford to continue without commercials, and the first one would come along in a few minutes. He did it live, and you have never heard a commercial delivered with such disgust and passion and despair, again through clenched teeth, for Hershey's Chocolate Bars. I don't think the station or the cool deejay ever recovered from that one, as it might have signaled the end of an era.

Once in awhile when everyone on the dock had a buzz on from the usual suspects or just from life, someone might say, "Let's do a Flaming Groovy!" All would totally agree, and would proceed to lie on their back in a circle, shoulders just touching. One would place a large bowl of water in the circle's center, while someone else took the clear plastic cover from their cleaning, tied a knot in it every 3 or 4 inches, and hung it by one end from a hook in the ceiling, directly above the bowl of water. The lights were then turned off and the lower end of the plastic was lit.

What happened next was just ethereal, and the higher you were, the better. Quiet, dark room, with just the small flame burning, until it came to a knot. As the knot burned and became superheated, it dropped off of it's own weight and *the assault on your senses began!* As it dropped, the blob looked like a fireball coming right at your eyes, and that, combined with the sound of a large caliber bullet whizzing by your head, was enough to send everyone into the cosmos. The room filled with "oooh" and "aaah" and "Jesus" and "far out," and other sounds of pleasure and wonder, and then came the disappointment as it ended. But for a while each person was transported to his or her own universe. The effect was just stunning.

Now, those times are gone, kids, so please don't try this yourself, as it could prove dangerous. Besides, neither it nor the words "groovy" or "far out" have actually been used in 40 years. Except by my groovy wife.

* * *

Our Officers' Club was a pretty nice facility. The Bachelor Officer Quarters (BOQ) was in the same building and consisted of rooms furnished with really "Early Navy" furniture, very plain but comfortable enough. Sometimes when I had The Duty (as Officer Of The Day, meaning an overnight stay) I would take a room here rather than sleep on the "duty" bed in my office, just for a change of scenery.

There was a restaurant decorated in "Early Navy Stuffy Formal," with carpet in neutral colors in a floral design, which was used mainly by the older officers and the many retirees who lived in the area. "Across the tracks" and downstairs was the bar and an informal restaurant used by the younger officers. In the bar hung a sign that read, "Whoever enters covered here, shall buy the house a round of beer." If an officer came in with his hat on, the bartender would ring a ship's bell several times, and serve everyone a beer, compliments of the forgetful officer. I believe I had to pay up one time, but thankfully there were only a few people there.

Once I had the bright idea to put on a Rock 'n Roll dance down there on a Friday night. There was a small stage and dance floor in the bar, and arrangements were pretty easy to make, including the CO's provisional okay, and I was able to get a very good band that I had heard once downtown.

Well, we had a great turnout, with even some more senior officers showing up, with lotsa beer and booze, lotsa beautiful girls, and everybody danced! With visions of making this a regular thing I went to see the Captain the next Monday, and he retracted the "provisional" part of his okay. He told me that he had heard what a lot of fun we had but regretfully he had to pull the plug because many of the retirees having dinner upstairs had complained about the noise. He *did* regret it, I know, he had no choice, but I was severely deflated and decided not to try anything like that again.

Probably not by coincidence, it was about this time that I began going to the Chiefs' Club more often. Chief Ron Walker had asked me over a few times but I had demurred because the other Chiefs may not like having an officer hanging around, limiting their conversation and their good time. But when I did finally start going for a drink or two after work, Ron would simply stand up, get everyone's attention, and announce, "There's an officer present but don't worry, he's one of us." He's one of us. I heard Ron say that many times when he introduced me to someone new. It was as if I were being let into a secret society, which, in effect, I was. Not many officers had such entrée to enlisted Navy people as I did. Some of it was due to Ron and some of it derived from the fact that I found them easy to get along with and liked them. It would have been quite a different story if my own Chief Berry were using the club, as we worked together every day, but Berry didn't drink, and besides he headed right home to "mama" at the end of the day.

There are many characters in the world of the Chief Petty Officer, and most of them belonged to that club. It was always great fun: sometimes boisterous and very comical. Many of us were Vietnam veterans, and so the stories flowed, most of them bullshit. As we had Army and Marine tenants on the base, the Sergeants would show up and join in. There was one guy, a black Army Master Sergeant, with ribbons from here down to there, who wore a Montagnard bracelet. He was Special Forces, in those days better known as Green Berets, who had served with the Montagnard people in the Central Highlands. He didn't talk about his missions much, but when he did it was enough to curl your hair. Speaking of curly hair, he was called "Buffalo Soldier" (a nickname given by American

Indians to black cavalrymen in the 19th century because their hair resembled the tuft of fur between the horns of a buffalo, and like the buffalo, were courageous). I never knew his name, just Buffalo Soldier. You could tell his peers respected him by their demeanor when he was around. But Ron always needled his funny bone and got him to telling some of the funniest stories I have ever heard. Buffalo Soldier's biceps were as big as footballs.

Off base, I could go out with my friends from the dock because, notwithstanding my military haircut, all of them were totally "local," therefore I blended in and there was never a problem. With military friends it was a different story, though. The base and its clubs offered refuge from the hostility of the anti-war people (which sometimes felt like just about everyone in Seattle), but there was one place we all could go to unwind and feel welcomed, and that was Vancouver, British Columbia, a couple of hours north on Interstate 5. No hassle, no problems, and a beautiful city. It was so nice that you could knock off work and run up there for dinner, even in uniform! I took a date there several times, and small groups of us would go regularly.

One afternoon we received word that Army Chief of Staff General William Westmoreland would be flying into the Naval Base by helicopter in a few days and we were needed over there to provide security for his arrival. Making the arrangements was pretty easy: we would circle the landing pad with four or five trucks with armed police to ensure his safe passage from the pad to a staff car. McCann would go to supervise his police officers and I would go to represent the Navy and, well, because I wanted to have a look at this guy.

On the appointed day we moved out to the Naval Base and set up our security perimeter, made radio checks, and we were ready. We had been advised that three Army helicopters would be coming in, and for security reasons we nor anyone else would know which one he was on. Also, we were told that he might be piloting his own ship.

Soon enough, we heard the distant beating of rotor blades and then this huge roar as three Huey choppers in a line came in low and fast over the treetops toward us and landed one, two, three. McCann and I were standing off to the right side. Almost as soon as it touched down, the first chopper's pilot door burst open and out bounded Four Star General of the Army William Westmoreland.

He was a tall, handsome guy who *looked* like a general should look, and had an aura of power about him that very few people can wear well. He moved very quickly, and was making a beeline toward his waiting car when he spied me and McCann standing at attention giving our very finest salutes. He broke stride and came toward us. He returned our salute and offered a firm handshake to me and said, "Hi, I'm General Westmoreland." In the back of my mind I'm saying, "No shit, sir" while in the front of my mind I'm stammering out something like, "Lieutenant Cook, sir." He then turned, said, "Hi, McCann, how're you doing," pumped his hand two or three times, turned away, bounded into his staff car and was gone in a cloud of dust.

I think the whole thing lasted about 45 seconds. I looked around at McCann, who had this goofy grin on his face, looking after the disappearing car. He was pleased no end, red-faced and beaming. He said, "Gee, how'd he know my name?" I said, "Well, chief, you've become pretty well known around here," as I surreptitiously looked down at the plastic name tag on his jacket. He never figured it out and I wasn't about to tell him. And I am quite sure that when that old Irishman was laid to rest, he still had that same grin on his face.

* * *

During my year in Seattle I was fortunate to know three lovely ladies. I met Stephanie at the "O" Club bar one afternoon. She was just about all legs, which mostly showed as she perched up on a barstool in a short skirt, and blinded me. She was a very sweet girl and we dated for a while but a problem developed when she fell really hard for me, and scared the daylights out of this 26 year old lieutenant. So I let another wonderful girl slip away. Peggy, the "girl with the green eyes" was introduced to me by Ron Walker. She was beautiful to look at, was really unconventional, and had these mesmerizing green cats' eyes that I often fell into, feeling like James Stewart in *"Vertigo."* Once we went to a club downtown and were dancing, and I guess my normal rigid dance style was showing. Peggy said, "You're not hearing the music, just look into my eyes." Well, I did, and went into what I can only describe as a trance. I not only could hear the music as never before, I lost all sense of time and space. It was wonderful, like taking a trip through a Stargate.

Peggy also often got up in the middle of the night in her own trance, went to her easel and frantically painted the loveliest oils you have ever seen. In the morning she couldn't recall anything except that her hand was guided by an Italian artist who had lived six centuries ago. These days whenever I see a good emerald I still think of those beautiful eyes and get a little dizzy.

Then there was the lovely Polynesian girl who came to work in the office of the BOQ. The minute word got around about her, officers from miles away began showing up, walking all over their tongue, ostensibly to have some of that great Navy chow. She was just about perfect, small with a great figure, dark skin and hair down to her waist. Since, in my job I knew everything that happened on the base, sometimes before it happened, I got to her first. I became delirious when she told me that by night she was also a Tahitian dancer. The first time I saw her dancing with three other girls, all decked out in costumes of red and white feathers, I thought she was so beautiful that I almost passed out. Something like what we would call today "sensory overload." There were certainly beautiful and interesting women in Seattle!

* * *

I discovered another social event on the dock called a "Food Trip." After partying for a while, the whole group would get really hungry and 2 or 3 people would go to the market and just buy everything in sight, literally filling a cart, and take the food back where it was "gang-cooked" and then everyone ate everything. It was a massacre, but much fun and the food was always quite good.

One of those Food Trips occurred, but not before Bill made a call to a friend of his to order a "two pack," or rather two joints of marijuana. His friend had a PHD in something or other, but had elected to drive a gasoline tanker truck for a living, and to grow the most mellowing marijuana imaginable in the mountains outside of Seattle. A "two pack" was enough to waste a roomful of people, which it did on this occasion, but he would never accept payment; rather, he enjoyed seeing people have a good time.

While the dinner was being cooked it became clear that a few ingredients were missing and I volunteered to go back to the market for them. On my return, as I was coming back down the dock with a bag of groceries, I did not realize that the cold and the drizzle had combined to create treacherous Black Ice on the wooden planks. My feet just disappeared from under me, and WHAM! I crashed exactly flat on my back, my whole body hitting at the same time. It must have made a loud noise, I think it echoed through the 55-gallon drums under the dock, and people came to the windows to see. I lay there for a little while trying to remember who I was and slowly moved one arm and then the other to see if there was any damage. Something had gone "crunch" on impact, and I checked my watch, which was smashed to bits. I got to laughing at my ridiculous self and the groceries lying all over the dock and in the water. But my friends came to the rescue, and we salvaged enough food to complete a very fine meal. The knot on my head went away after a week or so.

A group of guys were going on a ski weekend up to Crystal Mountain, about 75 miles from town. Being a Texas boy, I had never skied before but was game enough, and Gary said he would teach me the basics. The others were able to go on Thursday, but Bill and I had to work and so had to leave Friday afternoon.

We met at the dock to change and grab our gear. His girlfriend was there to see us off. She had baked some chocolate chip cookies for the trip, and put a brown paper bag full of them on the front seat. Bill drove, and we headed for the mountains.

We had wanted to leave earlier in the day to avoid driving at night, but were unable to. Darkness came quickly, and the road was slippery and dangerous. Plus, we didn't really know where we were going because once we got to Crystal Mountain, we had to find this small, *unheated* cabin somewhere out in the woods. So we were trying to be careful so as not to go off the road, and played some music on the radio.

About halfway up both of us realized we were hungry, and each ate a couple of the cookies. In a little while I began to feel really relaxed and the music was sounding good. When the lights going by began to move up and down and all around, and all four of the car's tires slipped their bond with earth and we began floating, I turned and said, "Uh, Bill," and he said, "I know, she must have baked some grass into the cookies." And he was really angry that she hadn't said so because he was working so hard trying to be safe and this only complicated things. We had to slow down further, and crawled up the mountain. Finally, very late, we found the ski resort but it took another 45 minutes to find the cabin. The other guys were there and it was *so cold* inside. Fortunately Gary had advised me to buy a "mummy" type sleeping bag, and I woke up next morning without much frostbite.

My first day of skiing was almost my last, as the old ego took a severe bruising along with my knees and rear end. Gary, true to his word, took me through the basics: snowplow, snowplow turns, snowplow stop, and elementary parallel skiing and stopping. (I couldn't help but notice that he was skiing down the hill backwards while teaching me). I didn't know then that there was such a thing as a baby slope, so I left to practice by myself on a medium difficulty slope. It was a mistake because I fell so often that frustration and a sore knee began to get to me. What took the cake, though, was when I was down, in various awkward positions, these little 24-inch tall children came schussing by me like Spyder Sabich. Finally retiring from the field, I salvaged the day next to a large, warm fireplace and with several cups of hot spiced wine. Deeelicious!

* * *

About mid-tour I made the rank of full lieutenant. Captain Scott officiated at the small ceremony in his office, and pinned the silver bars on my collar (another frocking), as he did for one other officer. The double bars on each collar look like railroad tracks, and that's what they are commonly called. There is an old Navy joke that rather than having your bars pinned on your collar, you should be tough enough to have them, with the two little spikes sticking out, driven into your body (I think the Marines really do that). There is a funny Navy photograph of Capt. Scott about to drive them into Lt. Cook with his fist. In the afternoon there was a gathering of officers at the "O" Club bar, for the frocking party for the two of us new lieutenants. There is nothing frivolous, despite outward appearance, about these events, as they reach far back into Naval history and lore, and signify the camaraderie and traditions of the Officer Corps.

Boatswain's Mate Chief Alcorn Berry was worth his weight in gold, both literally and figuratively. Besides being my able right arm he was a very interesting fellow. I had been to his apartment once where he introduced me to his wife, a small, shy Philippino woman. She was also the daughter of the Chief of Police of Olongapo City, The Philippines (if you remember, the city just outside the gates of the Naval Base at Subic Bay), which meant that he was a very powerful man, and that she was extremely influential. Chief Berry really didn't know how well he had married because one day he brought in a stack of papers and asked me if I could go through them and help him figure what they were all about. I started reading the first one, thankfully it was in English rather than Tagalog, and found that it was a deed to some property in Olongapo, in his wife's name. So I told Berry that he was the proud owner of a commercial building there. We both thought that was pretty good so I went to the next page and found that he and she also owned a bar on the main drag in town. I was getting the idea now, so I began flipping through the whole stack of papers and found that each one was a deed for something. The stack was over two inches thick! There were mainly commercial buildings, bars, apartment houses and vacant land. And I was totally impressed! I looked up at him and said, "Chief, you're rich!"

He smiled so large that I could see all of his teeth: "What? Naw! Really? Naw!" all in the same sentence, and he began laughing and I laughed along with him. He had suddenly discovered he was wealthy and I was really happy for him because he was such a good man. Even though these properties were probably not worth as much as they would be in the U.S. (or maybe they were), the sheer volume of those deeds would assure Chief and Mrs. Berry a very long and comfortable retirement in the Philippines.

I will always remember and laugh about an incident concerning Chief Berry and my step father. See, the Chief knew he was an Admiral but not that he was Commander, Naval Reserve Training Command. That meant he was head of Training and Administration of Reserves (TAR in Navy parlance) for surface ships, more commonly known as the Head TAR. Well, Chief Berry hated all TARS, who were designated USNR (reservist) as a career path. They had always been a thorn in his side for one reason or another, and when he vented about TARS I never said anything because I didn't want to ruin his fun.

So, one afternoon he came into the office all upset about something, and all he could say was, "Goddamn TARS, Goddamn TARS, Goddamn TARS!" I could see McCann beginning a grin (he knew what Zim did for a living) and pretty soon he burst out into his cackle, "Hee, hee, hee, Berry, do you know who his father is?" This caught Berry in mid-rant, and he looked from McCann to me and back to McCann and said, "No, who?" And McCann burst out laughing, "He's Admiral Zimmermann, the Head TAR for the Navy, hee, hee, hee!" Well, I swear Chief Berry blushed, really, it caught him so off guard. "Who? What? Naw! You're father's the Head TAR? Naw!" (Delivered in his great Southern accent). And we were all laughing including the Chief, who covered his face with his hands in disbelief that his mortal enemies (except for all Crooks, that is) "belonged" to my step father. He started to apologize but I just held up my hand and said, "Oh, no, Chief, that's your business, forget about it. But you should see the look on your face!" So it was okay. But I believe I have never seen anything to match this one moment of pure comic timing, before or since.

Note: Upon his retirement in 1972 after 32 years of Naval service, Rear Admiral Edwin J. Zimmermann, Jr. commanded a reserve force of approximately 52 ships, 150,000 personnel, and 250 training centers. This command was so stressful that he lasted barely three years into retirement before dying of a massive heart attack at the age of only 57 years. Upon Zim's death, Admiral Zumwalt, Chief of Naval Operations, sent a very personal and moving letter to my mother. I still keep it.

Besides normal base police business, there were many adventures to be had out on the vast airstrip complex, which was no longer in regular use. Due to its size it was regularly patrolled, as was the perimeter road skirting Lake Washington, since we were really vulnerable to trespass by boat. The entire year I was there we did battle with "The Phantom," the pilot of a small plane that practiced "touch and goes" on the main runway all the time. He was good, he was wily, and he would bait us and then get away at the last minute, before we could read the ID numbers beneath his wings. Of course, what he was doing was trespassing on federal property, and the FAA would have loved to talk to him, but he threw down his gauntlet early and must have enjoyed seeing our trucks speeding down the runway trying to read his numbers. Whenever he would cut it a little close, he would angle his wings so that neither top nor bottom could be seen, and flee into the ozone. We were very zealous in our pursuits, and never caught him (or her), but had we done so, we probably would have missed the game.

I thought we might have had The Phantom at last when, while out driving the perimeter road. I looked over at Lake Washington just in time to see a small plane literally cartwheel a couple of times by its wingtips and flop into the water right-side up. (I was never able to figure exactly how that plane had hit the water in order to perform this peculiar stunt.) The pilot scrambled out onto a wing and as I was calling in to the office to notify the Seattle Police, a private boat came over to pick him up before the plane sank into very shallow water. Whoever I talked to in the office eagerly asked if it was The Phantom, but I had to say no, the colors on the plane were all wrong. So our nemesis lived to fly and taunt another day.

Out on the field were old underground ammunition and fuel bunkers, long since welded shut, and several above-ground storage buildings which were used only by resident owls for roosting and pooping. A number of requests had come in to my office from guys who were going to Vietnam, for space to park their cars for 6 months to a year. They would normally have to find a storage company and pay a monthly charge while away at war, which could get expensive. I got approval from the CO to do a quick survey of any suitable buildings, and came up with a pretty good-sized one which, while very dusty inside, stayed dry and the owls weren't getting inside to poop on the floor. And we set up an informal storage garage for these guys so we could help them out a little. My guys would check out the cars a couple of times each month, and there was never a problem. I thought that was awfully decent of the Captain to approve.

* * *

As I have said, there was never a dull moment when Bill was around. On a day when he didn't feel like working (as the gas station inspector), he would call his supervisor to report on the stations he had (actually had not) visited, and during a lull in the conversation he would pick up one end of a black hose and blow into it. This produced the old "double bell" sound we would make when driving into a station in those days. The bell was at the other end of the hose, attached to the wall above his bed. You just had to be there to see and hear this insanity. He would get through this routine with a straight face, then roll over and go back to sleep. No one should ever underestimate the inventiveness and humor of this guy.

We all knew he was just treading water in this job, where he had to call in six times a day to report to some drone. He came pretty close to "early separation" one day when he was discovered in his car in the company parking lot, smoking a joint for lunch.

The last I heard of Bill, he was living with a beautiful girl on a mountaintop in Peru, raising llamas. It figures.

There was one more major food trip, only this time Bill's friend came by earlier with his two pack. A good-sized group of people got ripped and then got really hungry. It was one of those special times when everyone and everything were funny, in fact so funny that by the time dinner was ready, which was late, a large round table loaded with delicious food went totally untouched! We all had been laughing so hard and for so long, the appetite was gone. No one ate a thing! So about 20 lbs. of spaghetti and meatballs and garlic bread and salad and a fairly decent wine went begging for customers.

One enduring image I have is of Bruce in the bathroom trying to use the new-fangled Water Pic. Trouble is he was trying to use it 12" from his face and only succeeded in squirting himself in the eye and up his nose. We all had a look at this and the laughter never ended. Greg and Bill also introduced us to their "Old Time Movies," where one would flip the lights on and off very fast and the other would do a pantomime. It looked like a movie made in 1920, and in our condition, it was a riot!

Rick was one of those guys who was so quiet and unpretentious, you hardly ever noticed he was there. A thoroughly nice human being, he had not one ounce of aggression or anger in his whole body. He wouldn't hurt a fly. At least that's what we *thought!*

One afternoon I was driving home just after one of those "Seattle showers," and happened to see Rick walking home, up ahead of me on the same side of the street. He had on a raincoat, and was carrying a briefcase and a folded umbrella. Well, the car ahead of me went through a big puddle and splashed poor Rick from head to toe, and just kept on going. And Rick lost it. He became a wild man, running after the car and beating on it with his umbrella until the terrified driver was able to drive off. I was so shocked at this outburst of violence that I broke out laughing. It looked like a Charlie Chaplin movie. I pulled alongside to see if he wanted a ride home, but he said no, thanks, he was too upset and that he'd better walk it off. I never mentioned this episode on the dock because no one would have believed me anyway.

Rick was always a dark nut-brown color, which we attributed to his obvious Italian heritage. But I and the others came to find out that it was also a very good tan, which he must have worked on in great secrecy. The discovery was made when we all went to the beach for the day.

Now, the whole dock had been convinced that Bruce was our resident eccentric person, but we were to find out that wasn't quite true. Rick almost topped him by merely getting ready for a suntan.

From the car he took out his beach towel and his kit, a small case with a handle, sort of like a tackle box, and went down to the water's edge. There he spread the towel, sat down, opened the case and proceeded to set up shop. We watched in fascination as he took out different bottles, one by one, and methodically spread the contents all over himself. There were ten bottles. When asked what was in them, he was evasive, saying only that there was purified water, aloe, salt water, and some other things. I think he wanted to protect some secret formula. This ritual took a half-hour, and we were rolling our eyes and winking at each other. But, eccentric or not, it really worked because he always had the best tan this side of George Hamilton.

* * *

People came to us with all sorts of requests for use of the airfield. Goodyear submitted a request to base their blimp there so it could fly for the annual "Sea Fair" and hydroplane races. A deal was worked out, and part of the tradeoff was that base personnel who wanted to, would get a free ride on the blimp. So I, along with many others, got a float on this rather eccentric machine, and it was nice, and slow and smooth, and kind of like riding an old Greyhound bus. But moving so slowly through the air, you could really take in the scenery and realize how beautiful Seattle and the lakes really are. I think we attained a speed of about Mach Zero.

Due to Chief McCann's special relationship with the Seattle PD, we saw a lot of them. Part of our land was sort of hilly. The top of one hill was flat, and a perfect size for training police dogs. So on some days one could take a ride over there and watch these really professional policemen train their magnificent K-9 partners in the art of neutralizing bad guys. Even though the "crook" had on plenty of padding, it was plain scary to watch what these dogs were capable of. On our part, there were no tradeoffs for this evolution, as the only possible one would have involved taking turns in the padded suit. Forget that!

The police did offer, however, another interesting proposition: Chrysler-Plymouth was trying to interest the SPD in changing their entire fleet of police cars over to the Plymouth Satellite, and offered up two of them, brand-spanking new, for testing. Someone was using their head, and combined this testing with a high-speed driving course for new officers. All they needed was a place, and our main runway fit the bill. An arrangement was made, again with a proviso: I, LT. Beesley (my boss), and a couple of other officers were given the opportunity to go through the high-speed course. So we and a number of green police officers went through the class with a seasoned police instructor. There was a long, straight course laid out on the runway, and a curvy, very difficult one laid out on the outer roads.

When I was called away from the office for my turn, I went down there and the instructor handed me a crash helmet to wear. I thought, "Uh-oh," and asked if this was really necessary, and he said if I wanted to do the course I had to wear it. I soon found out why, as the instructor, to show me what was expected, drove over both courses, deftly handling the new car but punishing it terribly. What he did was a little scary but I thought I was such a great driver it would be a piece of cake. I found that I was slightly overrating myself as a road ace.

I got into the driver's seat, helmet on and strapped in. We were on the runway course, and the instructor told me to start rolling and then to accelerate to 95 miles per hour. I thought, *"all right!"* We practiced high-speed lane changes, as he yelled, "Right lane, left lane," I had to snap the car into that lane without losing control, such as rolling it. At the end, he told me to get back to speed, then he yelled, "Hit the brakes, *hard!*" So at 95 mph I slammed the brakes as hard as I could, fighting to keep the front wheels straight. Try that in the old family Buick Special sometime! I nearly ate the steering wheel and the screeching tires made my ears ring. The stench of burnt rubber filled the car. He said I did passably well at this, and now we drove over to the obstacle course.

The idea here was to drive through many curves and turns as quickly as possible without hitting any cones or anything else. The instructor held a stopwatch, as your time determined your grade. I was thinking I would show this guy, after all I was a Corvette driver, and proceeded to knock down a dozen or so cones and to spin out with my clumsy driving. He didn't even consult the stopwatch because of all the "pedestrians" I had killed, and told me I had flunked. It brought me down a peg or two, all right. By the time everyone had been trained, one of the Plymouths had burned a piston and the other had its brakes literally burned out. I do not know if the SPD ever switched over.

Now to get to my one big boner in Seattle. I had of course long known that to enter the base, each vehicle had to have a valid base sticker displayed on the front bumper, driver's side. My office issued these stickers, and they were supposed to match the government ID card of the driver. It had always bothered me a bit that we waved these cars through without periodically checking ID's; who knew who was coming on base in a legal car? Especially in Seattle? There were all sorts of people in that city who wished us harm.

So of my own volition, without informing my superiors, I ordered an ID check to take place one morning as people drove into the base. Simple, right? All they had to do was pull out their wallet, flash a valid card at the guard, and be on their way. Well, what a disaster! Half the people couldn't even find their card, and the other half took forever to dig around in their wallet or purse or their glove box and by the time we were ½ hour into the exercise, traffic was backed up so far on Sand Point Way in both directions and all of my phone lines were lighting up, that I had to take a big gulp and call the whole thing off. I realized that it's possible I could have issued an alert that ID's would be checked on a certain date, but that would have defeated the purpose of the thing.

Boy, were there a lot of angry people, all late for work. It didn't really bother me, though, because they *should* have had their ID ready at all times. I waited for a call from the Captain, or the XO, or even from my boss, but none ever came. I think they figured I was just doing what I was supposed to be doing.

But I did get a call from Captain Koenig, Commandant of the 13th Naval District, who was a tenant on the base. I had known a few people who had been called on his carpet (by the way, it was green and rectangular, about 4' by 12') and to this day still had burn marks on their rear end. I dreaded the call because he was one of the people on the base you really didn't want to fool with. So with much trepidation I went up to his office expecting a real bruising, but was greatly surprised by a gentlemanly reception followed by a lecture, which did not fault my intent, but rather my method. He made several suggestions as to how I might do this thing in the future without clogging up the traffic pattern of a good part of Seattle, and without having almost everyone on the base hate me. I actually found myself liking him, and assured him that I would do everything he suggested next time I did an ID check. I never did another ID check.

Chief McCann was a diabetic and would have forgotten to take his insulin most of the time but for his young daughter, a plump little redhead, very pleasant, who looked after him very diligently. They were a nice little family, and so when he asked if I wanted to go salmon fishing with them on a Saturday, I said sure. Up godawful early and into his old Ford station wagon, and the three of us drive to Port Angeles, stopping along the way for those delicious bear claws and coffee, and catch a ride on the boat of an old (of course) police friend of his. We had a pretty good day with the fishing, then traded our catch and a small fee for an equal weight of fresh-canned salmon, at one of the few canneries left in the area. All in all a very nice day with two very nice people.

One night a call came into the office that there was a disturbance at the Officers' Club. One of my cops responded to find that a disgruntled and very drunk Navy wife had missed her parking space and had come up over the curb to rest on the club's lawn. Coming inside she got hold of a glass of red wine, which she proceeded to throw and bounce off the chest of none other than Captain Scott!

Now, no one ever touches our CO, much less splatter his uniform with wine, and my guy got between them, quickly defused the situation with the Captain's help, and got her the hell out of there. She was taken to one of our holding cells to cool off before being picked up by a very embarrassed and contrite officer. He had his own problems with a wife like that and I hoped he wasn't looking forward to a long career in the Navy. I was particularly pleased with the professional way my guy handled a pretty dicey situation, and a very good letter went into his personnel jacket.

We had an aircraft carrier tied up at Sand Point, well, actually it was the brainstorm of some enterprising sailors who took an old motor whaleboat and turned it into a perfect 26-foot scale model of a contemporary "flattop." It could actually get underway, with the coxwain/captain sitting under, and able to see out of, the ship's "island" (the huge structure which juts up from the flight deck area, on a real carrier containing ship's operations and flight operations). It was a really good-looking ship, and was used in various public relations events. Amazingly, I had seen this carrier before, in Omaha of all places, where it was then under the aegis of the Naval Reserve Training Command.

But I digress. A reporter, probably from the Seattle Times, called one day and asked to come onto the base to do a story on our little ship. He was given permission and upon arrival was directed down to it, where a petty officer was waiting to show him around and explain its operation. Well, within twenty minutes the petty officer called to tell me that this rude and arrogant reporter had spent only five minutes on the carrier and was now busy poking around in places he didn't belong and was insulting to our sailors. I had a policeman go down and find that guy and bring him to the office, whereupon we got into an argument. He thought he was a hotshot investigative reporter, obviously did not like the Navy, and was just looking for dirt. I kicked him out of the office, telling him to get off my base. He made another smart remark and I leaned out the door and yelled to the guard at the gate to "get this guy's ass off the base *now!* " He did so and nothing ever appeared in the paper about it, thank goodness. Some people just rub you the wrong way, and that's when Navy public relations go right out the window. What an asshole!

* * *

As I mentioned, every summer Seattle paid homage to boats and water in the form of SeaFair. It is still a celebration of all that is good when the weather is warm and clear. Included is a parade of very beautiful yachts from the 20's and 30's, when boats had real lines and real style. There were also the hydrofoil races (I think they were called hydroplanes then), which Gary and Ben were hot about going to. Their uncle loaned them a really nice outboard boat which had just been refinished, and they brought it over and tied up alongside the houseboat.

There was a small conflict of fundamental beliefs here: motorboats had the unenviable and lowly nickname of "smudgepots," bestowed by those who loved nature and natural things, and who thought that only wind should power a boat. I think most people in Seattle then felt this way, but not during the Hydrofoil Races! Because if you didn't have a smudgepot, you couldn't get out to the "boom," a massive line of logs linked end-to-end across Lake Washington, to which you could tie up, watch the races, party and drink beer until you exploded! Which we proceeded to do. But not before taking a tour around the lake, going by actor Dan Blocker's magnificent home, and stopping at the marina where the hydrofoil crews were fine-tuning their boats.

This was a most interesting stop, as I learned from a mechanic that the engine that powered his boat was a twelve-cylinder Rolls Royce powerhouse, the very same engine that had powered the British Spitfire fighter of WWII fame (the Rolls Royce Merlin 45 engine was rated at 1,600 horsepower, and in brief bursts could go to 2,000 hp). He said if I wanted a demonstration, hang around for a few minutes because his driver was about to take the boat out. It was parked stern-to-the-beach, and I looked down to see that the single chromed propeller looked kind of small, with only two thin, knife-like blades. I wondered how such a puny prop could propel these boats at such high velocity.

Well, the driver got in, cranked it up, and with an explosion of power and noise, buried that stern in the water and was just *gone* in milliseconds. I found that they did it with RPM's (revolutions per minute). That Rolls Royce engine developed such high RPM's that there was no need for a gearbox, the engine directly drove the drive shaft and propeller. That's why the guy was gone almost as soon as he started the engine. The display of sheer raw power was a little scary, but you couldn't help but be amazed and thrilled!

The rest of the day out at the boom was anticlimactic, as we drank too much beer, partied too hard, and got terribly sunburned. What a great day.

One of the biggest events for hippies and longhairs and druggies came to be the "Columbia River Rock Concert and Lighter Than Air Fair," down on the Columbia River dividing Washington State and Oregon. It was to be a two-day blast of music and good times, and so a car full of us went down to have a look. We camped out overnight and awoke to rock music coming out of the largest speakers I had ever seen. It was no Woodstock, but the bands weren't too bad, there were plenty of people there but room for everyone. A lot of drugs were going around but our group stayed away from anything heavy, and I just wandered around and watched the people. There was a fat guy lying naked in a mud hole, dead to the world on something, and everyone just walked around him. There were a lot of nice looking girls to see--- mostly with some really tacky-looking guys. It was hard to figure the attraction. Maybe it was the skuzzier you looked, the more women were attracted to you.

Then came the Hell's Angels. They were there to sell drugs and just to frighten people. They were big and mean and carried chains and generally ruined the mellow feeling going around. The entire crowd became quiet and avoided making eye contact with these guys. Finally they left and the party resumed.

One remarkable thing happened: we heard a constant beat of some kind coming from the river and went down the embankment to investigate. The strangest sight and sound greeted us, hundreds and hundreds of kids, mostly naked, sitting on the riverbank and in the water, each with a rock, banging out a rhythm on the river rocks. It was mesmerizing, this noise, a beat every other second, a thousand kids in cadence. We looked at each other, shucked our clothes and joined in. We each grabbed a rock and got into the water.

After an hour or so of this it began getting late, so, in a very mellow mood we got dressed, picked up our camp and headed back for Seattle, feeling lighter than air.

* * *

It was my week to go over and inspect the brig, have lunch, talk to the guards and observe the prisoners. As winter was coming soon, all of the snowbirds who had been AWOL in Canada came south and turned themselves in to this brig because it was well-known among that "community" to serve the best chow. And it *was* good. I liked eating there.

The prison was full so it took me a long time to look into each cell and observe each man there. When we reached the top floor and the last cell, my escort of two petty officers warned me not to get too close to the window. They said this guy was a real "bad actor," the term they reserved for only the most difficult and violent prisoners. He was the worst hard case they had. He could become so violent that he was the only one there who had to be chained hand and foot and escorted by guards to chow and to the doctor, etc. He continuously cursed and spat on the guards, had tried to attack and bite them many times, and no matter how abusive he became, they could do nothing.

And these were very tough guys in their own right. They were terribly frustrated, though, that they couldn't do anything to get this guy's attention. They knew that I knew that they knew exactly what they really wanted to do to rehabilitate this guy, and that was to beat the living shit out of him. You could see it in their eyes. But it was a non-starter and we all knew it.

There was no elevator from this, the third floor, just two flights of concrete stairs. As we were leaving, I mentioned to them that the stairs could be a real hazard, and for the safety of the prisoner, to be very careful when escorting him down.

Two weeks later I did my next inspection, and upon reaching the top floor, noticed the empty cell.

"Where's your bad guy?"

"Sir, he had a pretty bad accident and will be in the hospital for six weeks."

"Gee, I'm sorry to hear that. Well, carry on."

As I have said, Ron Walker had gotten me to sign on to the Prisoner Delivery detail, and I did two trips during that year. The first was a run up to Anchorage to pick up a guy and bring him back to our brig. I had never realized how far Alaska was from the lower 48, something like 2,000 miles. There was a delay in my taking custody, so I stayed two nights in a fairly primitive hotel. In fact, except for a small downtown area with one 4-story skyscraper, it looked pretty much like the Klondike. Anyway, I had a little time to explore a new place.

The sailor I was escorting wasn't going to be much trouble. Legally, I could keep him in cuffs, and we made arrangements to board the (commercial) plane first and sit in the last row next to the restrooms. This kid was not going to run, so I took off the cuffs as we entered the terminal. I did warn him, though, that if he did run, I was faster than he was and it wouldn't do him any good. (Actually I have never been very fast on my feet, but what did he know?) The return to Seattle was without incident.

The second run was a little different. I had to take a sailor from our brig and deliver him to his ship, the carrier USS Saratoga (CVA-60), based in Mayport, near Jacksonville, Florida. He was a little older and angrier than the first guy so he remained handcuffed until we were seated, again in the back, he next to the window, me in the middle seat. I did throw a jacket over his cuffs in the airport, both to save him some embarrassment and to avoid frightening the other passengers.

When I got him out to the ship, we checked in at the quarterdeck, and the Officer of the Day called an officer to come up and take custody of the prisoner. It was a commander and I noticed right away that he had only one little decoration, the famous "geedunk" ribbon. He looked pretty pathetic. His eyes darted to my ribbons which, while not so numerous, were ones that counted, and his face fell visibly. I was embarrassed for him, but felt like telling him to get his butt off this huge ship and out to WestPac before the fireworks stopped, he obviously being a career officer. But maybe he figured that out for himself.

Note: USS Saratoga did make it to Vietnam in 1972, and did several tours on Yankee Station. Her pilots saw plenty of action. Hopefully our commander was still aboard and was able to earn some decorations commensurate with his rank.

I longed for a ride in an F-4 Phantom fighter. I wanted to see if it really shook the earth. As I have said, the airdales called it a Corvette with wings. There was a second seat behind the pilot, for the weapon system operator, and I wanted to ride in it. I knew it would probably scare me to death but I could not wait to feel that power.

I had made the acquaintance of a commander who happened to be the CO of a reserve squadron of Phantoms, and gradually worked our conversations around to asking him for a ride. He was a little cool to the idea at first, but after an evening at the 'O' Club bar he said, "Why not?" I needed several clearances and a checkup by a flight surgeon, and finally got through all of this when he called one afternoon to say sorry, he'd been transferred out of the area. What a bummer! As things turned out that was going to be my last chance to experience an F-4. In retrospect it was probably all for the best, as I am sure I would have had cardiac arrest. See, these days I won't even get on a roller coaster, or a single-engine plane for that matter.

I was hit by a bolt from the blue one day when I was summoned to the Captain's office, where he and the XO informed me that they needed a crack marching team to participate in the Veterans Day parade *two weeks hence!* They had obviously gotten a call from someone higher up. In my head I was saying, "Oh, shit, man," while I was telling them something they already knew: we had no men, no parade gear, no nothing, but an armory full of M-1 carbines.

They really were aware of the spot they were putting me in, because they gave me Carte Blanche to anything or anyone I needed on the base or elsewhere, just get the job done. For one of the perfect moments in my life where I was thinking on my feet, I asked the Captain if that included the Marines. He caught my drift right away, his face visibly brightened, and he said, "You've got 'em."

The significance of this request lies in the fact that sailors simply can't march, at least with any precision. This is not to be critical, as my step father used to say there is nowhere to march on a ship. In boot camp they come close, heck we even took a run at it in OCS, but never came near the Army or Marines. (We will leave the Air Force out of this discussion so as not to embarrass anyone.)

The U.S. Marines had an office on the base, as tenants of ours, manned by two men, a captain (two bars, same as me) and a master sergeant. They were expecting me, as my CO had already phoned ahead. Now, these guys were recruiters, and looked the part, so I will need to describe them for you. The captain was about 6'2", had that particular "jarhead" haircut: white sidewalls and a crew-cut or buzz-cut that sort of slanted down toward the forehead, was so muscular and with such a small waist that his uniform wouldn't *dare* have a wrinkle in it. His sergeant was a carbon copy at about 5'10", same jarhead haircut, with a little more beef but no less solid. Both had a chest full of Vietnam ribbons and others I didn't recognize, and just plain engendered *respect*. They could have easily been the poster boys for the whole Marine recruitment program.

We sat down and I described the dilemma, and asked the captain if either of them could help teach some sailors to march, and real fast! In answer to my most fervent prayer, he said, "My sergeant here was a D.I. at one time and I don't think he'd mind if I loaned him to you for a couple of weeks." As D.I. translates to Drill Instructor, I was about to jump out of my skin, but I tried to be calm, "Thank you, Captain," and then, "Sergeant?" and he replied, "No problem, sir."

We made the arrangement for about 2 hours each morning out on our newly-designated "grinder" (aprons and runway) for two weeks, excluding weekends. I had to necessarily give the sergeant his own Carte Blanche to do anything it took to whip these guys into a cohesive unit in that short period. By doing that I knew how popular I would not be in that same short period.

Now came the heartless part, where I went to each department and division and requisitioned (spelled s-h-a-n-g-h-a-i-e-d) the men I needed: a warm body in decent physical condition who looked sharp in uniform. I needed 25 people to report the next morning out on the grinder for 10 days of drill instruction prior to marching in the parade. It was left up to the head of each section whom to send.

I stayed away. You can imagine the consternation these sailors felt when they showed up to find a Marine drill instructor was going to be their new friend for two weeks. Most of them were already upset at being pulled off of their jobs to learn how to march! Particularly the guys who were yeomen and barbers and cooks who just didn't *need* this!

From the door of my building I could view the first session in the distance, for as long as I could stand it, that is----our guys looked pretty ragged, moving in column from left to right, right to left. You could hear the sergeant barking cadence from all that way, and he wasn't kidding. But he also had the good sense to know that these were sailors who didn't want to be there, not Marines, and he toned down the D.I. routine to medium decibels. He was perfect.

With manpower and training underway, I and Chief Berry turned to parade gear. We needed everything but rifles and black leather holsters. That meant helmets, parade belts in white webbing, and white leggings. The marchers would be wearing their dress blue uniform, and nothing looked better with white gear.

We scrounged Army helmets and liners and set our transient sailors to work cleaning and sanding and spray-painting them with several coats until they were a high gloss white. The parade belts and leggings we scrounged from old Shore Patrol stores and in dusty warehouses. Some of them were mildewed, and all of them were old and stiff and stale. Each piece had to be cleaned and then made white again with bleach and, in the hardest cases, by using the white liquid stuff we officers used on our white uniform shoes. Our offices looked like a Shanghai sweatshop with these things draped over everything while drying, and smelled of bleach and paint. It took most of the two weeks to manage this, but pretty soon we had our parade gear.

We needed to find a guide (to call cadence) for the parade. Using our Marine as a ringer would have been criminal, but it had briefly crossed my mind. No, we would need a Navy man who would impress, so I turned to Chief Ron Walker, who readily agreed. This spot would be highly visible and he was never very shy about that kind of thing. He would drill with the troops the last two days and would learn what he needed from the sergeant. Ron would wear dress blues with a white web belt and a holstered .45, and white leggings.

I was very nervous during those two weeks and kept looking down at the grinder at our people marching back and forth, back and forth. But even after a few days you could see the miracle being born: the lines were straighter, and their heels were beginning to hit the pavement almost at the same time. I couldn't believe how good this guy was. As days passed, people walking outdoors began to pause and watch the unthinkable.

The most subtle change came over the marchers. They noticed that people were beginning to watch them, and they knew they were getting better every day. The griping and resentment were slowly replaced by a certain pride, and their backs became straighter and, tired as they were, there was a new snap in their march. It was infectious and spread to the whole group. When I asked the sergeant about it, he gave me a knowing smile, saying, "Sir, I've seen this happen hundreds of times."

During the last week they marched with rifles, Ron came in on the next to last day, and the last day was a full-dress rehearsal, held is a closed hangar, in the greatest secrecy. I did not attend.

Come parade day, Ron saw to the assembly of the group and transportation downtown. He shepherded his flock to their assigned parade position, checked gear and uniforms, and lined 'em up. I went downtown by myself, merely as an observer. This was their show and their day. I had a camera with me. Walking down to the assembly point, I got a good picture of the group from the front, at attention. They looked really great except that Ron's white web belt was pulling down under the weight of his .45 (2 1/2 lbs. unloaded), but there was nothing to be done about it now. I always listed to starboard whenever I wore one (3 lbs. loaded).

I waved and wished them good luck and went down to the parade route to stake out a good vantage point in order to get some pictures. And, truthfully, I was not prepared for what happened next.

The parade started with military bands and color guards and VFW and American Legion units; a lot of color and fanfare and music, then came the marching units. There was no marching music here, as each service "marched to its own drummer," so the only noise was the cadence called and the marchers themselves.

There was a large crowd and they clapped in appreciation as the sharp Army and Marine units marched by, and politely clapped for the Air Force unit that came in front of ours. (I'm not picking on them, but they really weren't very good). But then there was a loud, collective "whoop" from the crowd as the Navy came into view. Loud applause and actual *cheering* erupted as they passed by, and I could see why: they looked so damn good! Ron was tall and impressive and was calling out perfect cadence to the best marching group I had ever seen. They looked so good in their uniforms and were so perfectly in unison. I was so proud! (I am getting goose-bumps again as I write this and remember). As they passed me I could see the perfect rows, perfect rifle position, white leggings rising as one, and heels slapping the pavement at the same instant. And, best of all, the pride that showed on all of those young Navy faces. What a day! I got so worked up that I forgot to take any pictures.

The unusual sight of a snappy Navy marching unit that electrified the crowd also caught the attention of the media, and there was coverage on TV that evening, and in the newspaper.

When the bus returned to Sand Point we surprised the guys by running it right into a hangar and closed the doors. Captain Scott was there to give a personal "thank you" and "well done" to each man, then he made a discreet exit as Ron and I uncovered an iced keg of beer, brought two cars in and cranked up the best rock station, and let in a number of wives, girlfriends and female enlisted sailors who had "volunteered" for the mission. And we had a really nice party for this tired but happy, very professional Navy drill unit.

The next day I called the Marines and thanked them profusely for their help, and the Sergeant received a commendatory letter from Captain Scott, which ended up in his permanent file.

Whenever dignitaries were coming in, we put our best foot forward in matters of security, protocol and the appearance of the base. We wanted them to see what we did and how we did it, and to have them leave with a good impression and a smile on their face.

One such occasion arose when we were notified that not one, but two United States senators and their wives would be visiting for a brief inspection. These men were the big boys who had hold of our purse strings, so we did our part with a security plan for their arrival, and had the trucks washed and a uniform inspection. Everything had to be "just so" for these men who helped govern our country. There was a feeling of excited anticipation throughout the base.

On the big day we were ready for them: the security perimeter was set and the Captain and his welcoming committee were assembled. At around noon they arrived, and the first one out the door was Senator Ernest F. "Fritz" Hollings of South Carolina. A fine looking man, tall, fit and tanned with a great head of white hair, this guy really looked like a senator should look! Everyone was plainly impressed, and were made even more so by his courtly manner.

The other senator then emerged and caught us all off guard. He was the exact opposite of Sen. Hollings: short, overweight, wearing a rumpled brown suit, his hair hanging down into his face, he nearly stumbled because he was so drunk! It was disgusting.

While we are on the subject of dignitaries, we had a visit from one who certainly did not disappoint: Admiral Elmo R. "Bud" Zumwalt, Chief of Naval Operations. He flew in one afternoon for a conference with the Captain, but first gave a short address to us "troops" out on the tarmac, then walked around our circle shaking every hand. My grandfather used to tell us never to trust anyone who didn't look you in the eye when he shook your hand. Well, when Admiral Zumwalt shook your hand, he not only looked you straight in the eye, he gave the impression that you had his full and undivided attention, even for that brief moment. Admiral Zumwalt left an indelible impression on everyone who saw him and shook his hand that day. He also left an indelible mark on the Navy. The USS Zumwalt (DDG-1000), a Land Attack Destroyer, is due to launch in 2013. The new Zumwalt Class will include up to 32 ships. There is no higher honor that can be accorded a Navy man.

And then there were the heroes. The quiet ones. I knew three in my year at Sand Point. I have already mentioned Captain Scott and his exploits in the air (and in the water) in the Solomon Islands in 1943-44.

I got to know another one, a quiet and dignified man named Gene Lacey. Gene was a Chief Warrant Officer and was my "opposite number" (security officer) over at the Navy Base. He had also been one of the officers on the bridge of the USS Pueblo when it was captured by the North Korean Navy on January 23, 1968.

Gene was so gentlemanly and calm, it was hard to picture him in the middle of such an omnibus action, one that humiliated the United States and resulted in 11 months of beatings, near starvation and mental torture for the officers and crew. By 1970 he looked no worse for the wear, but I knew there had to be some scars deep down. He did not talk about his captivity very much, only tidbits here and there. I do remember his telling me once that he couldn't stand the thought of fish heads and rice.

My memory of Gene Lacey is one of respect and admiration. And I think the last time I saw him was when he called to say I had better come over to the Navy Pier: One of my guys was over there on business, and a cargo crane had dropped a very large and very heavy wooden crate onto his (my!) truck and flattened it like a pancake. Luckily no one was in it at the time. Gene and I both agreed: it was crushed pretty good.

The third hero I met was Rear Admiral Robert W. Copeland, USNR. He was one of my step father's reserve Admirals, now retired, and they were also friends. Zim asked me to pay a call on him in Tacoma before I ended my tour in Seattle. He also recommended I read, or re-read, a history of the Battle off Samar in 1944 prior to the visit, so that I would be aware of the kind of man I was meeting. I did that, and was so thoroughly stunned by the story that I couldn't wait to meet him.

The Battle off Samar was part of the larger Battle of Leyte Gulf. Every American should read about this action, and learn of the heroics of so many ships and people like the then-Lieutenant Commander Copeland and his crew. He was the CO of the USS Samuel B. Roberts (DE-413). I urge you and everyone you know, to read the authoritative and definitive history, *"The Battle of Leyte Gulf, 23-26 October 1944,* by Thomas J. Cutler. You, too, will be thrilled and stunned.

For this action, LCDR Copeland was awarded the Navy Cross for heroism. After the war, he returned to civilian life and a law practice, but stayed active in the Reserves and rose to the rank of Rear Admiral.

By the time I met him he was in his early sixties, but I must admit, he looked much older. He was very cordial and, although his WWII exploits never came up, we had a nice chat about Zim and the reserve program, what I was doing at Sand Point, and the Navy in general. It was a very pleasant visit, no more than a half-hour (as dictated by Navy etiquette), and as he talked I imagined him as a young man, a totally fearless warrior putting his little ship up against Japanese cruisers and battleships, protecting his carrier group from them. Not giving up until the last shot was fired and helping turn the tide of a very important sea battle. He was a very special kind of man.

* * *

It came time for my fitness report, hopefully a good one because if I stayed in the Navy, I wanted to go to Destroyer School to be qualified as a department head on a destroyer. I thought there was a pretty good shot at it since I had been a division officer on a destroyer in a war zone, and a department head on an LST in-country, in even more of a war zone.

You will note that I said "if" I stayed in the Navy. I was at a real crossroads in my life, and could not decide whether to stay in or get out. On the one hand I liked the life well enough: it offered excitement and travel and the best comradeship I could ever ask for. On the other, I had begun to feel a little constrained in my thinking, in that there seemed to be no room for much creative thought, or thinking "outside the box," in the Navy. And that was beginning to bother me a little.

What would probably tip the scale toward staying in was acceptance to Destroyer School. It would mean major advancement in an elite force, and an excellent career move. I had already made application and Captain Scott had forwarded it with a hearty endorsement that I be accepted.

So I harbored high hopes that my fitness report would put some icing on the cake. Well, Ron Walker dropped by one day with his wolfish grin face on and I knew something was up. He said, "I've seen your fitness report." Of course my first question was, "How does it look?" After a few minutes of the obligatory downing of my talents as an officer, he said, "You got an Outstanding!" (An Oustanding fitness report was very rare and not to be taken lightly). After I whooped a couple of times and walked around in circles for a while, I came back to earth enough to ask him, "Wait a minute, how come you've seen my report?" The wolfish grin reappeared and he said, "I wrote it."

Sure enough he had, but my CO had made his modifications and signed the report, and so I came away with what I felt was my entrée to Destroyer School, should I decide to stay in the service.

When the day came, I picked up the phone and called my detailer and asked him with some confidence if I had been accepted to Destroyer School. He replied, "No, your application was denied." I was so stunned that it took a minute for things to sink in.

"What? Why!"

"You have one average fitness report."

"That's the reason? You've got to be kidding."

"No, I'm not kidding."

"Do you have my other fitness reports in front of you?

"Yes."

"What do they say?"

"There are two excellents, one high excellent, and one outstanding."

"Well?"

"It doesn't matter. You have one average fitness report."

"Did you read Captain Scott's endorsement of my application?"

"Yes, but that makes no difference. The Navy is hung up on that fitness report."

"Well, what would I need to do now to get into Destroyer School?"

"Go back to sea for another year as a department head on an oiler or supply ship."

"I've already done that!"

"I know, but that's the only way you can get into Destroyer School."

"Well, thank you, you have just made a decision for me."

Though this guy had not been unsympathetic toward me during this unbelievable conversation, I slammed the phone down so hard I thought it would shatter, put my head down on my desk and just began crying and couldn't stop. I wasn't crying because the Navy was being so damned unfair; I had seen this kind of blockheaded decision-making before, affecting good and decent officers and sailors. No, I was crying because the decision was made, and all too abruptly, that I was going to leave the Navy. I just couldn't and wouldn't do a year on an auxiliary ship after what I had been through on combatant ships. I would have felt too much like Mr. Roberts on the USS Reluctant.

When I was able to pull myself together, I picked up the phone and called my step father in Omaha. He was not happy about it, I could tell, but he was going to respect my position and was not going to interfere. He would give my mother the news and I would talk to both of them later.

Once I put in my separation papers things began to happen in quick succession: a Hail and Farewell party given me and some others at the Officer's Club, a farewell party given in my honor at Ron Walker's home, and a farewell party sort of given in my honor on houseboat row. As usual, when you leave a great bunch of people like this, you, and they, take names and phone numbers and addresses and earnestly promise to keep in touch. It just rarely turns out that way. Out of all those wonderful people I knew, my friend Ron Walker was the only one I saw and spoke with again over all the subsequent years. In my last days on the dock I became a little worried about Bruce, who looked pale and drawn and was just not on track. I thought he was really getting ill, but when I asked someone about it I was told that he had simply run out of marijuana. It turned out that he had been stoned every single day since we had met and this is what he looked like sober. I wished him well, as I did to every single character whom I had come to know and love in that special place. And now it was time to go.

A lieutenant commander was ordered in to replace me, which made me, just a lieutenant, feel pretty good. Conversely, I think he was really embarrassed to relieve a mere lieutenant because he wanted me out of there so quickly, with just a modicum of orientation from me. And that was all right, I was ready to go now. Just two things left to do.

I had a private meeting with Chiefs McCann and Berry, and gave them my thanks for their hard work and support during the last year. We had accomplished so much, and I told them that this was probably my most satisfying tour in the Navy. I then gave them the highest compliment I can give: I said that they were both good men and that it had been my honor to serve with them. With that, Bosun's Mate Chief Berry gave me a steel-trap handshake, and Police Chief McCann gave me a handshake that turned into a bear hug, and he got just a bit of a tear in his eyes. So did I. Sergeant Raines had assembled all of the men he could pull off of their posts, and I gave them my gratitude for a job well done. On my way out I signaled Raines to follow me, shook his hand and said, "Thank you for everything."

I then left my building, jumped into the Corvette, drove out to the airstrip, hung a right and raced through the gears at full throttle until reaching the end. I got out, stooped and picked up a small chunk of the runway that had broken off, and tossed it into the car.

Somewhere in my musty storeroom of Naval traditions I thought I remembered one where, upon leaving a ship for the last time, one removed one's shoes and threw them over the side. This was close enough, so I took my brown shoes off and tossed them in the drink. (To this day they are probably still moldering at the bottom of Lake Washington).

And then, in my sock feet, I got back into the car, and just left.

Note: Not too long after leaving Sand Point, I received word that Chief Jim McCann had died of insulin shock. I guess his little girl couldn't be with him every minute of the day to take care of him. I was very pleased, though, to hear that Sergeant Raines was now Chief Raines. He loved old McCann, as I did, and was the only one who could fill his shoes.

Epilogue

I don't dream about Vietnam, or think about it all the time. I was one of the lucky ones who was never placed in the position of facing the terror or fright or trauma that many of our people did. There are so many stories, from friends, from books, from the computer, and from veteran magazines and newsletters. I read an article in the Spring 2007 River Currents newsletter, written by Robert Clark, entitled, "*I Was There*." It is so poignant that it says just about everything there is to be said about Vietnam, and the effect that it had on an entire generation of young American men and women.

If you can't feel this, you have no feelings at all. I am going to quote twice from this story, written by a true hero. They need not be put in context:

"I recall the smells, too. Like the way cordite hangs on the air after a fire-fight. Or the pungent odor of rice paddy mud. So different from the black dirt of Iowa. The mud of Nam smells ancient, somehow. Like it's always been there. And I'll never forget the way blood smells, sticky and drying on my hands. I spent a long night that way once. That memory isn't going anywhere.

I remember how the night jungle appears almost dreamlike as the pilot of a Cessna buzzes overhead, dropping parachute flares until morning. That artificial sun would flicker and make shadows run through the jungle. It was worse than not being able to see what was out there sometimes. I remember once looking at the man next to me as a flare floated overhead. The shadows around his eyes were so deep that it looked like his eyes were gone. I reached over and touched him on the arm; without looking at me he touched my hand. "I know, man, I know." That's what he said. It was a human moment.

Two guys a long way from home and scared shitless. "I know, man." And he did.

And the other:

"A couple of years ago someone asked me if I still thought of Vietnam. I nearly laughed in their face. How do you stop thinking about it? Every day for the last twenty-four years, I wake up with it, and go to bed with it.

But this is what I said. "Yeah, I think about it. I can't quit thinking about it. I never will. But, I've also learned to live with it. I'm comfortable with the memories. I've learned to stop trying to forget and learned instead to embrace it. It just does not scare me anymore."

A psychologist once told me that *not* being affected by the experience over there would be abnormal. When he told me that, it was like he'd just given me a pardon. It was as if he said, "Go ahead and feel something about the place, Bob. It ain't going nowhere.

You're gonna wear it for the rest of your life. Might as well get to know it."

A lot of my "brothers" haven't been so lucky. For them the memories are too painful, their sense of loss too great. My sister told me of a friend she has whose husband was in Nam. She asks this guy when he was there. Here's what he said, "Just last night." It took my sister a while to figure out what he was talking about. *Just Last Night.* Yeah, I was in Nam."

* * *

My wife spent most of her working life as a flight attendant for Trans World Airlines, and volunteered to work charter flights ferrying soldiers between the US and Vietnam. They would take young, fresh looking men in and bring old men out. Going over, she said some of these kids spent the whole flight in the toilet, throwing up. And a good many of them gave her letters to mail to loved ones, along with money for stamps. She made 8 or 9 of these round trips during the fall and winter of 1968, into Tan Son Nhut, Da Nang and Bien Hoa. They were shot at many times, and bullet holes were sometimes found in the aircraft.

She was deeply touched by the experience, and had many memories of those days. But there is one incident that she simply could not get out of her mind, and it is one of the saddest things I have ever heard.

They were on the ground at Tan Son Nhut, December 1968, just days before Christmas, and soldiers were boarding the flight, ready to go home to the USA. The line stretched out onto the tarmac, four abreast. Just nearby was an Air Force transport plane, loading the most terrible cargo: body bags. They were stacked deep on pallets, and the cargo guys were having trouble with the loading, so one of them had to get up on one of the pallets to rearrange them.

And one of the guys in line just went berserk. He broke ranks and went running toward the Air Force guy, grabbing at him and screaming, "Get off of there, you son of a bitch, those are my friends you're walking on!" She said he wouldn't stop screaming and trying to attack the airman, and it took several people to pull him away. By this time the Air force guy was in tears, saying, "I know, I'm sorry man, this is a really crappy job and I'm doing the best I can!" My wife said there were maybe 150 body bags on those pallets. How very sad. She did not see the soldier on the flight home, and so doesn't know if he left that day or not.

* * *

Vietnam was such a terrible experience for so many. The people mentioned here, of course, are only a small example. But then they had to return to the United States, to a hostile reception, or really no reception at all. And that is one of the reasons so many veterans, men and women, have so many problems stemming from their service. It was so unfair, and it hurt so many people. Soldiers were actually advised to get into civvies as quickly as possible after they landed, in order to avoid having any problems. This, instead of the admiration and gratitude of their people after all they had been through.

An Iraq War veteran named Daniel Wadhams wrote a letter to the Vietnam Veterans of America magazine, dated November/December

2005, and it is one of the nicest and most unselfish things I have ever read:

"This letter is way overdue. I am a veteran of the current war. Since I have returned home, I cannot tell you how many people have thanked me. I really don't feel I deserve it. You guys are my heroes. You performed in conditions worse than I served in and did it for a country that was not grateful. You paved the way for soldiers of today and showed us what real courage is.

I am proud to have served my country, but the next time someone wants to thank me, I am going to ask them to do me a favor and thank a Vietnam veteran."

At the beginning of this book, I mentioned the Vietnam Service Ribbon, and it also appears on the front cover. The next time you see this on a baseball cap or a pin or a bumper sticker, or on a ribbon bar, you will know that person served in Vietnam. Maybe you should honk your horn and wave, or simply say, "Thank you."

Made in the USA
San Bernardino, CA
15 March 2015